I Suffer Not
a Woman

I Suffer Not a Woman

*Rethinking 1 Timothy 2:11–15
in Light of Ancient Evidence*

Richard Clark Kroeger
and
Catherine Clark Kroeger

 Baker Books

A Division of Baker Book House Co.
Grand Rapids, Michigan 49516

Published by Baker Books
a division of Baker Book House Company
P.O. Box 6287, Grand Rapids, MI 49516-6287

Sixth printing, May 2003

Printed in the United States of America

Library of Congress Cataloging-in-Publication Data

Kroeger, Richard Clark.
    I suffer not a woman : rethinking 1 Timothy 2:11–15 in light of ancient
  evidence / Richard Clark Kroeger, Catherine Clark Kroeger.
        p.   cm.
    Includes bibliographical references.
    ISBN 0-8010-5250-5
    1. Bible. N.T. Timothy, 1st, II, 11–15—Criticism, interpretation, etc.
  2. Women—Biblical teaching. 3. Women in Christianity—History—Early
  church, ca. 30–600. I. Kroeger, Catherine Clark. II. Title.
  BS2745.2.K76   1991
  277′.8306—dc20   91-31822

For current information about all releases from Baker Book House, visit our web site:
http://www.bakerbooks.com

For
Mary,
Marjorie,
Elizabeth,
Robert,
Paul,
and **Margaret,**
without whose patience
and support
this book would never
have come into being

Contents

Appendices

Abbreviations

ANET *Ancient Near Eastern Texts*, ed. J. B. Pritchard
b. Babylonian Talmud
BG Codex Berolinensis Gnosticus
frag. fragment
Gk. Greek
Heb. Hebrew
LB Living Bible
Mish. Mishnah
NHC Nag Hammadi Codex
NIV New International Version
PG *Patrologia Cursus, series Graeca*, ed. J. P. Migne
PL *Patrologia Cursus, series Latina*, ed. J. P. Migne
SIG *Syllogue Inscriptionum Graecorum*, ed. W. Dittenberger (1915–24)
TDNT *Theological Dictionary of the New Testament*, ed. G. W. Bromiley
y. Jerusalem Talmud

Preface

A physician in family practice was summoned to her pastor's study and there was informed that her chosen medical specialty is outside God's will for her life. The pastor insisted that only two specialties are open to her: obstetrics/gynecology and pediatrics. The electrified young woman asked why God could not see fit to use her gifts in implementing healing for families. The answer was that 1 Timothy 2:12 forbade her having any authority over men, and that therefore she could not enter into a patient/physician relationship with a man. The woman left the church, went to a developing nation, and took up service as a missionary doctor, ministering in Jesus' name to all who came to her clinic.

A beautiful and obviously intelligent young woman lingered somewhat shyly after we had given a lecture on an alternative interpretation of 1 Timothy 2:12. She approached us after most of the others had left, and her first few words evinced a deep desire to serve Christ with all of her talents. She was a member of an active but conservative church that severely restricted the scope of her Christian activities. "Maybe I shouldn't say this," she murmured. "But I have been absolutely *clobbered* by that Bible verse!"

An attorney was told by certain members of her family that according to 1 Timothy 2:11–15 she should be a waitress rather than a lawyer.

A church magazine announced that a dedicated laywoman would take over the leadership of a ministry to nursing homes in the Milwaukee area.[1] An indignant reader responded, "Exactly how does the 'headship' given her square with 1 Timothy 2:11–15?"[2]

If there is one verse in the Bible more than any other which is used to disbar women from proclaiming the Good News of Jesus

Christ and exercising their talents for his glory, it is 1 Timothy 2:12. Within its context this verse reads, according to the King James Version,

> [11]Let the woman learn in silence with all subjection.
> [12]*But I suffer not a woman to teach, nor to usurp authority over the man, but to be in silence.*
> [13]For Adam was first formed, then Eve.
> [14]And Adam was not deceived, but the woman being deceived was in the transgression.
> [15]Notwithstanding she shall be saved in childbearing, if they continue in faith and charity and holiness with sobriety.

On the basis of this translation of verse 12 women are denied a vote in church affairs, rejected as teachers of adult Bible classes, kept home from the mission field, disenfranchised from the duties and privileges of leadership in the body of Christ, and forbidden the use of their God-given talents for leadership.

While we were participating in a colloquium on this passage at a conservative theological seminary, a layman rose during the question period. "Is there any other major doctrine in the Bible," he asked, "which depends on only one verse?" He was assured by a member of the faculty that there is not. The layman persisted further, "And is it true that the understanding of this verse is dependent upon the translation of just one verb which is used only once in the entire New Testament?" Again he was assured that indeed this is so.

Many evangelicals view all biblical passages about the role and ministry of women through the lens of 1 Timothy 2:12.[3] It becomes the key verse on women, the one on which all others turn. Christ's explicit command that the women should proclaim to the male disciples the news that he had risen is given secondary importance in comparison to this one Pauline mandate. The spiritual leadership of Hulda, Deborah, Miriam, Priscilla, Phoebe, and others is denigrated or denied. Yet it was Priscilla who "instructed Apollos more perfectly in the way of the Lord" (Acts 18:26) at Ephesus, the city to which this command was addressed. The apostle Paul enjoyed warm collegiality in the gospel with the women he called "fellow laborers."

We cannot ignore the record that it was the judge and prophet Deborah who led the children of Israel into battle and trusted God for a great victory. Nor can we deny that the preaching of the prophet Hulda triggered the great revival under King Josiah, and that her identification of the book which was brought to her as the Word of God began the process of canonization. And what shall we do with the unnamed woman of Abel Beth Maacah who assumed the responsibility to deliver the city from siege (2 Sam. 20:14–22)?

English does not give us the clue provided by Hebrew in identifying the gender of the second person pronoun or of the third person plural. Thus we find, "The Lord gives the Word. Great is the host of women who proclaim it" (Ps. 68:11) and again, "O woman who is herald of good tidings to Zion, lift up your voice with strength, O woman who is herald of good tidings to Jerusalem, lift it up, fear not; say to the cities of Judah, 'Behold your God'"(Isa. 40:9). Such passages call women to a ministry of proclamation. How does this fit with the commonly accepted translation of 1 Timothy 2:12?

Let us consider a question which God asked through the prophet Micah. It occurs in a passage famed for the question, "What doth the Lord require of thee, but to do justice, to love mercy, and to walk humbly with thy God?" (Mic. 6:8). The beginning of the passage sketches a courtroom scene in which the hills and mountains act as judge and jury in litigation between Yahweh and the people of Israel. The Lord reminds Israel of the many acts of kindness and the great deliverance from Egypt and then asks, "Have I not sent before thee Moses and Aaron and Miriam to lead thee?" (Mic. 6:4). God is calling to Israel to give account of herself, and one of the questions at the judgment is this: Is she mindful of the gift of the leadership of Miriam?

What have we in today's church done with Miriam and with the gifts of so many other talented women? Have we allowed them to be used, or have they been turned away with the use of a particular translation of 1 Timothy 2:12? This verse causes us to ponder whether women are called to silence or to service. It is necessary to compare Scripture with Scripture to find the correct meaning. We must consider *all* that the Bible has to say about the activities of women committed to God's will.

For centuries Christians have struggled with this fundamental contradiction between 1 Timothy 2:12 and the passages in which women were bidden to tell of their risen Lord or were called to teach, to lead Israel, to rule over God's people. Mary Slessor, the great missionary heroine of Calabar, wrote in her Bible beside an apparently restrictive translation of a verse, "Nay, Paul laddie! This will na' do." It behooves us to ask, are there other avenues of interpretation, of translation?

For centuries women have raised these questions. A nineteenth-century novelist, Charlotte Brontë, has her heroine declare:

> He [Paul] wrote that chapter for a particular congregation of Christians, under peculiar circumstances; and besides, I dare say, if I could read the original Greek, I should find that many of the words have been wrongly translated, perhaps misapprehended altogether. It would be possible, I doubt not, with a little ingenuity, to give the passage quite a contrary turn; to make it say, 'Let the woman speak out whenever she sees fit to make an objection;'—'it is permitted to a woman to teach and to exercise authority as much as may be. Man, meantime, cannot do better than hold his peace,' and so on.[4]

Yes, translation and interpretation are crucial. The proper interpretation can release women to serve wherever God may call them, or it can consign one half of the church to leave its world-wide minstry to the other half.

Our purpose is to maintain on the basis of Scripture that both men and women are equally called to commitment and service, wherever and however God may lead. This book will seek to deal carefully and conscientiously with a controversial passage which has frequently obstructed the ministry of women. Since this text is so often the pivotal one in controversies over the role and status of women, we believe that seekers are entitled to an extensive amount of pertinent information. Much of the material in this book deals with the religion and culture of ancient Ephesus and is not readily available, even to the specialized reader. On the other hand, the enormous amount of supplemental material must not impede the progress of the general reader. In the main text, we will try to set forth our thesis in a straightforward manner. Those desiring more detailed information and explanation will find it in the endnotes and appendices. As the reader will note, some of the ancient texts are translated from Coptic. These texts were originally written in Greek, though only the Coptic versions are still extant. Some of the Greek words still remain embedded in the Coptic texts. These Greek words have been indicated but should not be an obstacle to those who do not read Greek.

The Chinese say that "one peep is worth ten thousand words." The pictures of archaeological data are an essential part of the argument of this book. Often the physical remains from a long-gone era demonstrate the realities of ancient Asia Minor far better than words. They draw us closer to a comprehension of the religion and culture of the communities to which the pastoral Epistles were addressed.

We believe that much of the problem over the difficult texts has arisen because so little is known in our churches and seminaries about the lives and outlook of the women to whom Paul wrote. This book is an effort to correct the imbalance. An understanding of the context can bring a new interpretation.

Introduction
Problems with a Traditional Interpretation

....

O ur interpretation of 1 Timothy 2:12 is critical to the manner in which we shall deal with other difficulties in Scripture as well. The Bible is an ancient and often perplexing
book, written by many different authors over many centuries, and
yet traditional Christians believe that this book is indeed the
inspired Word of God, our only infallible rule of faith and practice.
Those who maintain that the Bible contains a fundamentally consistent and coherent message must deal with the apparent dis-
crepancies between our target passage and the rest of Scripture.
The problems are of two kinds: theological and practical.

Theological Problems

It is essential that we face honestly the difficulties inherent in
a traditional understanding of 1 Timothy 2:12. Traditional interpretation has held that this verse forbids women to teach or make
decisions. The fact is that women did indeed teach men, that
women served as leaders, and that in doing so they enjoyed God's
blessing and won the praise of other believers. Priscilla instructed
the learned Apollos, Lois and Eunice taught Timothy, and Phoebe
is named as an overseer and a deacon in the church at Cenchrea.
Furthermore, believers are enjoined to teach and to learn from one
another, without reference to gender. There are yet other points at
which the traditional interpretation creates a theology at variance
with the major teachings of Scripture.

Eve as a "Secondary" Creation

One of the major perplexities in this passage is the curious inclusion in verses 13 and 14 of a description of Eve's creation and deception. Some have understood this to mean that man's superiority stems from his priority in creation, and that woman's secondary status is based upon her subsequent formation from the side of man. If being created first determines superiority, however, we must go back beyond the man to the beasts, the birds, the fish, and the creeping and crawling creatures. The Bible speaks of man and woman as being equally commissioned to have dominion over the earth and to fill it (Gen. 1:26–28) and as being equally made in God's image: "When God created humankind, he made them in the likeness of God. Male and female he created them, and he blessed them and named them 'humankind' [literally, Adam—here used generically] when they were created" (Gen. 5:1–2).

Eve as Gullible

Some scholars maintain that the reason for the prohibition is that women, like Eve, are gullible and easily deceived. They cannot lead or teach because they are so often led astray. This argument will not stand up to the weight of a biblical tradition that extols the wisdom of women. In the Book of Proverbs, Wisdom itself is extensively portrayed as a woman giving instruction to those who are willing to learn (Prov. 1:20–33; 8:1–9:6). The wisdom of women builds a house (Prov. 14:1), and the valiant woman of Proverbs 31 "opens her mouth with wisdom, and the teaching of kindness is on her tongue" (v. 26).

At a number of crucial points in the history of God's people, a succession of wise women appears to cope with problems which the men have been unable to resolve (1 Sam. 25:3–35; 2 Sam. 14:2–23; 20:16–22; Prov. 31:26). As we have seen, Deborah was appointed by God as a judge (Judg. 2:16; Neh. 9:27) and "the people of Israel came up to her for judgment" (Judg. 4:4–5). When the enemies obstructed the roads so that it was impossible for the people to assemble before the Lord, she decided upon military action. The male general was afraid to lead the hosts of Israel against so formidable a foe, and so Deborah marched with him at the head of the troops. As promised, God accomplished the destruction of the enemy general at the hand of a woman (Judg.

4:9, 21–22). The entire story emphasizes the superior wisdom and resourcefulness of the woman.

Another wise woman negotiated the lifting of a siege against Abel Beth Maacah which Joab had rashly laid without complying with the provisions of Deuteronomy 20:10–12. Once she had gained a concession from Joab, "she went to her people in her wisdom" (2 Sam. 20:22). The leaders of this city were very good at helping other people with their problems (2 Sam. 20:18), but in their own time of trouble, this woman was the wisest of all.

Abigail, "a wise and prudent woman," stopped David's anger when he was bent on a murderous mission; and he praised God for sending her as an emissary to keep him from committing a terrible crime (1 Sam. 25:33–35). After Joab's own efforts to secure forgiveness for Absalom failed, he summoned the wise woman of Tekoah to intercede with David for reconciliation with his son (2 Sam. 14:1–24).

Queen Esther was raised up when all seemed hopeless. God's providence had brought her to the kingdom for just such a time (Esther 4:14). Though fearful for her life, she devised a plan to save the Jewish nation, and she was given both the fortitude and the wisdom to execute that plan. As a result, many Gentiles turned to faith in the true and living God (8:17). In the end her injudicious husband expressed his pleasure at her prudence and good judgment; and she was vested with authority in her own right (9:11–12, 29–32).

Let us not forget that resourceful and courageous women managed to save the life of Moses when Pharaoh had ordered the destruction of all male Hebrew infants,[1] that Jael outwitted and slew Israel's enemy Sisera, and that Jesus delighted in the answer of a Syro-Phoenician woman who matched wits with him when he tested her faith and perseverance. She was desperate for her daughter to be healed, and neatly turned his words around to catch him. He declared, "Because of this saying, go; the demon has gone out of your daughter" (Mark 7:29). He commended her *logos*, not only the saying but the faith and the intelligence behind it.

Eve as Primarily Responsible for the Original Sin

Some would disenfranchise women from leadership because they hold that 1 Timothy 2:14 lays the fundamental responsibility for the fall upon Eve. This is in direct contrast to two important passages in the Pauline Epistles, where Paul assigns the guilt essentially to Adam:

> Thus, then, sin came into the world through one man, and through sin death; and so death spread to all men, because all have sinned. . . . Nevertheless from Adam to Moses death reigned as king, even over those who had not sinned after the likeness of Adam's transgression. Now Adam is a type of him who was to come . . . For if through the transgression of that one man, the rest of men died. . . . And it is not with the free gift as it was through the one that sinned; for the judgment came from one transgression unto condemnation. . . . For if through the transgression of the one, death reigned as king through the one, . . . it follows, then, as through the transgression of one man came condemnation unto all men, even so through the act of righteousness of One came acquittal and life to all men. For just as through the disobedience of one man the rest were made sinners, even so by the obedience of One shall all the rest be made righteous. [Rom. 5:12–19]

> For since by man came death, by man came also the resurrection from the dead. For just as in Adam all die, so also in Christ will all be made alive. [1 Cor. 15:21–22]

By our reckoning, Paul ascribes the guilt to Adam nine different times in these passages. It is noteworthy that just as Eve is said to be "in the transgression" in 1 Timothy 2:14, so we read of the "likeness of Adam's transgression" in Romans 5:14. *Parabasis,* the same Greek word, is used in both cases. It would perhaps be more just to postulate that Paul, when he speaks of Adam, has in mind both male and female, as does the writer of Genesis 5:1–2. Here "Adam" is a generic name for humankind, as it is in Genesis 1:27–28.

The text of the Hebrew Bible, as well as its Greek translation, the Septuagint, states that Adam was *with* Eve when she partook of the forbidden fruit (Gen. 3:6). Though many translations lack the statement, the Hebrew literally says, "She gave to her husband, who was with her." Furthermore, the Hebrew text indicates that the serpent is speaking to both the man and the woman, for the plural form of the second person is used. The account infers that Adam and Eve were equally responsible. We suggest that 1 Timothy 2:13–14 is concerned not with laying the blame on women but with a strong repudiation of a popular false teaching which glorified Eve and the serpent.

Women as Bearers of Eve's Guilt

Still others look at 1 Timothy 2:9–15 in a manner which may give a seriously distorted view of God's redemptive grace. Not long ago we heard a professor of New Testament declare, "The verse is not complicated, the argument of the passage seems clear, and the normal lexical meanings of the terms seem to fit well."[2]

This professor linked God's judgment upon Eve at the fall (Gen. 3) with our target verse and announced:

> As a result of her [the woman's] actions God tells her that she will bear children in pain, that her desire will be to her husband, and that he will rule (have authority) over her (Gen. 3:16). The punishments, subjection and child bearing, are the two issues in 1 Timothy 2:11–15. The woman's conduct in the fall is, according to Genesis, a primary reason for her universal, timeless subordinate relationship.[3]

His reasoning is very close to that of Tertullian, who wrote to women that they would go about still mourning the sin of Eve in order to expiate what each had received from Eve—the ignominy of that first sin and the hatefulness of human perdition. "Are you ignorant that you are an Eve? The sentence of God still lives upon your sex even in this present age, and of necessity the guilt lives on too. You are the devil's gateway, you are the unsealer of that tree, you are the first destroyer of divine law, you are she who persuaded him whom the devil was unwilling to attack directly."[4] Clement of Alexandria declared that a woman should blush for very shame that she was of the same gender as Eve—hardly a positive psychological suggestion!

Such an understanding of the reference to Eve in 1 Timothy 2:13–14 appears to be a dangerous interpretation, in terms both of biblical theology and of the call to Christian commitment. The consequences of an individual's sin may remain until the third and fourth generation (Exod. 20:5; Deut. 5:9), but God's mercy extends to a thousand generations (Exod. 20:6; Deut. 5:10; 7:9). There is a serious theological contradiction in telling a woman that when she comes to faith in Christ, her personal sins are forgiven but she must continue to be punished for the sin of Eve. To construe this passage as a perpetual condemnation of women puts a terrible burden of guilt and shame upon half of those redeemed by the blood of Jesus, which, according to 1 John 1:9, cleanses from all sin. Furthermore, both Old and New Testaments declare that each person must answer for her or his own sin (Eccles. 12:14; Rom. 14:10; 2 Cor. 5:10).

> A man shall not die for his father's wrongdoing; he shall live. . . . You may ask, "Why is the son not punished for his father's iniquity?" Because he has always done what is just and right and has been careful to obey all my laws. Therefore he shall live. . . . It is the soul that sins, and no other, that shall die; a son shall not share a father's guilt, nor a father his son's. [Ezek. 18:17–20]

Then follows a promise:

> But if a wicked man turns away from all his sins which he has committed and keeps all my statutes and does what is lawful and right, he shall surely live; he shall not die. None of the transgressions which he has committed shall be remembered against him for the righteousness which he has done; he shall live. [18:21–22]

If, as it is often charged, 1 Timothy 2:12–14 forbids women to teach because of Eve's sin, why are not men also held responsible? Are they not the sons of Eve as much as women are the daughters? Are men not held accountable for the sins of their forebears, while women must pay for the sin of their original ancestress? Most of all, what shall we do with the good news that there is now no condemnation for those who are in Christ Jesus (Rom. 8:1)? Do women indeed still bear the taint of Eve? Even the ancient pagan authors held it unjust that the gods or mortals should hold another generation accountable for the sins of the past. Shall we ascribe a lesser justice to our God of love, mercy, and grace?

The doctrine of the Bible is one of God's forgiveness and kindness in restoring a fallen sinner. Is there no restoration for women? Rather let us consider the possibility that 1 Timothy 2:13–14 is not a contradiction of God's loving and equal dealings with all of humanity from the beginning of time. Surely these dealings apply to women as well as men. The gospel is the Good

News of forgiveness for sinners and of freedom for those made captive by sin and oppression.

At the beginning of the First Epistle to Timothy, the writer declares that he has been given a ministry even though he was formerly blasphemous and a persecutor and insufferably insolent (1 Tim. 1:12–13):

> But I received mercy *because I behaved this way ignorantly in unbelief.* The grace of our Lord overflowed beyond measure with faith and love in Christ Jesus. Faithful is the saying and worthy to be accepted by all that Christ Jesus came into the world to save sinners, of whom I am chief. But for this I received mercy, so that Christ Jesus might reveal the entirety of his patience to me first, as a sort of prototype of all those who should come to believe on him unto everlasting life. [1 Tim. 1:13–16, emphasis added]

If Paul was forgiven for what he did ignorantly in unbelief and thereafter was given a ministry, why would the same forgiveness and ministry be denied women? Let us approach this epistle as being from one who knew what it was to receive abundant forgiveness and who had a concern to share with others redeeming love and inclusion within the family of God. In this book, we shall suggest that 1 Timothy 2:11–15 is not a decree of timeless and universal restriction and punishment but a corrective: a specific direction as to what women should not teach and why.

Practical Problems

Frequently we meet women who tell of their conviction that God has called them to ministry. Many have been deflected from their calling by other Christians who tell them that this cannot possibly be God's will. The women become bewildered, for they are eager to obey God, yet are thwarted by the determined obstruction of sincere believers who would gladly support the call to ministry of a male with equal talents. All too often the negative arguments are based upon a traditional interpretation of 1 Timothy 2:12.

We are commanded neither to grieve nor to quench the Holy Spirit of God (Eph. 4:30; 1 Thess. 5:19). An acquaintance of ours, a highly gifted professional woman, was touched one night at church as she heard of a specialized ministry with a need for workers. She approached the speaker after the service and explained that God had been tugging at her heart. The speaker, an officer in a large parachurch organization, asked about her husband. When he learned that she was unmarried, there was a long pause. At last he said, "I suppose you could work in our ladies' auxiliary." As the woman left in tears, she thought, "That just isn't like Jesus. The Bible said he would not quench a smoking flax" (see Isa. 42:3; Matt. 12:20). How often, from Bible times until now, have God's potential prophets and messengers been opposed, repudiated, and silenced!

The Division of Believers against Themselves

A traditional interpretation sets believers against their own prayer lives. Jesus commanded his disciples to pray that God would thrust laborers into the fields already white unto harvest. How can Christ's followers pray this sincerely when they are at the same time doing their best to deter half of those laborers? We once heard an evangelical leader declare, "The laborers are few, divided by two." Those who are committed to spreading the love of Jesus to every region of our world cannot with integrity reject those willing to give themselves for the effort. Married women with certain gifts are often considered acceptable; the single woman faces far greater rejection, especially if her gifts fit her for leadership. Women are told often that they may exercise their leadership abilities anywhere except in the church or in its related ministries.

The New Testament teaches that individual members, along with their gifts and talents, are God's gift to the church (1 Cor. 12:4–11; Eph. 4:11–13). There are many gifts of leadership and service, all from the same Spirit, all to be used according to their function (Rom. 12:4–8). Among these gifts are those of teaching and administration. No limitation with respect to gender is indicated (Acts 2:17–18; 1 Cor. 12:28). Persons endowed with the gift of teaching are expected to develop this potential to the glory of God, while those in authority should be scrupulously conscientious (Rom. 12:7–8). We are members one of another (Rom. 12:5), and we cannot deny our need for the gifts and functions of one another (1 Cor. 12:21). If this arrangement has been established by God, how do we dare to overthrow the divine order? If we prohibit the exercise of gifts which God has given, we can only weaken and distort the body life of all the members.

The Need for a Clear Message

We had been asked to tell about our work to a group of missionary wives in a foreign country; and as we started, we noticed that one woman seemed transfixed. We assumed that the intent listener was preparing an elaborate rebuttal.

No sooner was the meeting thrown open for discussion than she burst out, "You can't imagine how important this is to me! Last summer my husband and I were home on deputation and visited the churches that support us. In some churches I was forbidden to speak, on the basis of 1 Corinthians 14:34–35 and 1 Timothy 2:12. Other churches took an opposite position and insisted that I must go into the pulpit and tell about my work because they were supporting me.

"By the time I got back to the field, I was terribly confused. If it was wrong for me to speak about Christ and his work at home, then it must also be wrong over here. I wondered if I should even be here as a missionary. I started reading the biographies of great missionaries such as Mary Slessor, Gladys Aylward, and Lillian Dickson; and I wondered what would have happened if they had kept silent."

The woman's agony had been compounded because she served in a country whose government opposes Christian ministry, nor do women there enjoy as high a position as they do in America. Since the mission's mail was sometimes opened by postal officials, she dared not write asking for help with her dilemma. Furthermore, her mission specialized in the preparation and distribution of the Bible. Was she being unfaithful to a basic precept in the Word of God?

How tragic that the message of our churches had confused a missionary of the cross! Scripture calls us to communicate a clear message. Paul asks: "If a musical instrument, whether a flute or a harp, does not have a distinction in its tones, how will anyone understand what is piped or played? And if a trumpet gives out a confused sound, who will prepare themselves for war?" (1 Cor. 14:7–8). The same chapter declares that God is not the author of confusion (1 Cor. 14:33). If women have failed to prepare themselves for the war against sin, evil, unbelief, poverty, hunger, and injustice, often it is because they have received an unclear signal. Yet the call of Christ is clarion-clear. Women are called to give all of themselves—gifts, talents, training, intelligence, and aptitude—to his service. It is our obligation to wrestle with the apparently contradictory texts which act as a deterrent and to find an appropriate resolution.

A Practical and Theological Problem

Perhaps the most difficult of the perplexities attendant on this passage is verse 15, "she shall be saved by childbearing." Here the problems are both practical and theological. At the practical level, there is sometimes a connection made between Eve and the process of childbirth. Grantly Dick Reed, a pioneer in natural childbirth, maintained that the distortion of such Scriptures served to increase the anxiety and tension, and therefore the pain, of women during parturition. Deliveries are easier and safer if women do not feel that they are paying for the sin of Eve!

On the theological level, those who believe that salvation is by faith alone have a hard time explaining how women might be saved by childbearing. Timothy is told that the Scriptures can make him "wise unto salvation" (2 Tim. 3:15). Do not women also need the Scriptures to tell them of God's plan of redemption? Can they indeed find salvation in an obstetrical process rather than in the atonement of Jesus Christ? There is the further difficulty that many women pass into eternity without ever having given birth to a child. Are they not saved?

Some have suggested that the childbearing refers to Mary's having brought Christ into the world, or to the fulfillment of the prophecy that Eve's seed should bruise the serpent's head (Gen. 3:15). Both of these explanations may well have some validity, but they are not wholly satisfactory, especially as the text says "*she* shall be saved through the childbearing if *they* continue . . . " To whom does the text refer, what is meant by "childbearing," and how might the first readers have understood the saying?

An eminent and highly conservative New Testament scholar recently told us that he could not imagine that the apostle Paul or any other New Testament writer wrote verse 15. If we believe that this verse is part of the canon, it behooves us to address ourselves to its difficulties, along with those in the rest of the passage. It is possible to understand this whole section of Scripture in a positive and constructive manner.

PART 1

Approaching the Text in Its Context

Approaching the Bible with Faith

All of us need to be equipped to come to the Bible with our perplexities, especially when we do not know where to turn for human help. Blessedly, certain guiding principles can give us direction when we are bewildered as to God's will and purpose for our life. Any time that we are dealing with controversial issues, it is important to keep these principles before us.

The Bible's Basic Message

When we approach the study of Scripture, we need first to think of the scope of its message. The Bible is *not* a book of oppression—for women or anyone else. It has repeatedly proven to be an instrument of liberation for God's people. It records the deliverance of the children of Israel from slavery, it relates how Israel was delivered again and again from the hand of her oppressors, and it insists upon humane treatment for disadvantaged persons. It goes on to tell of our deliverance from the manifold bondage of sin. It offers hope for the poor, comfort for the afflicted, identity for the disenfranchised, and justice for the dispossessed. A stated purpose is to set the prisoner free.

The most powerful exaltation of the Word of God, Psalm 119, contains within it a corollary message of liberation. The psalmist describes again and again the oppression which he endures and states his confidence that he will find deliverance by means of the Scriptures. Those who dwell upon God's Word are encouraged to find liberation within it:

> Plead thou my cause and set me free, quicken me according to thy word (v. 154).
>
> Behold mine affliction, and deliver me, for I do not forget thy law (v. 153).
>
> I have done justice and righteousness; thou wilt not leave me to mine oppressors (v. 121).
>
> Be surety for thy servant for good; let not the proud oppress me (v. 122).
>
> Set me free from the oppression of man, and I will observe thy precepts (v. 134).

Though the psalm is a long one, the reader will be rewarded by studying it, especially verses 22, 44–46, 49–51, 86, 92–95, 117. The psalmist declares that the commandments of God vindicate themselves (v. 151), that they are righteous and faithful (v. 138), and that they bring deliverance to the oppressed (vv. 39–42). Is not our God a God of justice and love, and did not Jesus say that he came to preach liberty to those who were oppressed?

The twofold message of liberation and commitment to Scripture speaks directly to the dilemma that faces us in 1 Timothy 2:12. We are caught between the apparent contradictions with regard to women and our belief that all of the Bible is truly God's message to us. Often it seems that we must abandon either our view of the Bible as our only infallible rule of faith and practice, or else we must deny the full equality of all persons before God.

The Rule of Faith and Practice

Long ago, when we were students, Inter Varsity Christian Fellowship had introduced a one-month lay training institute to prepare Christian college students to deal with the attacks upon the Christian faith which were our daily lot in the secular classroom. Our instructor was Cornelius Van Til of Westminster Theological Seminary. He taught us that the Bible, if it is truly the Word of God, will hold up to intense scrutiny; that we can dissect it, shake it in a test tube, grind it fine, and analyze it carefully. If we find apparent contradictions, this is an invitation, not to discard the Bible, but to study further.

We need to come to the Bible with just such a faith when we deal with the hard issues—not only those of doctrine but also those of Christian behavior. If we can develop a hermeneutic of faith which will apply to the better understanding of gender roles in the economy of God, the same methodology may well serve us in circumstances which the church of Jesus Christ cannot now fully envision. The twenty-first century will surely bring theological debates of a nature different from any we have known, but the same Lord can guide us into all truth through the Word of God which shall not pass away.

In our own day, one of these legitimate questions concerns the biblical role and status of women. Some point to Genesis 3:16, 20 and to the restrictive statements of the apostle Paul and lay out a carefully circumscribed area of women's activities in church, home, and society. Others lay hold of Galatians 3:28 and claim the traditions of Deborah, Miriam, and Hulda, and of the women who at Christ's command first went to herald to the men their resurrected Lord. The issue is far from resolved and calls for commitments of which we would like to speak.

We are not dealing simply with a collection of ancient texts. This is the Word of God, given as light for our minds, cleansing for our souls, and nourishment for our spirits. We believe that in the Bible God has truly spoken to us. If that Word appears oppressive, contradictory, and unjust, then there are questions which need to be asked, alternatives which need to be pursued; but it is still the Word of God, still to be heeded as the words of life.

Here is where faith comes in. We believe that the Bible may contain paradoxes, perplexities, and problems but not outright contradictions. If God gave us a message, it is one which may be believed and acted upon, one upon which we may stake our very lives. And so we must travel with the faith that there is a resolution for this issue, even if that resolution is not immediately apparent.

David said, "Righteous art thou, O Lord, and right are thy judgments. Thou hast appointed thy testimonies in righteouess and in all faithfulness" (Ps. 119:137–38). We cannot abandon our belief that the Bible is indeed a message and not just a muddle. We do not denigrate Paul or his theology; rather, we must say that Paul deserves to be further studied.

Steps of Faith

What, then, are we to do? First, let us resort to the weapon of prayer, spread out our perplexities before God, and ask for the wisdom which is promised to any who will ask. We believe that the Holy Spirit is the one who gave us the Scriptures and that the Holy Spirit is our foremost teacher in understanding them.

A hermeneutic of faith also asks for commitment. We must be willing to be changed by what we read. In the conclusion to this book, we shall argue that 1 Timothy 2:9–15 has a positive, life-changing message of empowerment for women. Let us approach the Word of God with silence and submission (1 Tim. 2:11). The phrase *silence and submission,* a formula used in the ancient Near East, indicates readiness to hear the will of God and to obey it. God asks of us receptivity to heed and to obey.

This does not mean that we will be able to approach the Bible completely without preconceived notions. All of us bring our prejudices with us. It is important, though, to be honest about this. It is much better to admit to ourselves and others that we have certain viewpoints and to understand what presuppositions we have held as we read. We need to ask, have we read our own convictions into the text? Have we been fair to other viewpoints? Then we must be ready to alter our perspectives in accordance with light from the Word.

Loving God with Our Minds

The Bible tells us that God is love, and that the outcome of that love was a divine gift. When we read the Scriptures, it is because we love the Author and long for a deeper understanding of God. We are told to love God with all of our hearts, and in turn we may trust that marvelous and everlasting Love, even when we are confronted with a seemingly harsh passage.

The Bible further commands us to love God with all our minds. We must at this point get out our scholarly tools and apply them diligently. We need to obey the command to compare Scripture with Scripture. No less a thoroughgoing fundamentalist than the late L. E. Maxwell, president of Prairie Bible Institute, declared that more than a hundred passages in the Bible affirm women in roles of leadership, and fewer than half a dozen appear to be in opposition. We need to go through all of the relevant passages carefully. Could we be mistaken about Deborah, the prophet, judge, and general? Do we understand what it was that Jesus directed the women to do on Easter morning? Why does Micah say, "Have I not sent Moses and Aaron and Miriam before thee to lead thee?" (Mic. 6:4). Against these must be balanced the difficult Pauline passages, as well as all their exegetical problems, in 1 Corinthians 11:3–14; 14:34–35; and 1 Timothy 2:11–15.

It would be quite easy to give up, rather smug in our belief that the larger set of positive passages is quite direct, whereas the passages apparently representing a negative point of view are plagued with problems.[1] But they are still the Word of God, still God's message to us. We cannot deny the difficulties or ignore them. We believe that there is a resolution to the difficulties if we search for it with faith and diligent study. Jesus said, "Seek, and ye shall find." Part of our faith is that, like wrestling Jacob, we do not let go until we have reached a satisfactory conclusion.

Inspiration and Interpretation

We need to make a careful distinction between inspiration, the action by which God gave the Word to humanity, and interpretation, the human process by which we perceive its meaning. The divine message came through some ordinary people—farmers, fishermen, shepherds—but through them and their very human experiences, God spoke. Many types of literary endeavors were involved. Poets, dreamers, and prosaic chroniclers made their contribution, and editors played their part, all under the guidance of the Holy Spirit. That is God's side.

Then there is our side. We might think of our response to a work of art. It has been created by an artist, but we must respond with our own imagination, knowledge, and creativity to what we see before us. We might imagine something wholly fanciful, especially if we are looking at surrealistic art, but sometimes the artist supplies objective reality by labeling the work "Geraniums in the kitchen window" or "Portrait of the artist by himself." Then our interpretive response should include this knowledge. We may be helped further by an acquaintance with the artist's concerns and particular interests, teachers, family, nationality, period in history, sources of inspiration and influence, colleagues, and so forth.

If we read a book or hear a piece of music, we must expend our own energy to draw significance from it. The more effort we invest in the process, the better we shall understand the work and the intent of the author or composer. This is interpretation. It is not a purely subjective exercise, though it includes a personal element. Just so the Bible requires interpretation, and the process is a challenging one.

Some methods of interpretation appear more legitimate than others. One gigantic man tired of Cathie's efforts to deal with the original language and context of 1 Timothy 2:12. He pulled himself up to the full extent of his enormous height and said, "I think God has given an indication of who should have the power by giving one sex bigger muscles." This is not one of the preferred methods of interpretation, and we shall suggest other routes to understanding the text.

Interpretation

Essentially, this is a book about the interpretation of 1 Timothy 2:9–15. Most people are quick to tell you that the passage is a difficult one and requires careful interpretation. This is surely true, and not everyone will have the same perspective. The same might be said of many another passage of Scripture. We all know earnest, Bible-believing folk who may interpret a given passage differently from others and organize whole churches around their own interpretation.

Some Christians maintain that the correct interpretation of 1 Timothy 2:9–15 is the traditional one. They feel that no interpretation is necessary. Yet all of us interpret every passage of the Bible in one way or another. For instance, few of us understand Psalm 23 to mean that God is literally leading us through the Palestinian wilderness or causing us to feed upon vegetation suitable for sheep. Ordinarily we interpret this psalm as a beautiful allegory of God's loving provision for us. If we were to construe this portion of Scripture literally, we should gain a most bizarre comprehension of God's relationship with his people. Instead we look carefully at all the material we can assemble about sheepherding in the ancient Near East. The practices were quite different from modern American sheep-raising with its watering troughs, barbed-wire fences, and herding with a pick-up truck.

David had spent his own youth caring for sheep; about three thousand years ago, he composed a song based upon personal experience. As any Bible teacher knows, research into the ways of a Hebrew shepherd will give us a grasp of what David was describing. With this picture in our minds, we can then make a spiritual application to our own lives. God does not literally lead us as sheep, but the Lord's care is as tender and complete as was that of the ancient shepherd. Like sheep, we must follow the guidance of our heavenly Shepherd. The psalm is an extended metaphor, and we can comprehend it only if we accept it as such and understand something of its context.

In the same manner, the story of Jesus' arrest, trial, and crucifixion would make little sense to us if we did not understand something about Roman and Jewish systems of government and justice. We must comprehend the role of the temple and the Roman soldiers, what the Sanhedrin was, why three trials were involved before Jesus could be executed, the official status of Pontius Pilate, the nature of Herod's relationship to the Roman government, how crucifixion was carried out, and the accepted mode of Jewish burial. When we tell the story of Christ's death, we are careful to include these explanations so that people can understand the narrative as it appears in the Gospels. A knowledge of the context is necessary to clarify the biblical account. Otherwise the story might be open to serious misunderstanding.

Such a consideration of context is essential in approaching the Pauline passages on women. We need first to see Paul as one trained at the feet of Gamaliel in rabbinic tradition. As such, he was fully aware of the consequences of a Jewish woman removing her veil in a public gathering. But Paul was also a Roman citizen who was at home in the Greco-Roman world. He alone of the apostles appears to have been comfortable in dealing with non-Judaized Gentiles.

If we would understand the rationale of this missionary to the Gentiles, we must understand the worship practices of pagan women, for they differed extensively from those of men. We must also recognize that Paul had been born at Tarsus and retained a deep commitment to proclaiming the gospel in his native Asia Minor. His missionary travels repeatedly took him deep into the heart of Anatolia, to an intimate knowledge of those forms of religion which were practiced there, especially by women. We must look closely at the religious currents which swirled around Ephesus on the west coast of Asia Minor, to which 1 Timothy 2:9–15 is addressed.

Principles of Exegesis

Historical and cultural context is important, but there are many other considerations as well. As we begin, we need to examine the textual tradition. Is it reliable? For instance, 1 Corinthians 14:34–35 occurs at two separate points in some of the early texts. This raises a question as to whether it might not originally have been a gloss which slipped into the text. The mandate occurs in all versions of 1 Corinthians 14, however, and appears to be an authentic part of the epistle.

Next we should ask, "What does the text say?" Here a knowledge of the biblical languages is critical. Too often we leave mastery of the Bible in its original tongues to a rarefied and élitist group. We need instead a far stronger and more widespread competence in Greek, Hebrew, and other related languages. In each new generation, we must return to the texts to grapple with new situations which have arisen in our contemporary society. New questions must be posed of the old Scriptures.

When it really matters, we must get back to the fundamental text rather than putting ourselves at the mercy of translators. We must also be wary lest we be influenced by the unwarranted additions which some translators insert into the text. Most of the older versions at least italicized the words which had been added, so that one could be aware of the insertions; but modern versions and paraphrases often have no such italics to help the English reader discern what actually does or does not appear in the text. One widely-used paraphrase of 1 Timothy 2:14–15 adds these words: "And it was not Adam who was fooled by Satan, but Eve, and sin was the result. So God sent pain and suffering to women when their children are born, but he will save their souls if they trust in him, living quiet, good, and loving lives" (LB). Such a rendering inserts into the biblical text the notion that pain in childbirth is a punishment upon women for the sin of Eve. This misconception increases the fear of women as they approach the experience of childbirth and thereby intensifies the pain. This is simply not warranted by a literal translation of the Greek text, which reads, "And Adam was not deceived, but Eve being absolutely deceived was in the transgression. Nevertheless she shall be saved through the childbearing if they continue in faith and love and holiness with self-control." Even if the literal translation leaves the perplexities unresolved, accurate knowledge of the original text is essential if we are to deal with the problems. (For a discussion of this text, see chapter 16.)

Considerations of Language

Next comes the matter of language. Is there more than one meaning for some of the words employed in the passage? If there are other established meanings for a certain term, what sense would their utilization give to the passage?

A prime example is 1 Timothy 2:12, where a verb occurs which is used nowhere else in the New Testament. The problem is vexatious because in a case where a word occurs but once, the lexicographer often simply follows the translator and declares that it has such-and-such a value in New Testament Greek. *Authentein*, the verb in question, is defined in New Testament dictionaries as meaning to usurp authority or to dominate, although Greek writers used the term to imply other values such as to kill someone, to begin something or be responsible for the initiation of something, to lay claim to property as being one's own, to claim to be the author of something, and so forth. To translate that one verb differently changes the sense of the entire passage. This text, which causes women so much perplexity, can be rendered in a variety of ways. We shall explore the possibilities.

The Greek word for silence has at least five different meanings in the New Testament in particular and in Greek religion as a whole. What indication of this should we give in the passages dealing with women?

Considerations of Grammar and Context

Then there is the matter of grammar. Is there an unexpected construction which might give another interpretation? First Timothy 2:12 can perhaps be construed as an indirect statement with a redundant negative so that the emphasis is upon the content that women are forbidden to teach rather than upon their teaching or administrative function. We were explaining our interpretation and its grammatical basis to a friend who is a classicist. Suddenly she exclaimed, "Oh, I see! It can be an infinitive of indirect discourse—telling what it is that women shouldn't teach. Could it mean, then, that the Bible isn't blaming women for what

Eve did?" We nodded. She blurted out, "I couldn't stand the way the church has condemned all women for that. If what you are saying is true, then I might want to be a Christian!"

Loving God with Our Strength

If our love of God demands hard mental effort, let us not forget also to love God with all our strength. It is our responsibility to exercise the most serious scholarly endeavor of which we are capable. This means a thorough knowledge of the exegesis of other scholars, including those with whom we disagree. Lamentably, evangelical scholarship has not always been of a level of excellence that earned the respect of nonevangelicals. Let us acknowledge that we are called to a long-term effort. If we believe that there are solutions to our perplexities, let us commit ourselves to finding them. We cannot claim to have all the answers, but we can profess a faith that they are there if we continue to seek them.

Loving God with all one's mind requires time and energy and effort. There is a great deal of work to be done in language study and exegesis, and there are no shortcuts. In addition, this means gaining a mastery of materials which we may find repulsive—evidence about fertility cults of women or pagan rites, and impure literature. Worse yet, the path is often wearisome and tedious. Blessedly, God is our strength and can do for us what we cannot do for ourselves.

If we are to love with all our strength, we must have the courage to refute those interpretations which do violence to the Word of God or to the people of God. We must speak out against those who justify the abuse of women by citing Scripture; we must be very clear that the Bible forbids roles of leadership to those who strike another (1 Tim. 3:3; Titus 1:7). For example, a child protection worker in a Southern state was working with cases of incest. The families sometimes called on the pastor to remonstrate with her when she was seeking to establish a safe environment for a child. On more than one occasion, she was told that 1 Timothy 2:12 prohibited her from giving any direction to the child's father, the pastor, or the elders and deacons. When the weak are wronged by those from liberal or conservative camps, we must on biblical principles refute their actions.

The Transforming Power of God's Word

The second part of the Great Commandment bids us love our neighbor as ourselves. We love because Scripture has convinced us that all are made by God in God's own image, and that Jesus Christ came to redeem all. Surely this means treating all human beings with respect and seeking to bring each one to her or his highest potential. Gender, age, social condition, and racial considerations are all swept away by Galatians 3:28. The Great Commandment calls us both to respect the insights of other Christians and yet to bear to needy people our distinctive message. The Bible calls us to manifest the love of Christ in every dimension of life.

If the Bible calls us, it also transforms us. We believe that the Word of God is alive and powerful and capable of making us new. As we see the light of God's Word fall upon others, our attitudes toward them change. Let us illustrate with an experience in our own lives. As far back as Cathie can remember, an old piano had lain discarded in the dark loft above the barn adjoining the house which her great-great-grandfather built in 1799. As children, she and her sister used to squeeze behind the keyboard and marvel at the tinkly sounds which they could elicit. She once asked her mother why the piano was relegated to the loft, and her mother replied, "It just didn't work out in the house."

As the years passed, Cathie sometimes wondered whether we should not try to preserve the old instrument, but there really seemed no reason to accord it any better treatment than her parents had given it. It would surely pose a threat to our pocketbook and the established arrangement of our other furnishings. Then came Dick's retirement and a permanent move to Cape Cod, and he decided that the loft should be used for storage. It was time for the old junk up there to be carted to the dump, but it seemed only civilized to have someone who knew about old pianos check out the beloved childhood toy. We coaxed a conservator up the rickety ladder, and he flashed his torch beam upon the words above the keyboard. That one ray of light revealed that the piano had been made at London in 1821 by John Broadwood, a major figure in the development of the modern piano. There could be no doubt as to its historic significance.

Subsequently the piano was cleaned of mouse nests and other dirt, lowered, and brought out into the light of day where the gilt lettering and fine craftsmanship were clearly evident. We can never again treat the old piano as a third-rate piece of furniture, although the instrument is still decrepit. The conservator declared its restoration to be beyond his skill, nor was his old teacher willing to tackle the project. We came to the uncomfortable realization that something was required of us. Of course we could give the piano to a museum or sell it. But we are told that the Boston Museum of Fine Arts already has many such instruments waiting to be repaired. How can we consign our old friend to the museum basement? If we are to make the piano truly our own, the restoration will take a great deal of professional assistance and research and caring and expense and hard labor. We hope that some day it will again give forth the music for which it was designed.

The work of the conservator in illumination and cleaning resembles the work of the Word of God in teaching us to look at people in new ways, to ask new questions. Once we have seen the disadvantaged, the poor, the homeless, the afflicted, the fatherless, and the stranger within our gates in the light of their true worth as revealed in God's Word, we can no longer continue in our old heedless patterns. Nor will mere patronization suffice. Our hermeneutic of faith demands behavior transformed by the power of the Holy Spirit.

Do God's people call for less? How hard are we ready to work at freeing and enabling women for the service of Christ? Are we willing to risk the effort?

"I am thy servant; give me understanding that I may know thy testimonies! Redeem me from man's oppression, that I may keep thy precepts" (Ps. 119:125, 134).

The Pastoral Epistles
Who Wrote Them and Why

Suppose a man wrote to his son, "I am proud of you." If the boy had just written that he would be graduating *summa cum laude*, we could readily understand what the father meant. On the other hand, if the father had learned from the dean's office that the boy had gotten himself into a series of unfortunate scrapes, the words could mean something quite different. Perhaps the words were written in bitter sarcasm, or perhaps the father remembered his own college days and was amused. We would have to read the rest of the letter in order to determine the father's real meaning. In the same way, the meaning of an isolated verse of the Bible is best illuminated by its context.

When we address ourselves to a study of a passage which has occasioned so much pain, conflict, and bitterness, we must not expect that our task will be an easy one. It will require careful examination of both text and context. We need to understand as much as we can not only about the immediate situation but also about the wider circumstances that lay behind the epistle as a whole. We shall enter a world whose thought patterns were far different from our own, whose religious presuppositions may shock us, whose basic social and cultural organization will seem alien indeed. This very disparity is a major part of the problem in understanding Paul's message to women.

The Occasion

Our target verse occurs in the First Epistle to Timothy, one of three epistles which are often viewed as a unity. The Second Epistle to Timothy, as well as the Epistle to Titus, address the same problems and concerns, use the same language, and share a common point of view. Titus, often thought to have been written earlier, is a rougher and shorter version of much of the same material which appears in a more fully developed form in First Timothy. Titus purports to be addressed to Paul's associate of that name in Crete, while both epistles to Timothy are directed to the man described as Paul's son in the faith at Ephesus.

Churches under Siege

Although the documents which we will discuss are known as the pastoral Epistles, we have increasingly become aware that these letters address churches under siege. These churches are threatened by those within their ranks who endanger the Christian community with their false teaching and opposition to the truth. More than 20 percent of the material in these epistles deals with the false teachers and their erroneous doctrine, while much of the other content deals with setting the situation right and offering an antidote to heterodoxy. A. T. Hanson observed that the primary aim of the writer of the pastoral Epistles was "the instruction of contemporary church leaders in how to deal with the false teaching (probably incipient Gnosticism) with which they were faced."[1] Helmut Koester wrote, "In their fight against heresies, the Pastoral Epistles are designed to be a handbook, a manual for the church leader."[2]

Often we glorify the New Testament church, and it is hard to accept such a dismaying picture of heresy and bitter strife. The truth is that virtually every book in the New Testament warns of false prophets and false teachers, and that the churches of the New Testament were beset with many false doctrines and impurities. The behavior of some of their members was appalling and their church squabbles no better than those of today. The good news is that the same God who brought his people and his church through so many troubles is still able to guide, sustain, and deliver your church and ours in this present day.

The major passages in the Pastorals which refer to the opposition are 1 Timothy 1:3–11, 19–20; 4:1–10; 6:3–5, 20–21; 2 Timothy 1:1–15; 2:14–18, 23; 3:1–9, 13; 4:3–4; Titus 1:10–16; 3:9–11. Earnest Christians are often surprised to find that one of their favorite verses of Scripture actually occurs in one of these sections about false teaching.

> Call these things to people's mind, and charge them before God not to fight over words, which is a useless exercise that is destructive to the hearers. *Be zealous to present yourself as tested and proven to God, a laborer unashamed, rightly dividing the word of truth.* But avoid foolish babblings which are opposed to God, for they lead people to further ungodliness. And their teaching will spread like a cancer. Among them are Hymenaeus and Philetus, who have missed the mark concerning the truth by saying that the resurrection has already taken place, and they are upsetting the faith of some. [2 Tim. 2:14–18, emphasis added]

The servant of God was to provide an antidote to such sick teaching, to rightly divide the Word (2 Tim. 2:15), and to use it for doctrine, reproof, correction, and instruction in righteousness (2 Tim. 3:16).

Our conception of First Timothy is usually based upon the presupposition that it was written as a manual on ecclesiastical government for a church not much different from our own. The reality may come as a distinct surprise. The letter is addressed to a church in turmoil, threatened by heresy in its midst and fraught with bitter disputes over matters of faith and practice. That church was in dire need of practical and spiritual direction.

The author has departed but left Timothy behind with instructions to "stop certain people from teaching a different doctrine and embroiling themselves in myths" (1 Tim. 1:3–4). The epistle was initially a guidebook about how to cope with this specific problem. By the work of the Holy Spirit, many of its instructions are still relevant today and help believers to live, worship, serve, and make decisions in the Christian community.

Authorship

The writer claims to be the apostle Paul (1 Tim. 1:1), but the authorship and date of these epistles are hotly debated. Some scholars ascribe the work to Paul or to his amanuensis, for many of the Pauline epistles were written as a joint effort. Jerome Quinn, Walter Liefeld, and others[3] look to Luke as author, a possibility which is heightened by the note, "Only Luke is with me" (2 Tim. 4:11).[4] Others would assign the work to a more Catholic author at the beginning of the second century.[5]

Scholars have noted in the Pastorals the use of vocabulary that was current in the second-century emperor cult. This cult, however, flourished very early in western Asia Minor, and the only extant copies of the *Res Gestae* of the divinized emperor Augustus (d. C.E. 14) have all been discovered in the area.[6] The emperor Domitian (C.E. 81–96) built a temple to himself in Ephesus in the first century. It is sometimes charged that the pastoral Epistles reflect a more sophisticated form of church administration than would have been possible in the first century. In response, one might point out that while the Pastorals are quite specific as to the qualifications necessary to hold certain ecclesiastical offices, the duties are not spelled out with similar precision. The job descriptions may have developed later. Some have questioned whether the churches at so early a period would have had officers at all. Yet it does not take long for any new organization to select and install officers, and the appointment of presbyters attached to Jewish synagogues was already well established in the first century.[7]

The latest possible date for the composition of the Pastorals is the last quarter of the second century, when allusion is made to the work by Irenaeus, Tatian, and Theophilus of Antioch. Tertullian also knew these documents. Therefore they must be supposed to have been written at a time early enough to allow for so widespread a readership in the second century.[8]

We prefer a date in the first century of the common era and a writer who is well acquainted with the cultural and religious aspects of Asia Minor. A native of Tarsus in the province of Cilicia will do nicely, though we would argue for the involvement of at least one other hand in the composition. Possibly the epistle was written upon the instruction of the apostle Paul but completed after his death as his will and testament (*parathēkē*) to Timothy (1 Tim. 6:20; 2 Tim. 1:12, 14).

The author writes with the authority of Paul and offers two sources of reliable doctrine amid the confusion and bickering of a troubled religious community. Since the New Testament had not yet been codified, it was necessary to guide the reader in finding a base for one's tenets of faith. First, the author points to the Hebrew Scriptures as medicine for the sickness of false doctrine (1 Tim. 1:10; 6:3; 2 Tim. 4:3; Titus 1:9; 2:1). The second basis for faith which the writer offers is the instruction and example which he himself has given.

This instruction, to be sure, has been based upon the Hebrew Bible; but the writer has gone on to apply the gospel in a relevant manner to an emerging church. In contrast to the "fables and endless genealogies" which produced only bickerings, he, as a legitimate emissary of Christ, offers "godly edification (*oikonomia theou*) in the faith" (1 Tim. 1:4). *Oikonomia*, in the sense of God's plan or arrangement, is used several times in other epistles when Paul's appointment as an apostle is under discussion (Eph. 3:2, 8–9; Col. 1:25).

The author expects his audience to understand that he himself has interacted with this community and laid down a foundation for their faith. He writes in confidence to a "son in the faith," an appointed official of the church, but he nevertheless appears to expect others to recognize his concerns.

It seems to us that the state of emergency described in the letters argues for the involvement of Paul in their composition. In the swirling intensity of the bitter controversy, it would have been imperative for a young leader to make sure that he was well acquainted with the source of any advice which he received upon the matter. The letters address a specific crisis, with which the writer expresses familiarity.

While the same general aspects appear in the epistle to Titus, the two missives to Timothy contain some detailed specifics of the situation at Ephesus. Hymenaeus and Alexander have left the faith and have been repudiated by the writer (1 Tim. 1:19–20). Timothy is cautioned especially about Alexander the coppersmith, who treated the writer injuriously and withstood his words (2 Tim. 4:14–15). Hymenaeus and Philetus maintained that the resurrection was already past and turned others away from the faith (2 Tim. 2:17). In other words, the author maintains that he has had experiences of personal and specific interaction with at least some of his opponents. If these details did not correlate with actual conditions known to the original recipient, the letter would have been suspect and hardly likely to have been preserved.

Many other touches seem genuine, such as the identification of Eunice and Lois in the upbringing of Timothy (2 Tim. 1:5), the personal greetings and instructions (2 Tim. 4:9–22; Titus 3:12–15), and even the appeal for a coat and parchments which had been left behind (2 Tim. 4:13). These are nonpolemic and occur in the beginnings or the endings of the epistles, where they might more easily be added from another letter or manufactured by someone wishing to simulate an epistle of Paul. The names and characteristics of the opponents, however, form part of the basic argument against false doctrine and could far less plausibly be fabricated or inserted.

Nevertheless our argument is not tied to a specific system of dating or authorship but rather to an interpretation related to the dominant theme of First Timothy: how does a new church deal with members immersed in false doctrine and in misbehavior justified by muddled theology? Thus, our discussion is directed not at the authorship, but at the message and intent of the author. For convenience, the name *Paul* will at times be used to designate the writer of the pastoral Epistles.

3

Destination: Ephesus

The writer of First Timothy specifies that the epistle is being sent to a leader of the Christian community at Ephesus (1 Tim. 1:3). To be sure, scholarly opinion has not been unanimous in an opinion that the letter was indeed directed to this city. Nevertheless, the author intended his readers to understand his message within a situation specific to Ephesus, and the deliberate mention of this world-famous city evoked certain connotations. This literary imperative calls us to deal with the treatise against a backdrop of the city's social, cultural, and religious traditions.

The city of Ephesus, the fourth largest in the Roman Empire, lay on the western coast of modern Turkey, ancient Asia Minor (see map 1). It was not an easy place in which to bring the Christian message. In early times there had been a shrine to a female deity, and tradition held that the original image had been brought by Amazons, women warriors from the land of the Taurians on the Black Sea. This idol was first placed in an oak tree but was later removed to a sanctuary, about which the rest of the habitation grew. The original inhabitants were Lydians, Phrygians, Lycians, and Mysians; in about 1000 B.C.E., Ionian Greeks from the opposite side of the Aegean Sea invaded and then settled in the area.

The western coast of Asia Minor was known as Ionia, for the dominant civilization was Greek (see map 2). The epics of Homer and the works of many of the pre-Socratic philosophers were com-

47

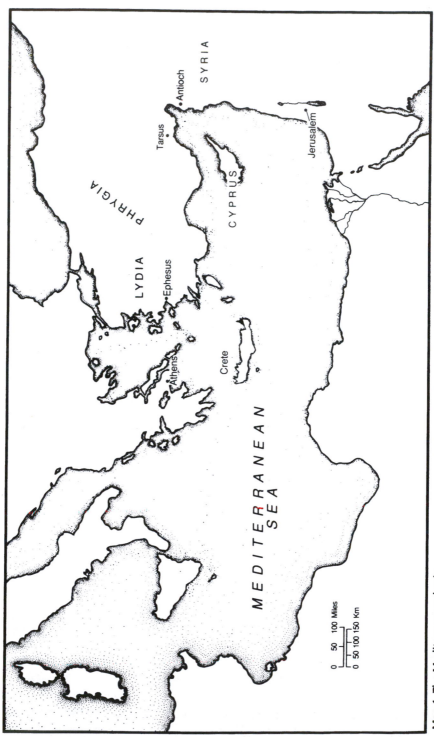

Map 1. The Mediterranean basin.

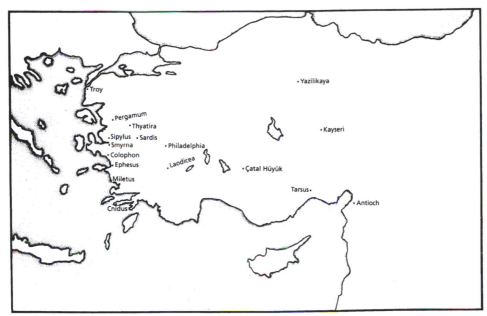

Map 2. Western Asia Minor.

posed in Ionia rather than in mainland Greece. From this Greek heritage first-century Ephesus still drew a love of philosophy.

> Who will destroy the safety of Ephesus, originally descended, as she is, from the purest Attic [i.e., Greek] stock, grown in size beyond all the cities which are in Ionia and Lydia, extending to the sea out beyond the land upon which it was settled, a city full of intellectuals, both philosophers and rhetoricians. The city derives its strength from ten thousand such citizens, rather than from cavalry, and makes a public commendation of wisdom. What sage, do you think, would abandon the cause of such a city?[1]

Such a boast reveals an intellectual snobbery and a zest for philosophical debate which we shall find refuted in the pastoral Epistles.

We must be mindful, however, that other elements were present as well. Ephesus was known as the gateway to Asia; and if it received Greek elements into Asia, it was also the portal through which oriental culture and tradition passed further west. The city had passed under the sway of the Cimmerians and the Lydians, had lain under Persian domination for nearly two hundred years, and had passed too under the rule of Sardis, Macedonia, and Pergamum, and, ultimately, Rome.[2] When we deal with the religion of Ephesus, we must not forget the importance of oriental strands in the tapestry. We shall argue that at least one element derives distinctively from the interior of Asia Minor—that of mother goddess cults.

The Great Mother of the Gods

In contrast to other parts of the ancient world, the primary deities in Asia Minor were female; and the maternal aspect was glorified in a manner almost unknown farther west. By 5000 B.C.E. Anatolian artists modeled heavyset mother goddesses from clay and depicted repeatedly the moment of birth (see illustration 1). For millennia the matriarchal goddesses reigned supreme, and their images are found in great abundance at archaeological sites (see illustrations 2 and 3). The Great Mother was given many names in different parts of Asia Minor, but she bore the same

Illustration 1. Clay figurine of a goddess giving birth (note the infant's head between the mother's feet). The figure is from a shrine at Çatal Hüyük.

Museum of Anatolian Civilization, Ankara

characteristics. Whether Great Mother of the Gods, the Mountain Mother, Ma, Bellona, Cybele, Demeter, or Artemis, she was the mother of gods and men, the mistress of wild animals. From her came all life, and the dead were gathered again to her womb. She stood guard over the tombs of her devotees.

These goddesses left their stamp upon successive generations and cultures. Neighboring Sardis, like Ephesus, was distinguished by its devotion to a strong mother goddess. In the first century C.E., Apollonius of Tyana wrote to the Sardians: "You have good reason to worship and honor the goddess of your ancestor. She is named 'mother of the gods' according to some, 'mother of humanity' according to others, and everyone agrees that she is 'mother of the crops.' But she is indeed the one common mother of all people. Why then do you alone,

Illustrations 2, 3. Images of mother goddesses from Horoztepe (end of the third millennium B.C.E.)
Museum of Anatolian Civilization, Ankara

being Demeter's own, have clans that are at enmity with law, nature, and established custom?"[3] We shall later see that most of the titles ascribed to the Great Mother were later given to Eve by heretical Gnostics in Asia Minor.

Artemis of Ephesus

The most famous shrine of the great mother goddess lay at Ephesus, where she was revered as Artemis, or *Oupis* as the earlier population had called her. The Romans knew her as Diana of the Ephesians. Pausanias reported that there was a shrine to the Ephesian Artemis in every Greek city throughout the Mediterranean world and that in private devotion she was the most worshiped of all the gods.[4] An official decree made by the people of Ephesus in about C.E. 163 proclaimed:

> Since the goddess Artemis, leader of our city, is honoured not only in her own homeland, which she has made the most illustrious of all cities through her own divine nature, but also among Greeks and also barbarians, the result is that everywhere her shrines and sanctuaries have been established, and temples have been founded for her and altars dedicated to her because of the visible manifestations effected by her.[5]

Her temple at Ephesus, where thousands of persons, both male and female, served the goddess, was one of the seven wonders of the world. (Illustration 4 shows an ancient coin that portrays the great temple and Artemis's image in it.)

The temple had been regarded as a sanctuary ever since the Amazons first took refuge there from Hercules. It was a place of

safety in an otherwise turbulent world—one conqueror even left his wife and children within the confines of the temple. When the Romans tried to demote the city, a delegation from Ephesus argued that the status of the city should be maintained because of the haven which the temple offered.

Illustration 4. Coin showing the Artemisium.
Drawing by Louise Bauer

Within this shrine stood a statue of the goddess herself. She wore a high crown, modeled to represent the walls of the city of Ephesus; and her breastplate was covered with breast-like protuberances. Above these she wore a necklace of acorns, sometimes surrounded by the signs of the zodiac; for Artemis controlled the heavenly bodies of the universe. On the front of her stiff narrow skirt were rows of triplet animals, and on the sides bees and rosettes—an indication of her dominion over childbirth, animal life, and fertility (see illustration 5). An elaborate system of magic developed upon the *Ephesia Grammata*, the six mystic words written on the cult statue of the goddess. The Book of Acts tells

Illustration 5. Artemis of Ephesus.
Drawing by Louise Bauer

us that newly converted Christians repudiated this system and burned their costly books of magic (Acts 19:19).

Religious conditions, the ancients maintained, were remarkably similar in Crete (the destination of the Epistle to Titus) and in Ephesus.[6] Strabo (64/3 B.C.E.–C.E. 21) spoke of the intermingling of Cretan and Phrygian rites.[7] Tradition held that some of the tribal groups of western Asia Minor, such as the Carians, had originally migrated from Crete. On that island Artemis was worshiped with the same rites as in Ephesus and had been given the title "the Cretan Lady of Ephesus."[8] "The Cretans worship Artemis most religiously, calling her according to their language Britomart."[9] The Ephesian celebration of Artemis's birthday borrowed discernible elements from the older Cretan rituals honoring the birth of Zeus.

Far more than most cities, the citizens of Ephesus derived their feelings of security directly from their goddess, for in the political realm the city had seldom known independence. On two occasions the inhabitants related the safety of the city directly to the intervention of the goddess. Once, when the city was under siege by the Lydians, woolen fillets were extended from the sanctuary of Artemis and drawn around the city.[10] The Lydians respected the protection of the goddess and spared the city.

The cult of Artemis also provided the city with economic security. Countless pilgrims, attracted by the sanctity of the goddess and the fame of her temple, poured wealth into shrine and city. Of even more importance financially, the temple served as a treasury for Asia Minor, the richest province in the Roman Empire. The watchfulness of the goddess guaranteed the safety of funds deposited in the Artemisium, and it was in fact an enormous banking center.

Ephesus stood as a bastion of feminine supremacy in religion. William M. Ramsay insists that it was no coincidence that the virgin Mary was first given the official title *theotokos*, bearer of God, at Ephesus, where Artemis herself had earlier borne the same title.[11]

Judaism at Ephesus

By the mid-third century B.C.E. Ephesus and surrounding parts of Ionia were already inhabited by Jews; and in the first century B.C.E. a vigorous Jewish community was able to contend successfully for its civil rights.[12] The Jewish population may have numbered as many as seventy-five thousand persons.[13] Many lamps bearing an inscribed menorah have been recovered, and there is evidence of the involvement of Ephesian Jews in magic.[14] The Jews of Asia Minor, especially those of Phrygia, had assimilated much of the culture of their surroundings, so that there was a saying, "The baths and wines of Phrygia separated the Ten Tribes from their brethren." Certain elements of Judaism, especially the biblical stories, were adopted by the larger society. At Apameia, coins minted in the reigns of three successive rulers showed Noah's ark.[15] The legend above the box-like ark says "Noah"; but the two persons standing outside the ark indicate that the biblical account has been embellished, perhaps from the Greek flood story of Deucalion and Pyrrha. We shall have much more to say about the embellishment of narratives found in the Book of Genesis. In particular we shall deal with strange distortions of the story of Eve in which she becomes the one who gives life to Adam. While such a view is consistent with Ephesus' strong emphasis on the maternal principle, it certainly does not conform to the message of the Bible and would therefore draw an attack from the author of the Pastorals.

Christian Confrontations at Ephesus

Not only Paul but also his missionary companions, Priscilla and Aquila, found it necessary to use the Word of God in a corrective manner at Ephesus. Apollos, a Jew from Alexandria, had been proclaiming Jesus but knew only the baptism of John. Acts 18:24–28 makes it plain that he was learned in the Scriptures and that his knowledge was accurate as far as it went. He was taken aside by Priscilla and Aquila and given a more accurate and complete understanding of Jesus. After this remarkable course of instruction, Apollos argued with great power that Jesus was indeed the Messiah, and thereafter the early church called Priscilla "a teacher of teachers."

Paul himself met a group of disciples at Ephesus whose knowledge of the gospel was so incomplete that they had not even heard of the Holy Spirit. His instruction and the laying on of hands soon brought them to a full realization of God's grace (Acts 19:1–7).

In these cases, there was a satisfactory resolution; but other religious encounters at Ephesus were not always so successful. A group of strolling Jewish exorcists decided to appropriate the name of Jesus into their ritual, with unfortunate results (Acts 19:13–16). The citizenry was so impressed by the power of the name of Jesus that some of those who practiced traditional Ephesian magic burnt their books in an enormous bonfire (Acts 19:18–19). Some, but apparently not all. We shall have more to say later of the continued use of magic among certain female members of the Christian community.

What Lay behind the Riot of the Silversmiths?

Then the silversmiths, makers of silver idols and fearful that the great Artemis of Ephesus might suffer dishonor or diminution, goaded the general population into a vehement demonstration against the teaching of the apostle, a demonstration that was curbed only with difficulty (Acts 19:23–40). What could Paul have said that produced so enormous a sense of outrage among the citizens of Ephesus that for two hours straight they shouted, "Great is Artemis of the Ephesians!" (Acts 19:28, 34)? Demetrius, the instigator of the riot, maintained that he was defending the goddess and her cult against discredit and defamation. Paul, he declared, had said that "they were no gods who were made with hands. And not only is there a danger that our trade will come into disrepute, but also that the temple of the great goddess Artemis will be judged of no account and that she who is worshiped by all Asia and the civilized world will have her sublimity pulled down" (Acts 19:26–27). Demetrius implied that the apostle was teaching something detrimental to both the goddess and her celebrated temple. We know of other first-century critics who deplored practices associated with the worship of Artemis. Despite their hard words, these critics seem to have been revered rather than repudiated.[16]

The words of the town clerk make it clear, however, that Paul had not leveled a frontal attack at either the goddess or her shrine: "You know that these men are not temple desecrators nor blasphemers of our goddess" (Acts 19:37). We suggest that Paul attacked the very basis of Ephesian religion. Rather than directing his opposition to a specific deity, he may well have engaged in a more widespread denunciation of the concept of the mother goddess as the source of all life. The silversmiths may rightly have perceived that he had launched an attack upon the divine maternal principle, the concept underlying the political, economic, and social existence of Ephesus. The God whom Paul proclaimed was indeed a God made without hands, above and beyond human sexuality, the One who had breathed into humanity the breath of life. The presence of a large number of Jews demonstrates that such ideas were not unacceptable in cosmopolitan Ephesus, but a direct repudiation of the maternal as divine may have been quite another matter.

Paul's Farewell to the Ephesian Elders

After the civic riot, it was deemed expedient for Paul to pursue his labors elsewhere. His concern for the establishment of a gospel witness at Ephesus remained, however. When he started along the coast of Asia Minor on his last journey toward Jerusalem, the elders of Ephesus were summoned for a farewell visit with Saint Paul at Miletus. He reminded them of his work among them and added:

> "Watch out for yourselves and for the flock over whom the Holy Spirit has placed you as overseers, to act as shepherds to the church of God, which he purchased with his own blood. I know that grievous wolves shall come upon you after my departure, and they will not spare the flock. And *from among you yourselves there shall arise men saying distorted things in order to draw away the disciples after them.* Therefore watch out." [Acts 20:28–31a, emphasis added]

The language and theme are so close to that of the Pastorals that some scholars have suggested that the passage was inserted by the author of the Pastorals. The passage demonstrates some very Lucan syntax, however, and is far closer to the writing style of Luke than of Paul. Conservatives see this as Luke's version of Paul's speech at Miletus. We are concerned here with its message—that deviant doctrine was a threat at Ephesus.

The theme of opposition at Ephesus is apparent too in the Pauline Epistles. He had written to the Corinthians: "I shall remain in Ephesus until Pentecost, for a great and effectual door is open to me, but there are many opponents" (1 Cor. 16:8–9). Clearly Paul was aware of intense opposition at Ephesus. The

Ephesians themselves were cautioned that they should not be blown here and there by every wind of doctrine, again an indication that teaching other than Paul's own was afloat at Ephesus (Eph. 4:14). Furthermore, they received a stern warning against those who might lead them astray (Eph. 4:17–24; 5:6–14). The church at Ephesus is commended in the Book of Revelation because, unlike some of the neighboring churches, it hates the deeds of the Nicolaitans—the hatred itself revealing some form of contact with a heterodox group (Rev. 2:6).

If we are to understand the purposes of the writer, we need to evaluate the environment in which he placed his directive to women. Let us examine the document with the premise that the destination of First Timothy was indeed Ephesus, one of the major religious centers of the ancient world and the bastion of a strongly developed theological system which could not easily be displaced. Our treatment will deal with the epistle as reflecting a troubled situation in the Christian community there, especially as it applied to women and their religious concerns.

4

Identifying the Problem
Evidence from the Pastorals

W hat can we learn from the Pastorals themselves about the nature of this false teaching? The First Epistle to Timothy begins as the writer explains that he left Timothy in Ephesus in order that the young leader might "admonish certain individuals *to stop teaching a different doctrine and not to give heed to myths* and endless genealogies which produce disputations rather than upbuilding of the household of God in faith" (1 Tim. 1:3–4, emphasis added). Some of the dissidents had missed the path to love which proceeds from a pure heart, good conscience, and unfeigned faith and had gone astray into fruitless discussions.

The author complained that although these people wished to be teachers of the law, they did not understand what they were saying or anything about the matters upon which they spoke so confidently (1 Tim. 1:6–7). They did not know that the law is directed to the unrighteous, the lawless, the unholy, the sacrilegious, murderers, slayers of men, liars, those who break oaths—indeed to those whose lifestyle is opposed to sound doctrine (1 Tim. 1:8–10). We know, then, that the author's opponents had some interest in the Jewish law, even though their knowledge of it was seriously distorted.

Few of the individuals who opposed sound doctrine are mentioned by name—only Hymenaeus, Alexander, and Philetus (1 Tim. 1:20; 2 Tim. 2:17; 4:14). We shall suggest that at least one

59

of the individuals who was teaching a different doctrine was a woman, and that 1 Timothy 2:12 forbids her to teach a heresy which was creating serious problems for the church. She is certainly not the only one whose teaching must be stopped, however.

At 1 Timothy 1:19–20, the writer speaks of those who have slipped anchor from their faith and good conscience and made a shipwreck of their faith. Among them are Hymenaeus and Alexander, who have been given over to Satan in order that they may learn not to blaspheme. This is our first indication that the false teaching may involve an attack upon the very nature of God, for blasphemy is to declare God less than mighty, holy, good, or wise. The mention of Satan as an instructor raises the possibility that the dissidents looked upon the devil in a positive light. We do not have far to look in the ancient world for a religious system which held in contempt the God of the Hebrew Scriptures and glorified Satan.

Enter Gnosticism

That system was Gnosticism. It was characterized by just such an opposition to traditional Jewish Scriptures, especially the first few chapters of Genesis. It distorted Bible stories in a most radical way. According to Gnostic thought, all matter was evil. The Creator, the God of the Hebrew Bible, was evil because he had made the material world. The serpent was beneficent in helping Adam and Eve to shake off the deception perpetrated on them by the Creator, and Eve was the mediator who brought true knowledge to the human race. Cain and Esau were heroes, while Abel richly deserved the fate which was his.

Until fairly recently, most of our information about Gnosticism came from the writings of the church fathers, who opposed the heresies with bitter ferocity. Their information is anything but unbiased! The accounts are interesting for our purposes, however, as they describe the Gnosticism of Asia Minor. In 1945 the discovery in Egypt of a whole library of Gnostic texts astonished the scholarly world. Now it became possible to read materials written by the Gnostics themselves. The documents are vehemently partisan, though no two are written from exactly the same theological perspective. In this book you will be introduced both to Gnostic ideas and to excerpts from Gnostic and anti-Gnostic texts. (For a more extended reading of certain texts, see appendix 7.)

Gnosticism has been called a religion of rebellion. Its mythology constitutes an "upside-downing" of the Bible as we know it. The writer of First Timothy called for readers to beware of "nonsense which sets itself against God" as well as of "oppositions of so-called knowledge (*gnōsis*)" (1 Tim. 6:20). Gnosticism gained its name from *gnōsis*, the Greek word which is used here to indicate knowledge. Gnostics claimed that they had special secret knowledge.

The mention in 1 Timothy 1:6; 6:20; and 2 Timothy 2:16 of fruitless discussions, drivel, and nonsense which oppose God is interesting because Gnostic writings do indeed contain material which appears pure nonsense. Sometimes there are long strings of repetitious nonsense syllables, sometimes there are riddles and paradoxes; and yet they conveyed significance to the initiate.[1] Many of the early Christians who tried to refute Gnostic theology found this use of nonsense particularly exasperating. Certainly nonsense is one of the hallmarks of Gnosticism. To this day the reading of Gnostic texts can be a frustrating experience because of the deliberate obfuscation in them. Other similarities between Gnostics and the false teachers referred to in the Pastorals include denial of the resurrection, genealogies, quarrels over words, wrackings of the mind, and speculation (1 Tim. 1:3–6; 6:4; 2 Tim. 2:14, 16, 18, 23; Titus 3:9).

The Epistle to Titus begins, like the First Epistle to Timothy, by explaining that Titus is to set right a bad situation and to appoint elders (Titus 1:5) "who must be able to rebuke the opponents by the teaching of sound doctrine" (Titus 1:9). There are many who have become involved in the babbling of nonsense and the perpetration of deceit, especially "those of the circumcision" (Titus 1:10). Just as the false teachers (1 Tim. 1:3–7) had an interest in the Jewish law, even if they did not fully understand it, so Jews are involved in the problem here. Titus should "reprimand them sternly so that they may be made whole in their faith and stop giving heed to Jewish myths and the commandments of people devoid of truth" (Titus 1:13). It is imperative that they be silenced because they "upset entire households by teaching what they should not for the sake of financial advantage" (Titus 1:11).

As we can see, the importance of silencing exponents of false doc-trine is a major motif of the Pastorals.

The Involvement of Women

We cannot cover all of the material in the pastoral Epistles dealing with the proponents of false doctrine, but let us next turn to 1 Timothy 5, where attention focuses on widows. Older wid-ows, known for their faith, piety, and good works, are to be enrolled in an ecclesiastical order, but, the writer continues,

> Refuse younger widows; for when they have gone astray from Christ, they will wish to marry, having this judgment that they abandoned their first faith. At the same time they will learn to be idle, going about from house to house, not only idle but babbling nonsense, workers of magic, speaking what they ought not. I wish therefore that the younger widows marry, bear children, rule the house, and give no occasion for slander to the adversary, for some have already gone astray after Satan. [1 Tim. 5:11–15]

This group of troublesome women carries its destructive doctrine and practice into the very homes of the congregation. Possibly these are the homes in which the house churches meet. Gordon D. Fee wrote, "It seems certain from 2:9–15, 5:11–15, and 2 Tim-othy 3:6–7 that these [false teachers] have had considerable influ-ence among some women, especially some younger widows, who according to 2 Timothy 3:6–7 have opened their homes to these teachings, and according to 1 Timothy 5:13 have themselves become propagators of the new teachings."[2] These widows may actually be followers or admirers of Satan; for there were those "who gave heed to deceiving spirits and the doctrines of demons" (1 Tim. 4:1). Certain groups of Gnostics did indeed venerate Satan as a benefactor of the human race. The letters to the seven churches of Asia Minor mention those who live where Satan has his throne, those of the synagogue of Satan, and those who learn "the deep things of Satan" from a woman called "Jezebel" (Rev. 2:9, 13, 24; 3:9).

We cannot rule out the possibility that some of the younger widows had been attracted to such a philosophy. They speak non-sense, a characteristic of Gnostic communication, and are called *periergoi,* often translated "busybodies"; but the Greek word might well be translated "workers of magic." The same term (*tōn ta perierga praxantōn*) is used in Acts 19:19 for "those practicing magic." Some Gnostics, as we know, were heavily engaged in magic; and in the ancient world women in particular were thought to be purveyors of magic. The things which they ought not to be speaking might be incantations or magical curses. (For this practice among the women of Asia Minor, see appendix 5.) They are also said to speak "nonsense"—a term "often used in contemporary philosophical texts to refer to 'foolishness' that is contrary to 'truth.'"[3]

We again find linkage of women with the false teaching in 2 Timothy 3:6–9. Paul warns his reader to turn from those who have a form of godliness but deny its power:

> Of such are those who sneak into private houses and lead forth silly women as captive, women loaded with sins, driven by various lusts, always learning and never able to arrive at a knowledge of truth. In just this way Jannes and Jambres withstood Moses, so these people oppose the truth, with their minds corrupted, their faith reprobate; but they shall not progress further, for their folly is evident to all, as was that of Jannes and Jambres.

Women are once more connected with the false doctrine, this time in the role of learners; but again there is a reference to the false teachers who go surreptitiously from house to house. This is reminiscent of the manner in which the priests of the goddess Cybele were reputed to gain entrance to private houses in order to subvert women.[4] It is all the more interesting because Eve, as depicted by the Gnostics, bore a pronounced affinity to Cybele.

Opposition to the Tradition of Moses

The false teachers incite people to withstand the truth of Moses, just as did Jannes and Jambres. The allusion to Jannes and Jambres is a curious one. These are the names assigned in Jewish tradition to Pharaoh's magicians who produced snakes in opposition to Aaron's rod-turned-serpent (Exod. 7:9–13). Pharaoh had asked for a sign in order that he might believe, and Moses had given one; but the magicians succeeded in persuading Pharaoh not

to heed the warnings of Moses. Both pagan and Jewish sources
mention Jannes and Jambres as magicians par excellence. Pliny
the Elder, who died in the first century C.E., wrote of a Jewish
group which practiced magic and believed itself to have derived
from Moses and Jannes.[5] If indeed they were considered forefa-
thers of a sect, then the warning against them is appropriate. The
author of the Pastorals declares that the heretics are stupid, just as
were Jannes and Jambres in their opposition to Moses. He then
cites the biblical account in order to repudiate the legendary figures and all of the spurious lore that had grown up around them.
This, we shall argue, is precisely what is happening in 1 Timothy
2:13–14, where the writer is dealing with contemporary lore
ascribed to Eve.

Another significant clue that the deviant doctrine may be tied
to women occurs in 1 Timothy 4:7, where Timothy is told to
avoid the stories told by old women. Interestingly enough, some
English translations fail to note the Greek word *graōdeis* (pertain-
ing to old women). In antiquity old women had a reputation for
storytelling which sometimes put the gods in an outrageous
light.[6] From earliest times in Anatolia, female religious officials
known as "old women" kept alive the ancient myths.[7] The tales,
or myths, are said to be *bebēlos* (opposed to God; 1 Tim. 4:7).
Translators usually manage to give the impression that the tales
were harmless, but the writer of the Pastorals viewed them as a
serious threat. The ancient power of the "old women's" myths
was pitted against the power of the gospel.

Myths as Part of the Problem

The problem of the stories referred to in 1 Timothy 4:7 did not
lie in the gender of their tellers. Curiously, the charge that the
false teaching involved myths is repeated several times in the Pastorals. Second Timothy 4:4 brings a complaint about those who
turn away from hearing the truth and go astray after myths.
These are not simply pleasurable stories. The tales have a religious content which diverts hearers from the truth. At Titus 1:14
we read that Christians should not give heed to Jewish myths and
commandments of those who had rejected the truth. As we have
seen, First Timothy begins with a command to stop those who
taught another doctrine and gave too much heed to myths which

engendered argumentation rather than edification. Such people supposed they knew the Jewish law, but in this they erred greatly (1 Tim. 1:3–7).

These Jewish myths or stories cannot be the traditional biblical stories, for again and again the writer maintains that wrong teaching must be combatted with the use of Scripture. The norm is the Word of God—what we would call the Hebrew Bible or the Old Testament, as the New Testament was still being written. The traditional Bible stories are not what Paul has in mind. We must look for some other form of Jewish myth which might draw people away from the truth.

Ancient writers attest that distorted stories, including perversions of the Adam and Eve saga, were already circulating in the first century of the common era. Recent scholarship suggests that Gnostic-like myths opposed to traditional biblical values may have been afloat in Alexandria as early as the second or first century before Christ.[8] Philo, who died in C.E. 45, utilizes the very theme which was to draw rebuttal by Paul: namely, mythologizing Eve as the one who brings knowledge and meaningful life to Adam.[9] His treatment of the story indicates that he is thinking along the lines of Gnostic myth, and he uses the same type of imagery which is frequently employed in Gnostic thought. He speaks with disapproval of certain Alexandrian Jews who allegorized the Scriptures to the exclusion of their literal meaning.[10] We can only conclude that these Jews must have been considerably less orthodox than he.

Apparently Ephesus itself was not immune from the infection. An amusing story was told about a Gnostic teacher, Cerinthus, who was said to be promulgating his blasphemous doctrines in Ephesus at the end of the first century.[11] The elderly apostle John once entered a bathhouse and left it precipitately when he discovered Cerinthus inside. John considered the man so wicked that he feared to remain under the same roof lest it fall in upon the heretic instantly!

A substantive discussion of the sources, dating, and origins of Gnosticism is outside the purview of this book. However, we are here less concerned with demonstrating the presence of Gnosticism than with showing that specific ideas associated with Gnosticism and certain other theologies were present. Our hypothesis will deal with the possibility that the false teachers were indeed

Gnostics, proto-Gnostics, or some group with a mythology remarkably like that of the Gnostics. There is within the Pastorals abundant evidence that Gnosticism was in a formative stage, though the hotly debated strands of theology were surely less developed than that known to us from second-century writings. We maintain that those involved with the false doctrines included both men and women, and that the women were involved in telling stories which contradicted the Scriptures.

An Examination
of 1 Timothy 1:3–2:11

Let us now proceed to an examination of the second chapter of the First Epistle to Timothy. At times it will be slow and tedious work, but only so can we discover the rationale of the writer.

"Therefore I exhort that first of all supplications, prayers, intercessions, and thanksgiving be made on behalf of all people." Why does the writer say "therefore"? To what line of argument does he refer? We have already discussed the command to stop the opponents from teaching their false doctrine (1 Tim. 1:3–4), and we have seen that Hymenaeus and Alexander had made a shipwreck of their faith and had been turned over to Satan for instruction (1 Tim. 1:19–20). Paul has mentioned false teachers whose doctrines only engender profitless bickerings that do nothing to build up the body of Christ (1 Tim. 1:4, 6). He speaks too of those who hold to no law and are unruly, even though they profess to be teachers of the law. Their conduct includes a list of appalling behavior patterns that are unfitting for Christians (1 Tim. 1:7–10).

We shall notice throughout chapter 2 a series of connecting adverbs which indicate that the author is drawing his argument from what has preceded. He wishes prayer to be made because of the spiritual danger, both to people's faith and to their personal lives. He asks that prayer be made for everyone, but also "for kings and for all those who are in authority" (2:2). Remember that Gnosticism was a religion of rebellion, and Paul wishes Christians to be responsible and loyal citizens of the state. They are to pray for others in a spirit of love, and to pray for those in authority as part of their civic duty. Paul then leads us to the purpose of these prayers: "that we might lead a peaceable and quiet life in all piety and reverence" (1 Tim. 2:2). This is quite the opposite of the disruptive and quarrelsome crowd mentioned in chapter 1!

Let us comment for a moment on the word *hesuchios*, an adjective used here to describe a quiet and peaceful life. In 1 Peter 3:4 this adjective describes "a meek and quiet spirit which is precious in God's sight," while the verb form occurs in 1 Thessalonians 4:11 to indicate a lifestyle which is quiet, orderly, and industrious. The word is important because later in 1 Timothy 2:11 and 12 the noun form will be applied to women, and most translators understand it to mean that women should keep silent. In 1 Timothy 2:2, it has to do with quality of life. It implies compliance with the law rather than resistance, and harmony with one's neighbors rather than wrangling and hostility. Paul calls for peace rather than argumentation. This meaning, we suggest, might well apply to the use of *hesuchia* in 1 Timothy 2:11–12.

The writer next goes on to say this decent, quiet, and orderly life is "good and acceptable before God our Savior who desires everyone to be saved and come to a knowledge of the truth" (1 Tim. 2:3–4). Here again there is a hint of the wrong doctrines which keep people from arriving at this knowledge of the truth. The phrase *knowledge of truth* occurs four times in the Pastorals. The foolish women who are led astray by the false teachers are always learning and never able to come to a knowledge of the truth (2 Tim. 3:6–7). In 2 Timothy 2:25 the writer advises that the servant of God must not engage in argumentation but rather teach those opposed to the orthodox message with meekness, so that God might give to them repentance unto a knowledge of truth and they might be saved from the snare of the devil. Opponents, then, need repentance unto a knowledge of truth. Repentance from error leads to knowledge of truth, and a knowledge of truth leads to salvation. Paul himself is a servant of Jesus Christ according to a knowledge of truth in godliness (Titus 1:1), and he writes to confirm the church in the will of God as revealed by the Scriptures.

Paul sticks to his theme of providing truth as an antidote to error. Then he turns to an important doctrinal issue: that of one

God and one mediator. "For there is one God, and one mediator between God and people, the human being, Christ Jesus" (1 Tim. 2:5). Frequently this verse is rendered "For there is one God and one mediator between God and man, the man Christ Jesus." There are two common words for "man" in Greek. One is *anēr*, and it means specifically a male person. The other is *anthrōpos*, from which we get English words such as "anthropology." This word connotes a human being and does not specifically denote gender. This is the word that is used twice in this verse. Jesus is described as an *anthrōpos* who brings together God and humanity.

One God

Paul states that he has been made a herald and apostle and teacher to the Gentiles to proclaim the truth of one God and Mediator (1 Tim. 2:7). He wrote to a city and culture where there were many gods and many mediators. Contemporary readers find it difficult to imagine the easy manner in which people in the first century adopted many elements from various religious systems. In today's world, Christians are not ordinarily Buddhists, nor do Mormons borrow ideas from Roman Catholicism. For the most part, individuals choose the religious system which they find most satisfying and adhere to its maxims. In the ancient world it was possible to be a priest in several cults; an individual could enjoy a fusion of paganism, Judaism, oriental religion—and even Christianity—while at the same time honoring the Roman imperial cult. This eclecticism harbored an enormous multiplicity of deities and of pathways to salvation.

Paganism abounded with gods and mediators. "Virtually everyone, pagan, Jewish, Christian or Gnostic, believed in the existence of these beings and in their function as mediators, whether he called them daemons or angels or aions or simply 'spirit.'"[1] All properly cultured persons understood the value of the traditional mediator. Plutarch (ca. C.E. 100) wrote of the *daimones* and demigods who stood midway between gods and humanity. He suggested that it may have been Phrygian influence which first produced the system of mediators.[2] If this system did indeed develop in Asia Minor, it may well account for the particular emphasis in an epistle directed to Ephesus.

Plutarch described Isis, a popular goddess at Ephesus, as a mediator of divine grace. Through her marriage to Osiris, she led the devotee to a knowledge of the ultimate and thus fulfilled human aspiration for communion with the divine. Plutarch identified her as "the feminine spiritual principle" of which Plato had spoken.[3] It is this feminine spiritual principle which often served as mediator.

Gnostic religion teemed with celestial beings who ranged themselves in ranks, as many as 365 in number. In many Gnostic systems, the God of the Old Testament, creator of the world, is not the highest deity. Rather he is the craftsman who made the universe. Ptolemy wrote to Flora: "He is the creator and maker of the entire world and of those things which are in it, being different from the natures of the other two [i.e., between a higher 'perfect' god and the material universe] and is rightfully set in the midst of them, so that he might appropriately take for himself the name of middle position."[4]

It is indeed shocking for today's conservative Christians to discover an ancient religion which relegated Jehovah to the status of intermediate. Paul would allow no such latitude of belief. For him there is but one God, and he is the Most High. Here Paul mounts an attack on the heart of the opposition. It was necessary to affirm the one God and the one Mediator who had "given himself as a ransom for all, as a testimony at the right time" (1 Tim. 2:6). The witness proved that there was only one God and one Mediator.

One Mediator

Mortal women could serve as prime movers and mediators in religion. The cult personnel of the great temple of Artemis of Ephesus numbered into the thousands, some of whom certainly stood in an intermediary position between the deity and her worshipers.[5] Lydian women appear to have been especially active in the cult of the Ephesian Artemis. A poet of the fourth century B.C.E. wrote: "As the girls of Lydia, beloved maidens, dance nimbly, leaping back and forth, their hair swaying, striking their hands together beside Artemis, the most Beautiful, at Ephesus. Now they squat on their haunches and now leap up just as the dabchick does."[6] Aristophanes (fifth century B.C.E.) wrote: "And you, blessed Lady of Ephesus, who have a temple of pure gold in which Lydian maidens honor you greatly . . ."[7]

The priestesses passed through three ranks, the honeybees (or postulants), priestesses, and senior priestesses. We can see the honeybees, alternating with actual bees, carved into the statue of the Ephesian Artemis (illustration 6). By the first century C.E. the high priestess had replaced the high priest as the chief functionary of the cult, both at Ephesus and at neighboring Sardis.

Women were assuming greater status as principal mediators of the gods, though the process had begun far earlier. In the early third century B.C.E. at Miletus, there were women who were officially enrolled to "perform initiations for Dionysius in the city or in the country."[8] "Always in Dionysian initiation scenes, it is women who act as the leaders and initiators."[9] Women were credited with having introduced his mysteries into both Greece and Rome. When the cult of Sabazios reached Athens from Asia Minor, the mother of Aeschines performed the initiations. Strabo, a native of Asia Minor, declared: "All regard women as the prime movers when it comes to religion. It is they who incite the men to the more devoted worship of the gods, to festivals, and to wild

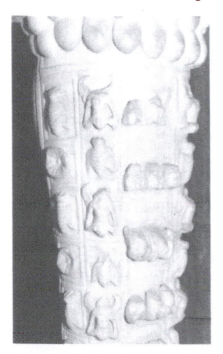

Illustration 6. *Melissai* (bee women) depicted on a statue of Artemis of Ephesus.
Photographs by Dick Waters   Used by permission of Ephesus Museum

outcries. One rarely finds such a behavior pattern in a man living by himself."[10]

One of Euripides' heroines claimed special religious privileges for women:

> Moreover in matters pertaining to the gods—
> I judge them foremost.
> There we have the greatest share. For women prophesy
> In the oracles of Phoebus, the mind of Loxias,
> And likewise at the holy pedestal of Dodona
> > by the sacred oak the female sex provides the counsels
> > of Zeus to all in Greece who wish it.
> Whatever holy rites are performed unto the Fates
> > or Nameless Goddesses—
> These holy offices are not appointed to men
> But entirely among women are they promoted to honour.
> Such is rightly the feminine role in matters
> > pertaining to the gods.[11]

Here we have a suggestion of something very like a female monopoly on certain types of religion. Feminine mediation of the divine had become in some instances a necessity. One of the first manifestations was the use of women to be the mouthpieces of the gods in the oracles at Delphi, Dodona, and Didyma. Only through them was the will of Zeus and Apollo revealed. They alone could serve the Fates and Furies.

Apparently the role of mediator and prophetess was sometimes assumed by Jewish women, for the Roman satirist Juvenal (ca. C.E. 60–128) speaks of a Jewess who was "a mediator of highest heaven, the interpreter of Jerusalem's laws."[12] Her orthodoxy is questionable, for she purported to be "the high priestess of the tree" (of knowledge). Surely the lady had Gnostic leanings.[13] She would for a price divulge the arcane secrets of Judaism to her clientele. Christian literature too made use of the woman who dispenses mystic knowledge.[14]

Gnosticism placed even greater emphasis upon the role of the feminine mediator. Many of these women had originally played a part in an older, traditional story and were later transformed into special religious emissaries. For instance, in one Gnostic text

Peter said to Mary, "Sister, we understand that the Saviour (σωτήρ)[15] loved [you] more than (παρά) the rest of the women.

Speak to us the words of the Saviour (σωτήρ) which you recollect, those which you know and we do not, nor (οὐδέ) have we heard them." And Mary answering said, "I shall explain to you what has been hidden from you," and she began (ἄρχεσθαι) to speak to them.[16]

The men can learn this hidden knowledge only from a woman. In other Gnostic writings, the prophet Marcos was instructed by Sige (Silence), while in the Nag Hammadi texts Norea, the wife of Noah, was particularly favored in the revelations. Celsus speaks of a number of Gnostic groups who drew their names and traditions from female leaders.[17]

Mary of Bethany, Mariamne, the sister of the apostle James, Philoumene, Sophia, and Eve all served as mediators of truth. The Carpocratians declared that their revelations had come from Mariamne, Martha, and Salome.[18] "The Ophites honored Mariamne as being the apostle designated by James, the Lord's brother, to carry on his teaching."[19] Of Helena, the consort of Simon Magus, it was said that she had been Helen of Troy and that her revelation passed from one feminine body to another.[20] She was termed "the mother of all," and from her name derived a group known as the Hellenians.[21] Other groups as well maintained that divine revelation had come to them in feminine form "because the world was not able to bear the masculine one."[22] One Gnostic deity declared: "I am the mother of the voice which is speaking in many ways, and completing the All. Within me is knowledge, the knowledge of the things which have no end. I am the one who speaks within each created being. And I am known by the All. . . . And (δέ) I have come a second time in the form of a woman and I have spoken to them."[23]

This mystic knowledge resided not only in feminine figures of sacred literature but in actual Gnostic women who were willing to share their arcane secrets. Epiphanius speaks of the women who tried to seduce him, while the Marcosian women enlightened the men, as did the Phibionite women. Marcellina, in Rome under the episcopate of Anicetus, led multitudes astray (multos exterminavit).[24]

In 1 Timothy 2:5–15 Paul addresses the notion that women were necessary to communicate ultimate truth. He is as well combatting the willingness of women to assume that they had a monopoly on divine enlightenment. He is committed to Jesus

Christ as the sole mediator and to the illumination afforded by the Holy Scriptures which could make one wise unto salvation. He points to Jesus as the one who "gave himself a ransom for all, a witness in due time" (1 Tim. 2:6). Christ's own sacrifice is vindication of the efficacy of his mediation. For this witness Paul himself had been commissioned.

Appropriate Behavior for Men and Women

After declaring himself to be "herald and apostle and teacher of this truth to the Gentiles" (1 Tim. 2:7), Paul becomes specific about the implications of this manifesto in verse 8. Since Gentile men and women often worshiped quite differently (different gods, festivals, temples, modes of worship), Paul addresses the problem of how men and women should pray appropriately.

Again he prefaces his directive with "therefore." A concern for the personal comportment of newly converted Gentiles is part of his apostleship. He asks that "men everywhere pray with holy hands raised up, and without wrathful passion or dispute" (1 Tim. 2:8). The word used here, *dialogismos* (dispute), is sometimes translated "doubting," but in view of many other references to the arguments and strife entailed in encounters with the opposition—and the specific instruction that the servant of God should not strive but behave with meekness—we think this is again a word deprecating hostility toward others.

Verse 10 begins, "Likewise also the women"—apparently meaning that women are to pray in the same manner but are to be careful of the impression which they are creating by their personal appearance. It is not surprising that women should be thus concerned in a culture which so often kept them cloistered. To be sure, they were more liberated in Asia Minor than they were in mainland Greece; but these injunctions serve notice that there must have been much fastidiousness in dress. John Chrysostom seized this passage to inveigh against ladies whose tiny gold shoes peeped beneath their elegantly pleated skirts.

This enjoinder might also have been a warning to women who sometimes disrobed during worship. A magnificent fresco in the Villa of the Mysteries at Pompeii shows a group of naked women participating in a celebration of the mysteries of the god Dionysus. Furthermore, it was sometimes an act of of piety and blessing for a pagan woman to raise her skirts to the waist. By contrast, modesty, rather than fertility, was a priority in Christian services of prayer.

Paul suggests that "modesty and good sense" are the "fitting apparel" of women when they pray (1 Tim. 2:9). He goes on to delineate both appropriate and inappropriate adornment. He begins with braids—although we generally consider braids dowdy, Apuleius considered them seductive, and apparently he was not alone. Furthermore, the elaborate hairstyles adopted by some women of the era required a special hairdresser. Juvenal describes how ladies of fashion had one slave to arrange their hair while a second slave stood by with a whip to lash the unfortunate beautician in case a cowlick proved stubborn.

"Gold, pearls, and costly clothing" are all condemned (1 Tim. 2:9)—although too often they find their place in even the most conservative Christian circles today. Ostentation in dress was frequently considered a sign of promiscuity in the ancient world, and the enormous expense was unjustified in view of the plight of the poor. Paul goes on to mention yet more precious array which is surely "suitable for women who profess godliness" and a knowledge of Jesus Christ—"the adornment of good works" (1 Tim. 2:10).

He turns from the prayer life of women to their study of the Word of God: "Let a woman learn in silence with all submission" (1 Tim. 2:11). The women are to be well taught in the Word. This was not ordinarily the practice in Jewish tradition. Although Beruiah, a second-century woman, was famed for her erudition in the Torah, her case is somewhat unusual. In view of typical rabbinic reluctance to teach women the Torah, Paul's decree that they should learn is an enlightened one.

Indeed, the rabbinic scholar himself was required to learn in silence. This was how one gained a knowledge of God. The people of Israel were told to keep silence before the Lord (Isa. 41:1; Hab. 2:20; Zech. 2:13); and they were instructed, "Be still, and know that I am God" (Ps. 46:10 NIV). Silence was a wall around wisdom, and Rabbi Isaac asked, "What should be a man's pursuit in this world? He should be silent. Perhaps he should be so with regard to the words of the Torah?"[25] Silence, then, was the duty of the learner. The phrase *silence and submission* is a Near Eastern formula implying willingness to heed and obey instruction—in this case that contained in the Word of God.

The Greek-speaking Jews who prepared a Greek version of the Hebrew Bible (the Septuagint) saw a remarkable correlation between "silence" and "submission." There are three places in the Psalms where the Hebrew text speaks of being silent unto God (Ps. 37:7; 62:1, 5). In each case, the Septuagintal translators rendered this by the Greek verb meaning "to submit oneself." The original implication is certainly one of attentiveness and receptivity to God.

The command in 1 Timothy 2:11 that women should learn is in marked contrast to the foolish women (2 Tim. 3:6–7) who are ever learning and never able to arrive at a knowledge of the truth. Paul would arm women with truth so that they might stand against error. Such is the route by which the author leads us to 1 Timothy 2:12. His concerns have been for peace, propriety, and a knowledge of the truth.

PART 2

The Prohibition
(1 Tim. 2:12)

A Closer Look at Our Target Verse

We come at last to our target verse, 1 Timothy 2:12. Here it is essential that the examination be most detailed. We shall study both grammar and vocabulary. A distinctive characteristic of First Timothy is the use of terms which have more than one meaning.[1] It is not always possible to be dogmatic about which meaning the writer intended by his use of a given word. Possibly he wished to evoke more than one image. The word *authentein* occurs only at this one point in the Greek New Testament, nor is it to be found in the Greek version of the Old Testament, the Septuagint. Yet its translation is crucial to an understanding of this text. More than one rendering is possible, and an alternative translation alters the entire sense of the verse.

Furthermore, the word order is unusual, and we shall analyze the vocabulary in the order in which it occurs in the Greek text. We might render the verse literally, "To teach, on the contrary, to a woman I do not grant permission, and not *authentein* but to be in silence." This verse contains three infinitives: to teach, *authentein*, and to be. The separation of "to teach" from the other infinitives is most interesting and may indicate that one or both of these two infinitives deal with the *content* of a woman's teaching. For example, a woman at neighboring Thyatira taught "the deep things of Satan." She instructed Christ's servants "to fornicate and to eat things sacrificed to idols" (Rev. 2:20). The two infinitives in this verse are used with *didaskein*, the same word for teaching as in 1 Timothy 2:12. Just as we are told in Revelation 2:20 what the woman was teaching, we may in 1 Timothy 2:12 be afforded a definition of what it is that a woman should *not* teach.

To Teach

The verse begins, then, with *didaskein,* the Greek word normally used for the activities of a teacher. In the First Epistle to Timothy, the use of *didaskein* is always accompanied by that of another verb. Each of the verbs in the doublet qualifies and helps to sharpen the focus of the other. The first use of *didaskein* in one of these doublets employs a compound form in the command "not to teach another doctrine nor to become preoccupied with myths" (*heterodidaskein mede prosechein,* 1 Tim. 1:3–4).[2] Next the writer urges Timothy to "proclaim these things and teach them" (*paraggelle tauta kai didaske,* 1 Tim. 4:11) and then to "teach these things and exhort" (*tauta didaske kai parakalei,* 1 Tim. 6:2). First Timothy 6:3 contains a warning against anyone who teaches a different doctrine and does not agree (*heterodidakalaei kai me proserchetai*) with wholesome words. The second verb is bound with the first in the total thought. Thus the *authentein* in 1 Timothy 2:12 may well qualify the *didaskein.*

A concern over teaching is a distinguishing characteristic of the Pastorals. Only the accurate transmission of God's message could combat the appalling errors raging in the troubled world depicted by the author. There was a desperate need for truth to be proclaimed by those who maintained an unswerving loyalty to the Holy Scriptures. Emphasis is placed upon the function of teaching (*didaskein*), the teaching itself (*didaskalia* and *didache*), and the actual teacher (*didaskalos*). *Didache* is defined in terms of the truth which it bears (2 Tim. 4:2; Titus 1:9).[3] The teachers are clearly categorized according to the truth or error of their message (1 Tim. 1:7; 2:7; 2 Tim. 1:11; 4:3–4; Titus 2:3). Those who are *didaktikos* (able to teach) must be prepared to instruct those in opposition (1 Tim. 3:2; 2 Tim. 2:24). The communication of the opponents, identified as a "teaching (*didaskalia*) of demons" (1 Tim. 4:1), is at direct variance with "the teaching according to godliness" (1 Tim. 6:2–3; 2 Tim. 4:3). If Timothy persevered in this teaching, he and his hearers would be saved (1 Tim. 4:16).

The crucial point is the thrust of the teaching and the results which it produces (1 Tim. 3:10; 4:6, 13, 16; 5:17; 6:3–4; Titus 2:7–8).

In the pastoral Epistles *didaskein* is used in contexts which express or imply the content of the teaching, whether the word is used of the false doctrines which the opponents promulgated (1 Tim. 1:3, 7; 4:1; 6:3; 2 Tim. 4:3; Titus 1:11) or of instruction in the truth (1 Tim. 1:10; 2:7; 4:11, 13, 16; 5:17; 6:1–3; 2 Tim. 1:11; 2:24; 3:10, 16; 4:2–3; Titus 1:9; 2:1, 3, 7, 10). In 1 Timothy 6:3 we find both a positive and a negative connotation: "If anyone teaches another doctrine and does not agree with the wholesome words of our Lord Jesus Christ, and the teaching according to holiness, he is blind and has no understanding." The writer offers "sound teaching" (*hē hugiainousa didaskalia*, 1 Tim. 1:10; 4:16; 5:17; 6:1; 2 Tim. 3:10; 4:3; Titus 1:9; 2:1, 7) with which to combat the sick teaching of the opponents.[4] Jerome Quinn, noting that there are eight related "dida-terms" which recur thirty times in the pastoral Epistles, maintains that *didaskalia* in the singular is a technical term "denoting apostolic instruction."[5]

Timothy must stand fast against the proponents of a strange teaching and follow instead the doctrine of Paul (2 Tim. 2:1–2; 3:1–10). Scripture itself is profitable for teaching as well as for reproof and correction of those who have deviated from the truth (2 Tim. 3:16). Teaching (*didaskalia*) of the truth must not be blasphemed (1 Tim. 6:1), but rather ornamented by the lives of believers (Titus 2:10).

If the context of 1 Timothy 2:12 is neutral and refers only to the activity of teaching rather than to its positive or negative content, then it is the only time that *didaskein* is so used in the Pastorals. The writer has made it clear that women were somehow involved in the false teaching (1 Tim. 4:7; 5:11–13; 2 Tim. 3:6–7; Titus 1:11), and it is in keeping with the other uses of *didaskein* to find in this directive a condemnation of their heterodoxy. We believe that the verb here forbids women to teach a wrong doctrine, just as 1 Timothy 1:3–4 and Titus 1:9–14 also forbid false teaching.

If we were to understand the use of *didaskein* as a prohibition against all women instructing men in any manner, we would find difficulties with other materials in the Pastorals. First, Titus 2:3 says that older women should be "teachers of what is excellent." While their instruction certainly was to include young women (Titus 2:4–5), it was not necessarily limited only to women. Secondly, Paul writes in 2 Timothy 2:2, "The things which you have heard from me in the presence of many witnesses, these entrust to faithful persons who will be able to teach others also." Here the word for "persons" is *anthrōpos*, which is used to designate persons of either sex. Far from prohibiting them from teaching, it appears to be a strong exhortation that responsible women should make the proclamation of the truth a very high priority! Those of either sex who are able to teach hereby receive a summons to make known the unsearchable riches of Jesus Christ.

The same epistle says,

> I have been reminded of your sincere faith, which first lived in your grandmother Lois and in your mother Eunice and, I am persuaded, now lives in you also. [2 Tim. 1:5, NIV]
> Continue in what you have learned and have become convinced of, because you know those from whom you learned it, and how from infancy you have known the holy Scriptures. [2 Tim. 3:14–15 NIV]

It was his mother and grandmother who had taught him the Scriptures. The same epistle mentions Priscilla, who, according to Acts 18:26b, "explained to Apollos the way of the Lord more accurately."

Other Pauline material contains commandments that women as well as men should teach. Colossians 3:16 says, "Teach and counsel one another," and 1 Corinthians 14:26 observes, "Whenever you come together, each one has a psalm, a teaching." Five verses later (1 Cor. 14:31) Paul says, "You all can prophesy one by one so that all may learn and all may be encouraged."

Women were specifically granted permission to prophesy, provided that their heads were appropriately covered (1 Cor. 11:5). Prophecy, according to 1 Corinthians 14:3, consists of "edification, and exhortation, and consolation." Surely these are basic elements in Christian instruction. Thus it becomes evident that a number of other Pauline passages support the concept of women sharing instruction with men as well as vice versa. We must therefore consider whether a specific sort of teaching is prohibited, rather than all teaching of any kind.

"I Do Not Allow"

The next word over which we should pause is *epitrepo*, usually translated "I allow or permit." It can also mean to turn to, to give up to, to commit to one's care, to entrust to, to trust to, to give way to, to suffer, to permit, to refer to, to concede, to agree to, or even to command. In classical times the verb could also mean to play the part of a mediator. The title of a play by Menander uses the participial form of this term to indicate the individuals entrusted with arbitrating a disagreement. Professor John Toews suggests that when the word occurs in the Septuagint, it speaks to a specific and limited situation rather than a universal one (Gen. 39:6; Esther 9:14; Job 32:14; see also Wisd. of Sol. 19:2; 1 Macc. 15:6; 4 Macc. 4:17–18).[6] This accords with the thesis that the apostle is here addressing a particular circumstance rather than laying down a widespread interdiction against the leadership activities of women. His use of the present tense may also indicate that his decree had to do with a situation contemporaneous with the writing of the epistle. The verb should probably be rendered "I do not permit."

Epitrepo is preceded by the first negative of the sentence, *ouk*. Two words, *ou* and *me*, were normally used to introduce a negative thought in Greek. When *ou* was followed by a vowel, it became *ouk* (as it does here before *epitrepo*). Just as in English we can form negative compounds such as nowhere, no one, nothing, so *ou* and *me* can form compounds. In 1 Timothy 2:12 the negatives are *ouk* and *oude* (a compound meaning "and not," "nor," or "not even"). Thus there are two negatives in this sentence, and they are usually translated "I allow a woman neither to . . . nor to . . . " A few versions read "I do not allow a woman to . . . nor to . . . "

Oude, however, often has a particular flavor as it is used by Paul. Philip Barton Payne points out that in the Pauline corpus *oude* is usually employed to bring together two closely related ideas. He maintains that its use falls into three major categories:

1. To join two expressions which are roughly equivalent in meaning. Galatians 1:1 has "Paul, an apostle, not sent from man, nor (*oude*) by men."
2. To specify with greater clarity the meaning of one word or phrase by conjoining it with another word or phrase. Romans 3:10 reads, "There is no one righteous, not even (*oude*) one." *Oude* emphasizes the total absence of a righ-

teous human being (other than Jesus) who can meet God's
standards.

3. To join together a naturally paired expression, as in 1 Thes-
    salonians 5:5, "We have nothing to do with night and (*oude*)
    darkness."

Payne argues, then, that the two expressions *didaskein* and
authentein, linked as they are by *oude*, together convey the
meaning of the decree.[7] The *oude* indicates that *authentein*
explains what sort, or what manner, of teaching is prohibited to
women. For instance, if we should say, "I forbid a woman to teach
or to discuss differential calculus with a man," it becomes clear
that the subject in which she should not give instruction is higher
mathematics.

Authentein

The second prohibition is that women should not *authentein*.
Most English translations render this word "to bear power over,"
while the King James Version has "to usurp authority over." Ordinarily the New Testament word for "to bear power" is *kurieuein*
or *exousiazein*; but here a different term is used, one that has
other meanings as well. This is not unique to Greek vocabulary,
for some English words can have a variety of meanings. For example, the noun *play* can mean recreational or children's activity, or
a theatrical performance; the verb can mean to engage in a sport,
to give a musical performance, to pretend, and so forth. In the
same way, *authentein* has a wide variety of meanings. Within its
significant range of meanings are the following:

1. To begin something, to be primarily responsible for a condi-
    tion or action (especially murder),
2. to rule, to dominate,
3. to usurp power or rights from another,
4. to claim ownership, sovereignty, or authorship.

If we are to be thorough in our inquiry, we must look at each of
the meanings and see if they may indicate alternate possibilities
of translation which we have not always recognized.

The earliest usages of *authentein* and related words mean to be responsible for something, usually murder. The word occurs at first usually in its noun form, *authentēs*. The word often connotes the one who is to blame. In one Greek tragedy, the father of Achilles, the mightiest Greek warrior, accuses Menelaus of being the *authentēs* and foul despoiler of his son.[8] In point of fact, Achilles was slain when a Trojan spear struck the only place where he was vulnerable—his heel. Menelaus was guilty only of having summoned all the Greeks to war against Troy after a Trojan prince had stolen away his beautiful wife, Helen. In retrospect, Achilles' father holds Menelaus responsible for the tragic death of his son and considers him an *authentēs* and a *miastor* (crime-stained wretch who pollutes others).[9]

Herodotus tells the story of a king who was fearful of an ominous oracle concerning his daughter's newly born son. He commanded one of his distant kinsmen, Harpagus, to put the child to death. The man pretended to obey, but actually delivered the infant to a shepherd to execute the deed. The shepherd, however, substituted his own stillborn child for the little prince and raised the live baby as his own. In the manner of many another Greek myth, grandson and grandfather at last recognized each other and were reunited. The king sent for the disobedient Harpagus and demanded to know why the child had not been slain. Harpagus replied that he had been unwilling "to be an *authentēs* either to your daughter or to you yourself."[10] There was no question of this loyal subject killing either the king or his daughter, but rather of doing away with the baby who was their descendant. He hesitated to perform an act which, though directed toward the child, would still bring blood-guilt toward parent and grandparent and place himself in the position of being responsible for the slaughter. In this case, that is the meaning of *authentēs*.

A law case preserved from the fifth century B.C.E. contains a debate as to who is actually the *authentēs* in a gymnasium accident. Someone must bear the blood-guilt for a situation in which a youth steps into the path of a moving javelin and is slain. Is the *authentēs* the lad who threw the missile or the one who encountered it? Who bears the primary responsibility for the death? The father of the dead boy tearfully begs that he should not have to bear the pain both of bereavement and of hearing his son pronounced an *authentēs* by the jury.[11] He urges that it would be an act of wickedness to declare both himself and his deceased son *authentēs*.[12] Here it becomes evident that the stigma of being an *authentēs* might be communicated to one's kin. Closely bound to the word was the concept of pollution, so that the term might be applied to those associated with the murderer as well.[13] To be the sexual partner of an *authentēs* was also a matter for reproach.

So important was the notion of ultimate responsibility that Athenian murder cases were tried under the open sky in order that the relatives of the victim might not have to come under the same roof as the *authentēs*. Sometimes *authentēs* was applied to one who had murdered his own blood kin.[14] By the New Testament period, *authentēs* also at times implied one who took his own life.[15] The verb *authentein* occurs in an ancient gloss on Aeschylus' *Eumenides* as "one who has recently committed a murder."[16]

Ceslaus Spicq, one of the most illustrious of modern commentators on the Pastorals, suggests that beside the notion of dominance in 1 Timothy 2:12, there may also be an intimation of woman bringing death to man. He notes the meaning of murder and adds that it was a murderess, drawn from Adam's side, who induced him to sin.[17] Ben Sirach, a Jewish author of the second century B.C.E., observed that it was woman who began sin and because of her all die (Ecclus. 25:23). It is also possible that *authentein* refers not to spiritual murder but to symbolized or actual murder.

Both in pagan and in heretical Christian tradition, there were rites in which a woman might be responsible for the murder of a man. Such a gesture would more likely be symbolic than actual, but this would not detract from its religious significance. Women frequently served as the officiants in the initiations of males into the mysteries, and the initiations were said to consist of three elements: things spoken, things shown, and things done. Elements of both sex and death were portrayed. (A discussion of sham murder as part of Greco-Roman and Gnostic religion is found in appendix 1.)

Within a framework of initiation, there would be ample room for both teaching and simulated slaying. Whether pagan or Gnostic, real or representational, such a cultic action, together with the recital of a myth or other instructional material, could have no place in a Christian community. Any evaluation of 1 Timothy 2:12 should recognize the possibility that the author forbids such cultic practices. It is by no means the only possibility, however.

That Strange Greek Verb *Authentein*

It is strange indeed that our target verse should include a pivotal word which has implications of killing, beginning, and copulating, as these all were elements of the mystery religions practiced in Asia Minor. Several words derived from the same stem as *authentein*. So far we have mostly discussed the form *authentes*, a noun that refers to a person who performs an action. (One of the definitions of the verb *authentein* is simply to be an *authentes*.) Another noun, *authentia*, denotes an abstract concept such as power, force, initiative, or even presumptuous license. There is also an adjective, *authentikos*, meaning original or genuine, from which we derive our modern English word *authentic*. There is as well an adverb, *authentikōs* (originally, genuinely, authoritatively). All of these forms may help us develop a fuller understanding of the values inherent in the verb. Which meaning we should select for the best rendering of *authentein* in 1 Timothy 2:12 is not a conclusion easily reached.

Translation is not an exact science. One has only to compare different translations of the Bible to see that at some points the sense has been understood differently. Competent scholars may render a given text by a variety of expressions, and each in its own way may be correct. Many Greek words have more than one meaning, and the translator's task is to choose the expression which in her or his understanding is most congruent with the sense of the entire passage and best fits the context.

Since the rendering of *authentein* is crucial to an understanding of 1 Timothy 2:12, it is only proper that we should look at the sweep of meanings and examine the possibility of each as the meaning correctly to be assigned. Since the material is not easy to come by, we shall set forth various possibilities. In view of the unusual religious and cultural conditions in Asia Minor, none of the possibilities can be ruled out categorically. (An expanded explanation of some of these conditions will be found in the appendices of this book.) It is important for the reader to understand that none of the translations suggested in this chapter fit in as well with the complete sense of the passage as the interpretation which we shall offer in chapter 8.

The Possibility of Usurpation of Power

The King James Version renders *authentein* as "to usurp authority," and usurpation is certainly one of the meanings which the verb may hold. The most interesting such usages occur in legal documents from Egypt. A wealth of papyri have been preserved in the dry climate and serve to give us insights into many mundane sorts of problems in the ancient world. In matters of jurisprudence, *authentein* assumes a more technical meaning. The great papyrologist Friedrich Preisigke offered *verfügungs-berechtigt sein*, the German implying to have the legal right to a piece of property and to the disposal thereof.[1] He gave two sixth century C.E. inheritance cases as examples in which the right to possession of certain property is contested.

In the first papyrus, heirs lodged a legal complaint that their older brother had deprived them of all the inheritance from their mother and father. Furthermore, once he had rented out the houses which formerly belonged to their parents, he had even gone so far as to claim them as his own (*authentein*).[2] He had collected the rents and appropriated these too for himself even though his actions left the others in uncomfortable straits (perhaps both financially and in terms of a place to lodge). Their complaint is in itself proof that the oldest brother did not have an undisputed right to the property. He had most certainly seized control of the houses, and the indignant tone of the Greek (*ou mēn alla kai authenthēsai*, even gone so far as to claim as his own) indicates that the *authentein* is the ultimate injury. The arrogance of the action is clearly implied. He had wrongly usurped that in which they rightfully had a share.

The second papyrus is the will of a physician named Phoibammon who is giving directions as to that share of the estate to which his widow will be entitled. It is very little:

> I will and decree that my most noble life-partner, my wife, have jurisdiction over those things which are hers and only those wedding presents which were given her by me in the hour of her auspicious nuptials before our union; and that she be content with these and not be able to demand more than these from any heir of mine whatever or of a joint-heir, nor to claim as her own [*authentein*] in any manner anything of my various possessions to detach it altogether from my estate. It is likely that she may wish to appropriate to herself something of mine, ill-naturedly to take it away from my estate. May it not be so with her after my death. [I will that] as she leaves my house she be able to take with her only those things which she inherited from her parents, whatever will be clearly manifest as those things which were brought to me as marriage portion from her parents' estate.[3]

The testator wishes to restrict his widow from demanding or claiming as her own (*authentein*) any other possessions.[4] In both of these legal situations, *authentein* is used in the matter of laying claim to property to which others feel they are entitled. The problem consists in other interested parties perceiving the action (*authentein*) as wrongful usurpation.

It is possible that the mandate in 1 Timothy 2:12 forbids the usurpation of power by women, especially as in the New Testament period there had been important transferals of religious power at both Ephesus and Sardis. By the first century C.E., it appears from inscriptional evidence that the function of the male high priest had been supplanted by that of the high priestess. Two inscriptions tell of the performance of the mysteries in the cult of Artemis by a priestess, but we know of none in which the officiant is a male. In one case from the early third century, the high priestess "renewed all the mysteries of the goddess and established them in their ancient form."[5] In Lydian Sardis, where there was a branch of the Ephesian cult, the high priestess of Artemis also seems to have taken over the duties of the high priest.

The Traditional Meanings of *Authentein*

The traditional rendering, "to have authority over," is justified as one of the widely-used meanings of the verb. *Authentein* and *authentēs* were originally applied to murder, but by the second century after Christ there is adequate documentation for the sense of having power or authority. To use it with such a meaning was considered vulgar among purists, however. A grammarian of the late second century wrote: "The word should never be used for the despot as certain court speakers do, but for the one who kills with his own hand."[6] Another ancient commentator also noted that *authentēs* meant "murderer" but that some of his less-educated contemporaries were using the word to mean "ruler" or "master."[7] A modern scholar commented: "I find it difficult to believe that the word meant 'ruler' in the classical period. Certainly much Greek literature has been lost to us, but the Atticists, who could read more of it than we do, would not have been so emphatic on the incorrectness of this meaning if there were other examples of this sense in classical authors."[8]

Moeris, who wrote in the second century C.E., states that the proper Attic form is *autodikein* (to take justice into one's own hands) rather than *authentein*, while Thomas Magister, a grammarian of the thirteenth and fourteenth centuries, advises the use of *autodikein* rather than the more vulgar *authentein*.[9]

The question of politeness and vulgarity aside, *authentein* was most certainly being used by the second century C.E. in a sense that implied dominance. This became pronounced in the centuries which followed the New Testament era. John of Damascus wrote of the power (*authentia*) of the King of Heaven.[10] Eusebius commented on Isaiah 40:10, "Your God is here. Here is the Lord God, coming in might, coming to rule with his right arm," and he added the explanation, "as if he said more plainly, with majesty and power (*authentia*)."[11] Eusebius tells how God initiated Jacob into an understanding of the powers (*authentia*) of the Father.[12] *Authentēs* came to mean master or lord and was in time corrupted into the Turkish word *effendi*.

The church fathers used *authentein* to mean rule or bear authority but gave to it other values as well. John Chrysostom, for instance, maintained that Mary came to see her son (Matt. 12:46–50) not because she wanted to visit with him but rather to demonstrate to the people that she wielded power and authority (*authentein*) over her child.[13] Philip deferred to Andrew because his older brother had precedence over him (*authentein*).[14] Yet Chrysostom used the same verb in a negative sense when he wrote, "If your wife is subject, do not tyrannize over her" (*authentein*) and again, "Do not try to have everything your own way" (*authentein*).[15]

The Possibility of Domination

Unquestionably "to dominate" is a valid meaning of *authentein* and one which may or may not be appropriate in 1 Timothy 2:12. If the directive is understood as forbidding women to rule over men, what are the implications? One immediate problem is that the command would then stand in direct variance to other Pauline material.

First Timothy 5:5–10 speaks of widows who are to be enrolled as members of the clergy, and Titus 2:3 requires female elders to be "worthy of the priesthood." First Timothy 3:11 gives the qualifications required of female deacons.[16] Romans 16:1–2 speaks of Phoebe as a deacon (or minister) of the congregation at Cenchrea, and she is also called a *prostatis* (overseer, guardian, protector). A verbal form drawn from the same stem is used by one of the early church fathers to indicate the person presiding at communion (*tō proestōti adelphōn*).[17] The verb is used also in the New Testament at 1 Timothy 5:17 for elders who "preside" (or rule) well, and at Romans 12:8 (rule) and 1 Thessalonians 5:12 (hold authority over). Phoebe's office as *prostatis* appears to imply authoritative responsibility similar to that of an elder.

A scholarly suggestion has been made that Phoebe was appointed or ordained to this post by Paul himself.[18] The verb (*genesthai*) is identical to that used when Paul says, "I was made [or ordained] minister" (Eph. 3:7; Col. 1:23) and to indicate that Christ was appointed (or ordained) high priest (Heb. 5:5). Thus the sentence may mean, "For she has been appointed, actually by my own action, an officer presiding over many" (Rom. 16:2).

Junia is called a "noteworthy apostle" (Rom. 16:7). Efforts by translators to turn this common feminine name into a masculine one (Junias or Junianus) simply cannot be substantiated. Paul mentions several women, including Priscilla, as "fellow laborers" and asks that Christians be subject to such as these (Phil. 4:2–3;

Rom. 16:3–4, 6, 12; 1 Cor. 16:16, 19). A number of Christian women appear to have presided over churches which met in their homes (Acts 12:12; 16:13–15, 40; Rom. 16:3–5; 1 Cor. 1:11; 16:19; Col. 4:15; 2 John); and women were involved in the first decision made by the early church (Acts 1:14–26).

The Scriptures themselves, as well as the vigorous leadership provided by the women of Asia Minor in the first few centuries of the church, cause us to question the traditional interpretation. A prohibition against women assuming positions of authority is inconsistent with the strong evidence demonstrating that in the early Christian communities women were most certainly engaged in leadership. Presumably they did not consider this Scripture to be a deterrent. How, then, might they have understood it?

There are other aspects which might be considered. Ancient tradition in the area around Ephesus, as we have seen, was based on legends of the Amazons as foundresses of the city and its cult. Amazonian worshipers of the original cult, that of the Tauropolian Artemis, were said to rule over men, to subject them to humiliation and slavery, and to assign them female tasks.[19] Widespread tradition maintained that the women of Asia Minor continued to display these characteristics. Certainly they enjoyed far greater freedom and exercised far more leadership than was the case in most other regions of the ancient world. Women might preside over official games or serve as magistrates and emissaries of the city. One coin has the name of the mint-mistress struck upon it. Nevertheless there is no evidence that women took an ascendant role over the men in civil life.

Religious affairs were significantly different, however. William M. Ramsay speaks of a special social system which existed in the religious realms of Asia Minor. About the great shrines, including that of Ephesus, were "sacred villages" where life was organized far differently from life in the secular world.[20] Within its temple systems and especially in the mysteries, matriarchy prevailed. He held that Lydian social institutions were "more of the matriarchal type, which seems to have been native to Asia Minor."[21]

In the summer of 1988, we were visiting Miletus with a group of tourists. We had finished our inspection of the ruins and boarded the bus, when suddenly the guide appeared and pointed a finger at Cathie. "You! Come quick!" She scrambled down from the bus and panted along behind him as he led the way to a group of men working at an excavation. He showed her a pillar which had been uncovered that morning. On it was a lengthy inscription, still partially covered with mortar. "Read it," he commanded. "Quick!" Since inscriptions have no breaks between the words, it was not possible to decipher much in such haste; but there stood a phrase in Greek that meant HIGH PRIESTESS OF ASIA. This is by no means the only inscription to accord a woman the high-priestly office, which historian James Donaldson called "perhaps the greatest honor that could be paid to anyone."[22]

The Amazons, according to Ramsay, belonged to an "old religion" in which women ruled and assigned to men traditionally feminine roles. Appendix 3 demonstrates the extraordinary strength of the tradition in Asia Minor. Such a pagan element, based upon sex hostility and reversal of gender roles, may well have found a place in a cult practice among the dissidents in the congregation at Ephesus. The apostle who taught that in Jesus there is neither male nor female would surely have condemned it. If this is the case, the condemnation is not directed against women participating in leadership but rather against a monopoly on religious power by women. Such a monopolistic attitude in the church is wrong, whether arrogated to themselves by men or women.

Authentein in Accounts of Promiscuity or Reversal of Gender Roles

A description of the reversed behavior of women, using the verb *authentein*, occurs in the writing of a Byzantine historiographer, Michel Glycas.[23] The material is by no means original with Glycas and may be traced through the Treatise of Bardesanes, the Clementine Recognitions of Peter, Eusebius, Caesarius, and Cedrenus.[24] In each case there is a lengthy discussion of the habits, largely sexual, of various groups ranging from Brahmins to Britons. In one society (bearing differing names in the descriptions of the various authors) women engage in men's work, fornicate freely without arousing their husbands' jealousy, and dominate the males. Much the same material is also found in descriptions of Amazon society.

Glycas may well have found *authentein* in one or more of his sources, even though the verb does not occur in the earlier forms as we now have them. It is noteworthy that the verb appears in a literary pattern characterized for over a millennium by sex reversal, female dominance, and promiscuity. This pattern, as we have seen, was said to be characteristic of the women of Asia Minor. Paul, a native of Tarsus in Cilicia, would have been well acquainted with the tradition and may have been firmly outlawing it in the Christian community.

Ritual Castration

One other aspect of sex reversal is worthy of mention. This is the reversal experienced by men who castrated themselves in the service of the mother goddesses, most notably Cybele, the Syrian Goddess, and Artemis of Ephesus. Ritual castration was a violent and bloody practice; in the case of Cybele's worship, it was specifically called "depriving of power." Those who had sacrificed their manhood were said to have been transformed into women and thereafter were considered feminine.[25] They wore feminine attire and jewelry. One Christian writer testified, "They wish to be thought women."[26] Another added that it was not possible for a man to serve as priest of the Mother of the Gods until he had been transformed into a woman.[27]

A first-century philosopher wrote about the priest called Megabyzos who served the Ephesian Artemis:

> How superior are wolves and lions to the Ephesians! They do not make slaves of one another, nor does one eagle buy another eagle, nor one lion become the cup-bearer of another lion. Neither does one dog castrate another as you do to the Megabyzos of the goddess, out of fear that her virginity should have a man as priest. Do you really show reverence for a wooden image when you commit such sacrilege against nature, when the priest robbed of his manhood is the first to call down curses upon the gods? And you have laid a charge of incontinence against the goddess as if you are fearful to have her attended by a man.[28]

It is possible that some vestige of this brutal practice still lingered in the Christian community. Castration was not unknown among Christians. Origen (C.E. 185–254), for instance, made himself a eunuch both "for the sake of the kingdom of heaven" (Matt.

19:12) and also so that he might instruct the women in his famed catechetical school without fear of scandal.

Sex and Murder

Authentēs and *authentein* sometimes occur in contexts in which both sex and murder are present. The word is seldom used at all in the classical period, and therefore it is the more remarkable that so many of the surviving usages occur in a sexual context. There are three instances in Attic tragedy in which widows are said to sleep with an *authentēs*, the one responsible for or associated with the murder of their former husbands. Euripides' Andromache laments: "The son of Achilles wishes me as concubine. I shall be a slave in the house of murderers" (*authentēs* in the plural).[29] The legitimate wife taunts her because she sleeps with the one who slew her husband and bears a child to an *authentēs*.[30] Sophocles, who uses the variant *autoentes*, has Electra lament that her mother shares her bed with an *autoentes*, indeed the murderer of her father.[31]

There is also a Euripidean fragment which deals with whether or not the gods will be lenient in certain equivocal situations.[32] One phrase is often understood as sharing a house with a familial murderer, but certain vocabulary terms—*paides* and *koinoneo* (a term for sharing but also for sexual intercourse)—suggest having intercourse with the *authentēs* boys or slaves (*paides*) of the house.[33] Here the objects are the *authentēs paides* (the word from which we get "pederasty") of the house, while in Euripides' *Suppliant Women* the objects of the *authentēs* are young men. In the latter play there is a discussion of the relative merits of tyranny and democracy. Theseus remarks that in a tyranny the ruler becomes jealous and slays youths while in a democracy the people as *authentēs* take delight in the youths who stand under them.[34]

Authentēs also appears in the words of the seducer of Alexander the Great's mother. The rascal is trying to persuade her that she is about to receive a visit from a god. In reality the priest will himself play the role of the god. Alexander's mother asks how she may prepare herself for the embrace of her divine bridegroom. The scoundrel replies, "When he himself comes upon you *authenti*, he will do to you what is necessary."[35]

From the ruins of Herculaneum came charred fragments of the work of the epigrammatist Philodemus. Certain letters are missing in the damaged text but the poet uses either *authentein* or *authentēs* in proximity to the phrase *those terribly wounded by the arrows of love.*[36]

The Mingling of Sex and Death

Another Greek epigram describes a wedding in which the bride is raped, and wedding guests and bridal couple alike die when the house collapses. Blood and roses are mingled in what the writer calls an *authentēs* wedding.[37] Just as *authentēs* can modify *phonos*, slaughter,[38] so here it modifies *gamos*, marriage or sexual union.

In early Greek literature, there are erotic references to death and slaughter. "There is an ambiguity to killing, as to love, and a verb like *meignumi* with both connotations, mingling in battle or mingling in sex, helps the poet in his play. . . . *Damazo* or *damnemi* have similar values, working in three related spheres of action: taming an animal, raping a woman, killing a man. . . . Homer's habit of playing on sex and war is not new with him, one imagines, but is common war talk and wartime humor. The idea is equally popular in Greek art."[39]

Both Greeks and Jews, for different reasons, associated sex with death. Among the Greeks, there was a belief that sex sometimes brought death to men. The god of marriage, Hymenaeus, was said to have died in the first moments of wedded joy.[40] Death was often the lot of those who mated with a goddess. The gods slew Iason when he lay with Demeter on Crete.[41] Artemis as queen bee and her bee-priestesses were also dangerous, for to mate with a bee brings extinction to the male.

Sex and Death in Jewish and Christian Literature

Jewish wisdom literature, both canonical and otherwise, views the promiscuous woman as one who leads a man to death. She slays him by luring him into intercourse (Prov. 2:19). Wisdom can keep a man from such danger, but a lewd woman sets her victims on a path leading to death and hell. "No one who resorts to her finds his way back or regains the path to life" (Prov. 2:19). Death lurks in the house of the strange woman (Prov. 9:18). The writer of Ecclesiasticus considers a married woman "as a mortuary for her lovers" (26:22); she leads to a "fatal disaster" (9:9).

The notion of sexual impropriety as causing death was current in Christian circles as well as Jewish ones. In the *Clementine Homilies*, Peter gives a long discourse on the value of a chaste wife and concludes:

> A single adultery is as bad as many murders, and the dreadful part is that the fearful impiety of its murders goes unseen. When blood is shed, the body is laid out, and the horror of the deed stuns everyone. Spiritual murders produced by adultery, since they are unseen, provide an unbridled incentive to the reckless.[42]

Sex and Mystery Religion

If illicit sex was seen by Christians and Jews as occasioning spiritual death, it was viewed more positively by pagans. Mystery religions certainly offered illumination and salvation through sex. Union with a surrogate of the deity prefigured the marriage with the gods which was anticipated in the afterlife. A second century C.E. writer specified that "marriage is called initiation and those who are married are called initiates because of this, and Hera the goddess of marriage [is called] the Initiated One."[43] Both the words and rituals of the marriage ceremony were used in the mysteries, and the initiate was greeted, "Hail, bridegroom, hail, new person!"[44]

Theon of Smyrna (a neighboring city of Ephesus) declared that the final stage of initiation was to know oneself beloved of the gods. Many tomb paintings and funerary offerings show the dead persons as bride or bridegroom of various deities, assured of immortality because of their initiation. Beyond death, a divine marriage awaited them.

A literary tradition has been handed down of mingled sex and death in connection with the cult of Artemis of Ephesus.[45] One finds these twin themes repeatedly in ancient novels—those documents which Reinhold Merkelbach, C. Kerenyi, E. Rohde, and others have held to be vehicles of mystery instruction. Appendix 4 discusses the frequent treatment of this motif as related to Artemis of Ephesus in the romances.

Artemis was called "a dear saviour-goddess, accessible to every initiate;"[46] and her devotee, Artemidorus of Ephesus, held that rites of initiation displayed both death and marriage.[47] He wrote that marriage and death were both "fulfillments," as was initiation. In initiation rites mortals played the role of a deity and introduced worshipers into a wedded state with the immortals. If a sick person dreamed of sexual union with a god, it was a sign of death, for "when the soul approaches the time to leave the body which it inhabits, then it foresees union and intercourse with the gods."[48] Sacred prostitution was widely practiced in the temples of Asia Minor and also offered the worshiper a ritual union with the divine.

Gnostics too introduced initiates to divine knowledge (gnōsis) through sexual activity. They were keenly aware that the biblical term to know was a euphemism for intercourse. Frequently there were elements of both sex and death in the rituals of some of the Gnostics (see appendix 6 for the sexual practices of Gnostics). Interestingly enough, in several Gnostic writings feminine figures "stripped a male of his power" through sexual intercourse! It was also the way in which some bestowed spiritual grace or power on men.

It seems important to lay out these possibilities, along with at least a limited amount of evidence of known conditions which might allow certain alternative understandings of 1 Timothy 2:12. The reader has a right to know that there is more than one plausible way to translate this verse. Nevertheless, there is one more alternative which fits most completely with the entire message of the Pastorals, and especially with the two verses immediately following 1 Timothy 2:12. We turn to this in the next chapter.

Is Another Translation Possible?

We have reviewed some of the meanings of *authentēs* and the related *authenteo*. We have projected alternative understandings or interpretations of its use in 1 Timothy 2:12. In each case we have indicated that there might be some possibility of such an understanding, but we believe there is a further group of meanings which can be translated into a sense more consistent with the letter as a whole and with Paul's continued argument in verses 13 and 14.

Pierre Chantraine, a French etymologist, wrote of *authentēs*: "The original sense is 'one who accomplishes an act, who is its author, who is responsible,' from which comes its use to designate a chief. . . . The sense of 'murderer' stems from the former [author]. . . . The only way to cover the obviously differing meanings of *authentēs*, as is necessary, is to note that the term expresses the responsibility of the subject in the accomplishment of an act or function."[1] Let us turn to the value which Chantraine held to be most basic, that of originating something or being responsible for it. The related adjective, *authentikos*, like the English "authentic," means something original or genuine. By the second century B.C.E., *authentēs* was being used to denote an originator or instigator. Polybius, about 150 B.C.E., wrote of a culprit as "the author [*authentēs*] of the deed."[2] Both Jewish and Greek authors used the term to designate "the real perpetrator of that crime," "the author of these crimes," and "the perpetrator of these evils."[3] The Vulgate rendering of *authentēs* as it occurs in the Wisdom of Solomon is *auctor* (author, procreator; 12:6). M. Pischari, another etymologist, wrote, "*Authentēs* here implies a nuance of pure responsibility, of the originator responsible [for the act]."[4]

A Greek rhetorician who lived about fifty years later than the apostle Paul also used the word in this sense. Discussing the ways in which different types of rhetoric were used and the differences in the responsibility of the hearers, Alexander the Rhetorician explained that

> in a deliberative council, the listeners are responsible to take action (*authentēs*); for they decide what they themselves should do and not do. In lawcases the judges, as though they were examining their own private affairs, decide whether the deeds of others have been done righteously or not. But the literary form of the panegyric requires neither those who are responsible to do something (*authentēs*) nor judges, but only hearers.[5]

In early Christian writings, God is called the architect and builder (*authentēs*) of a tower.[6] In a second century C.E. Christian novel, the term is used for "the sole creator."[7] Christ is elsewhere called the *authentēs* (author) and introducer of a new law of salvation, *authentēs* (originator) and leader of the work of the gospel, the teacher and *authentēs* (prime mover) of laws and teachings whereby the power of our Savior is revealed.[8] "Before the earth and starry heaven, he was the originating [*authentēs*] Word, along with the Father and Holy Spirit."[9] An early pope wrote, "He came and made, as being himself creator [*authentēs*]."[10]

Authentia, the noun form, has connotations both of primal cause and of power. At one point in the Septuagint it seems to imply "original status" (3 Macc. 2:29). Eusebius speaks of "the wholly-creating power [*authentia*] of the Father."[11] Poimandres, an important deity in Hermetic writings, declares, "I am Poimandres, the intellect of the Absolute Beginning (*Authentia*). . . . That light is I, the Intellect, your god, the one who was before the moist nature appeared out of the shadows. . . . You have seen the archetypal form, the first principle before the infinite beginning."[12]

From the concept of originality and creation sprang other usages, especially in the Egyptian magic papyri of the third and fourth century C.E. *Authentikon onoma* denoted the genuine, valid name, a name of primal origin—a name which might be used as part of a magic charm to call up a god.[13] *Authentēs* is applied to the sun as the real, primordial lord.[14] Sevenfold offerings and feasts of the new moon are called *authentikos*.[15] In nonmagical documents there are many references to documents which are *authentikos*, original or genuine, written with the author's own hand, as opposed to *antigraphon* (a copy).

The writer of 2 Clement speaks of Christ as male and the church as female. "The church, of heavenly origin, is spiritual, was manifested in the flesh of Christ. Those who keep her without corruption in the flesh shall have a share in the Holy Spirit, for the flesh is a copy of the spirit. The one who corrupts the copy (*antitupon*) shall have no share in the original (*authentikon*)."[16]

Like the other derivatives, *authentia* can mean both absolute power or the ultimate creative force. A. Dihle, a German etymologist, pointed out that it was an important technical term in early Christian doctrine. He observed that "in its first meaning *authentia* has as a synonym *exousia* [power, authority], in the second there is a transposition in *authentikos* to the meaning 'original.'"[17] Cerinthus, a first-century Gnostic in Ephesus, used "Authentia" to denote the Primal Deity from which all else derived.[18] Proklos spoke of God as *authentēs demiourgos* (primal Creator).

Notions of origin and "authenticity" could also give rise to concepts of authority. An interesting papyrus from the first century B.C.E. tells of a dispute over the fare to be paid to a boatman. In the haggling, the writer stuck to his original price (*authentein*), and thereby gained consent for the ferrying service to be provided at the specified rate within the hour.[19] A document from the middle of the third century C.E. uses the term *authentēs* to refer to persons originally appointed to collect taxes as distinct from their representatives or deputies.[20]

The verb form *authenteo* (the infinitive is *authentein*) could mean to take something in hand or to take the initiative in a given situation. A government initiated (*authentein*) "a renewal of public works to improve the cities."[21] Basil wrote to ask that the Bishop of Rome take the responsibility (*authentien*) for appointing legates to deal with a crisis since a general synodical decree would be too ponderous and time-consuming.[22] An Egyptian bishop was asked to take in hand (*authentein*) a particularly ugly matter of a divorce.[23] In the sense of to begin something, to take the initiative, or to be primarily responsible for something, the verb *authentein* is even used by the early church fathers for the creative activities of God.[24] John Chrysostom (late fourth century), when he was discussing the replacement of Judas in the Book of Acts, wrote, "He was primarily responsible [*authentein*] for the matter [of Christ's betrayal]."[25] In a treatise dealing with lapsed brethren who had renounced the cause of Christ during a time of persecution, Athanasius (mid-fourth century) suggested leniency for those who defected under compulsion but had not themselves instigated (*authentein*) the problem.[26]

Guillaume Budé, citing Theodore of Gaza's *De mensibus*, declared, "He asserts by such a vocabulary term that this once meant 'the one who murders with his own hand.' Later indeed, and for over a thousand years, *authentein* in Greek began to signify that which among the speakers of Latin means 'a doer, one that puts [something] in motion.'"[27]

In the late Renaissance, an era when scholars studied classical texts more thoroughly than is customary today and had at their disposal materials to which we no longer have access, another definition was cited by lexicographers: *praebeo me auctorem*, to declare oneself the author or source of anything. *Authentein*, when used with the genitive, as it is in 1 Timothy 2:12, could imply not only to claim sovereignty but also to claim authorship. "To represent oneself as the author, originator, or source of something" was given in various older dictionaries, such as the widely-used work of Cornelis Schrevel and the still-fundamental Stephanus' *Thesaurus Linguae Graecae*.[28] The earliest of these entries dates back to the Renaissance, the latest to the last century.[29]

The differentiation between being an originator and professing to be one is a valid point. In several texts the meaning is strengthened by the sense of asserting oneself to be the author or source of something. Basil, in a letter written close to 370, appears to use it in this sense. He had been deeply pained when his friend, Bishop Dianius, subscribed to the Arian creed in 360. In 362 the breach was healed when Dianius, at death's door, sent for Basil, confessed that he still embraced the Catholic faith, and died in Basil's arms. Later Basil was incensed because the rumor went out that he had anathematized his old friend. Where was he supposed to have proclaimed such an anathema? he asked. In whose presence? Was he merely following someone else's lead or did he himself instigate the outrage or even profess himself (*authentein*) to be its author?[30] *Authentein* is the climax of this carefully constructed progression. It moves from a passive role to an active one and then to claiming responsibility for the role of instigator.

Constantine's edict speaks of God who proclaims himself to be the author of judgment.[31] Pope Leo wrote to Pulcheria of Eutychus, the self-avowed author of the dissension in the church at Constantinople.[32]

An Alternative Translation

If we were to read 1 Timothy 2:12 as "I do not allow a woman to teach nor to proclaim herself author of man," we can understand the content of the forbidden teaching as being the notion that woman was responsible for the creation of man. We recall that a preoccupation with controversial genealogies, the matter of origins, was one of the principal characteristics of the opponents in the Pastorals. In this case, we would understand the *oude* as linking together two connected ideas. Then the thought might flow thus:

> I do not permit woman to teach nor to represent herself as originator of man but she is to be in conformity [with the Scriptures] [or that she keeps it a secret.] For Adam was created first, then Eve.

"To be in silence" can mean "to keep something a secret." Secret knowledge was an important part of ancient mystery religion and of Gnosticism. There was a Gnostic notion of Eve as creator of Adam, which was part of the "secret knowledge" that was available to adherents. Other people were not let in on the secret.

The word *hesuchia*, however, can also mean "peace" or "harmony" (see also 1 Thess. 4:11; 2 Thess. 3:12; 1 Tim. 2:2). This, we believe, is the preferred translation here for the term. Just as the writer asked that women learn in conformity to the Word of God, he now asks that they express their views in harmony with the revelation of the Scriptures: in this case, that woman did *not* create man nor did Eve bring spiritual illumination to Adam.

Throughout the Pastorals, the Word of God is represented as the antidote for false teaching. The women needed to make sure that both their study and their instructing accorded with sacred writ. They should cease from promulgating a deviant doctrine and bring themselves into accord with God's Word.

In New Testament times, *hesuchia* also denoted a disengagement from public life and debate.[33] Politicking and heated emotion were considered incompatible with serious study.[34] The writer has already called on all those who are engaged in unedifying controversy to desist (1 Tim. 1:4). This may constitute a specific appeal that the women who had become embroiled should stand aloof from the conflict and give themselves instead to learning the truths of the gospel.

There is another manner in which *oude* might be used here, though it would not change the sense appreciably. Appendix 2 is offered for those who desire to review certain technicalities of language. Those not so inclined may safely go on to the next chapter. It is important for every reader to understand, however, that it is possible to translate this difficult verse in more than one way, and that the Greek construction lends itself to more than one interpretation. We need to bear in mind that one of the distinctives of the Pastorals is the use of expressions which may be construed variously.

The Feminine as Primal Source

There are certainly implications of such a translation (see chap. 8) in a society that looked upon the feminine as primal source. In Anatolia, all life was thought to stem from the Great Mother; inquiry into the origins of things was important throughout antiquity but had special relevance in western Asia Minor. To this day, little girls in Anatolia have maternal values inculcated into them at a very early age. Instead of Barbie dolls, they have mother dolls. A traditional Turkish doll represents a woman with full breasts, capable of supplying abundant nourishment. Her arms are actually two babies, each with bonnet and tiny face where the doll's

Illustration 7. Anatolian mother-doll, whose arms are infants.
Photograph by Dwight Baker

105

hands should be (see illustration 7). The concept of maternity is deeply entrenched in the land; even the modern name for Anatolia, Anadolu, is said by Turks to mean "land of mothers."

We have already spoken of the birth-giving, life-supplying goddesses who dominated religious thought for millennia. Artemis was the goddess of birth and as a newborn had assisted her own mother at the delivery of her twin brother, Apollo. On the breastplate of one cult statue, a birthing scene is depicted: a feminine figure is in a position often assumed in delivery, while nearby stand two attendants (see illustration 8).[1] Ephesians explained that the great temple had burned because the goddess was in attendance at the delivery of Alexander the Great and unavailable to protect her sanctuary.

Illustration 8. Birthing scene on the breastplate of a cult statue.
Photograph by Heather Billings
Used by permission of Israel Antiquities Authority

Cybele, the Mountain Mother

At Ephesus Artemis was not the only mother goddess. Another was Cybele, sometimes known as the Mountain Mother, worshiped in mountains, caves, and wilderness. Her most imposing representation was executed four thousand years ago. To the northeast of Ephesus, an enormous Hittite carving of the goddess looks down from Mount Sipylus upon the surrounding countryside. The seated goddess wears a high crown similar to that of the

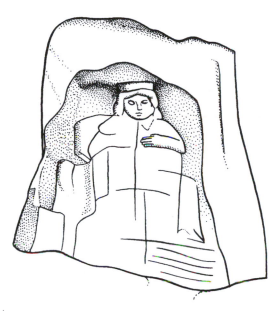

Illustration 9. Representation
of Cybele, the Mountain
Mother.
Drawing by Louise Bauer

Ephesian Artemis, and holds her breasts with her hands (see illustration 9). A sanctuary of Cybele stood on the northeastern slope of Panajir Dagh (Mount Pion) above Ephesus. Along the side of the hill were a rock altar and a multitude of niches dedicated to her, many containing terra-cotta statuettes of the goddess. Even

Illustration 10. Artemis (l.) and Cybele;
two worshipers (r.) are also shown.
Drawing by Louise Bauer

the remains of a sacrificial meal in her honor have been discovered in Ephesus.[2]

Her power as Great Mother of all Asia Minor was not to be disputed. While Artemis held sway in the great temple, Cybele maintained her stronghold on the mountain overlooking the shrine. The two goddesses increasingly shared the same characteristics and attributes but for the most part preserved separate identities (see illustration 10, with Artemis holding a hind and Cybele a panther).[3] Together with the effeminate young lover who was also her son, Cybele was worshiped in wild, orgiastic rites which were in time assimilated to a veneration of Adam, Eve, and the serpent.

Isis

The Egyptian mediator and savior goddess, Isis, at times became virtually indistinguishable from Artemis of Ephesus, and was even addressed as Artemis-Isis.[4] Both goddesses were lunar deities, well acquainted with magic and expert in delivery at childbirth. Indeed, Isis was popular all over the Mediterranean world. At Dicte in Crete she bore the name of Artemis and in Asia Minor she was worshiped, like Artemis, at crossroads.[5] She even claimed a shrine for herself in the Artemisium at Ephesus.[6] At Corinth she revealed herself as

> the procreator of all that is in nature, the mistress of all elements, the first offspring of the ages, paramount among the divine powers, Queen of the dead, greatest of those in the heavens, the unifying form of both gods and goddesses. I am she who administers by my will the luminous heights of heaven, the health-giving winds of the sea, and the doleful silences of the underworld. My sole divinity is honored throughout the whole world in many aspects, with varied rites, and by diverse names. Thus the Phrygians, first born of men, call me the Mother of the Gods, she who reigns at Pessinus.[7]

Here there is a specific identification with the Mother of the Gods.

Through her marriage to Osiris, Isis led the devotee to a knowledge of the ultimate and thus fulfilled human aspiration for communion with the divine. She was, asserted Plutarch at the end of the first century C.E., "the feminine spiritual principle." He further identified her as "nature's feminine principle" of which Plato had spoken, and she was receptive of all generation.[8] She was "the creative principle" of the universe and a mediator of divine grace.[9] Like the goddesses of Asia Minor, she was considered a primordial mother.[10] She had even given birth to Horus without the biological aid of Osiris.[11] As we shall see, Eve, the mother of all living, became closely identified with Isis in Gnostic stories.

Human Motherhood

The primordiality of motherhood extended to mortal women as well as goddesses. The Lycians, like the legendary Amazons, claimed their descent from their mothers rather than their fathers. Herodotus (ca. 480–425 B.C.E.) reported that among the Lycians a man told who he was by giving his own name, that of his mother, and that of his female ancestors.[12] Nicholas of Damascus, the court historian of Herod the Great, declared that they "honour women more than men, take their second name from the mother's side, and leave their property to their daughters, not their sons."[13] Nymphis of Heraclea in the third century B.C.E. noted "it was the custom of the Xanthians to take their names not from the father's side, but from that of the mother."[14] On certain Lycian tombstones, the name of the mother replaces that of the father, and sometimes there is the added notation, "Father unknown."[15] Those of unknown paternity could occupy high positions of public office, even that of senator. The parentage in this case was carefully scrutinized to determine the eligibility of the candidate. This accords with Herodotus' statement that the son derived his official status from the condition of his mother, so that if she was of aristocratic lineage, that status accrued to him as well regardless of his paternity. In more remote areas, the proportion of mother-only tomb inscriptions was sometimes substantially higher.[16] William M. Ramsay wrote, "The religion originated among a people whose social system was not founded on marriage, and among whom the mother was head of the family, and relationship was counted only through her. Long after a higher type of society had come into existence in Phrygia, the religion preserved the facts of the primitive society; but it became esoteric, and the facts were only set forth in the mysteries."[17]

From the Bronze Age onward the divine aspects of birth-giving were emphasized in Asia Minor (see illustration 8, p. 106).

Others in the ancient world also viewed woman as the ultimate source of life. Against those who regarded the mother as merely an incubator of the father's child, the pre-Socratic philosophers in Asia Minor, and even Hippocrates, insisted on the woman's part as an integral component of reproduction.[18] The role of the father in procreation was frequently downgraded and sometimes ignored outright. Even in the New Testament era, there was a harking back to the maternal element. Plutarch spoke disapprovingly of those who viewed the seed of woman as "a power or origin."[19]

Gnostic Pursuit of Origins

Gnostic literature contained references to "the generation of the female" (gennēma thēleias),[20] though beings generated solely by the female were not always given the highest acclaim.[21] Both Tertullian and Irenaeus rebuked the Gnostics for their belief that a female could produce a living being without aid of the male.[22] According to Hippolytus, the Naassenes "placed the originative nature of the universe in causative seed."[23]

The question of origins was desperately important to the Gnostics. One Gnostic tractate called Authentic Teaching tells how the Word was applied to the soul:

He gave the word (λόγος) to her eyes like a medicine so that she might see with her mind (νοῦς) and take notice (νοιεῖν) of her kinsfolk (συγγενής) and gain knowledge about her root, so that she might cling to her branch (κλάδος) from which she first issued forth so that she might take that which is hers and leave matter (ὕλη) behind.[24]

Knowledge of origins brought salvation. Ptolemy wrote to Flora: "Next you will learn, God granting, their origin and generation, when you are deemed worthy of the apostolic succession, which we also have received by succession."[25] The need to understand one's origins produced the interminable genealogies of which the Pastorals speak (1 Tim. 1:4; Titus 3:9). It was the knowledge of one's origin that brought salvation. Theodotos wrote: "[Knowledge] makes us free, . . . It is not only baptism which is freeing but knowledge. Who we were, what we became, what we were, into where we have been thrown; to where we hasten, from where we are redeemed, what birth is, and what rebirth."[26] The Gospel of Truth echoes the same thought: "He who is to have knowledge . . . understands from whence he has come and where he is going."[27] Another Nag Hammadi text declares:

> But (δέ), my son, return to your first father, God, and Wisdom (Σοφία) your mother, she from whom you issued forth from the beginning, so that you may fight against all of your enemies, the powers (δύναμις) of the Opponent (ἀντικείμενος).[28] . . . Know your birth. Know yourself, that is, from what substance (οὐσία) you are, or from what race (γένος) or from what tribe (φυλή).[29]

A knowledge of one's mother as source of life was important if the soul of the dead was to pass by the hostile archons, or lower powers, as it ascended to the higher realms. The Marcosians were given a formula by which they might gain a safe passage:

> "I am a vessel more precious than the female who made you. If your mother does not know her own root, yet I know myself and understand whence I am, and I call upon the incorruptible Sophia who is in the Father, but is the mother of your mother, not having a father, nor even male consort; But a female being born from a female made you, while not knowing her own mother, and thinking that she existed alone; but I call upon her mother." When they hear these things about the Demiurge, they become enormously agitated and condemn their root and the stock of the mother.[30]

In this passage we may be struck with the primacy of the female producing life. Like Isis, the Mother produces life without the assistance of a male consort and is herself the product of the female only. For the soul to obtain salvation, it is necessary to understand the feminine essence from which it derives its being. Some Gnostics defined their knowledge of divine mothers, and thus of heavenly reality, in terms of earthly obstetrical processes.[31]

One Gnostic, a worshiper of the serpent, left an account of an ancient ritual which he said formed an important part of mystery ritual. In the words of Walter Burkert, this Naassene (*Naas*, the Hebrew word for serpent) "claims the basic identity of all mysteries with Gnostic Christianity."[32] The most ancient rites were those of the Phrygian mysteries, but rites from other cults were adopted freely. The Naassene author describes one of these Phrygian rites which had been borrowed from Eleusis. During the sacred night of initiation

> by the light of a bright fire the high priest performs great mysteries which cannot be spoken and cries out with a loud voice, saying, "The divine Lady has borne a holy child, Brimo has given birth to Brimos," that is, a strong Female is source of a strong male. The birth, says [the Naassene] is revered, spiritual, heavenly, and from above. Mighty is the one who is thus generated.[33]

Part of the innermost secret, preserved here in the words of the ritual, was that of birth from an august mother. This knowledge had lain at the heart of Anatolian religion for millennia, ever since the moment of birth was portrayed upon the walls at Çatal Hüyük. Jane Ellen Harrison wrote, "In the old . . . religion, preserved in its primitive savagery in Asia Minor, the Mother, by whatever name she be called, whether Kotys or Kybele or Rhea or the Great Mother, is the dominant factor; the Son is, as is natural in a matriarchal civilization, at first but the attribute of motherhood."[34]

We suggest that the writer of the Pastorals was opposing a doctrine which acclaimed motherhood as the ultimate reality. Our Bible maintains that God, who far transcends all limitations of gender, created the heavens and the earth, and that all things are of God.

Didymus the Blind, a late-fourth-century biblical commentator, seems to have understood 1 Timothy 2:12 as focusing on the concept of man as source of women. (In Greek, unlike English, the word for "head" was ordinarily used in a metaphorical sense to mean "source" rather than "authority.")[35] Didymus wrote,

> The Apostle says in First Timothy: "I do not permit women to teach," and again in First Corinthians: "Every woman who prays or prophesies with uncovered head dishonors her head." He means that he does not permit a woman to write books impudently, on her own authority, nor to teach a false doctrine, because by doing so, she does violence to her source, man: for "the head of woman is man, and the head [source] of man is Christ." The reason for this silence imposed on woman is obvious: woman's teaching in the

beginning caused considerable havoc to the human race; for the Apostle writes: "It was not the man who was deceived, but the woman."[36]

If 1 Timothy 2:12 is translated as prohibiting women from claiming the power of origin, it fits with the refutation which follows. Women are forbidden to teach that female activity brought man into existence because, according to the Scriptures, Adam was created first. Eve, for all her desire to bring enlightenment, did not bring gnosis but transgression. This would gainsay the tenet held by some Gnostics that certain women had a special revelation. Such an interpretation harmonizes with other instances where Paul first indicates a heresy and then refutes it: 1 Corinthians 15:12–57; 2 Timothy 2:17–19; 1 Timothy 4:3–5; and Romans 3:8.

The Prohibition's Rationale

(1 Tim. 2:13–15)

Condemnation or Refutation? (2:13–14)

If verse 12 forbids a woman to teach that she is the originator of man but urges her rather to conform her message to that of the Hebrew Scriptures, how are we to understand verses 13–14?

For Adam was first created, then Eve; and Adam was not deceived, but the woman, being absolutely deceived, was in the transgression. [1 Tim. 2:13–14]

We suggest that these verses are not intended as the rationale for prohibiting a gospel ministry for women, but rather they constitute a refutation of a widespread heresy. Specifically, we consider this to be directed against Gnostic or proto-Gnostic mythology glorifying Eve. We have already mentioned the preoccupation of the false teachers with stories which they distorted.

Gnostic Ideas of Origins

If we expect an orderly account in Gnostic myths, we shall be greatly disappointed. Irenaeus remarked that no two Gnostics could be found who agreed on an issue, while Celsus declared that these sects could not come to any sort of agreement in their teaching.[1] Gnostic accounts had an extraordinary fluidity, a piling of one metaphor upon another. Often there are no clear-cut boundaries. In keeping with the paradoxical treatment of mythic material, a story may be told differently twice in the same document. Do not be surprised, then, if at times the myths are contradictory.

Most Gnosticism—and there are many varieties—presents an explanation of the beginning of the world which features a supreme being far higher than the God of the Hebrew Bible. Interestingly enough, he is sometimes identified as Authentia. Sometimes the supreme figure is female rather than male. There are, in fact, a number of spiritual beings, both male and female, usually called "powers." In most versions, each pair procreates other, lower powers.

Ialdabaoth, as the god of Genesis 1–3 is sometimes called, is one of the lower powers. He creates the physical world, and that is a grievous mistake. According to the Gnostic view, the material universe is evil, manufactured by a third-rate spiritual being. Thus the God of the Old Testament comes off very badly indeed, both for his creation of a world composed of matter and for his view that he is the supreme sovereign. Ialdabaoth is so blind that he does not even know of the existence of the higher powers: "Ialdabaoth in his arrogance boasted that all these things were under him and said, 'I am the Father and God, and there is no one above me.' However his mother heard him and shouted out against him: 'Do not lie, Ialdabaoth.'"[2]

When Adam and Eve are placed in the Garden of Eden, they believe that Ialdabaoth is the supreme deity. Here Satan, another of the powers, appears as a great benefactor. He realizes that Adam and Eve, caught in the deception perpetrated by Ialdabaoth, have no knowledge of the Supreme Being of the universe. They cannot attain to him because they do not even know of his existence. Their problem is lack of knowledge, and yet they have been forbidden to eat of the tree of knowledge. Assuming the form of a serpent, Satan communicates this wonderful *gnōsis*, or knowledge, to Eve, who then shares it with Adam. The two of them can now seek the Supreme Being who is far above the material world, seek to rise above the earth to his abode in pure spirituality, and seek to escape the unfortunate influence of Ialdabaoth.

"But Ialdabaoth, [the Gnostics said], did not wish the mother above nor the father to be remembered among men. But the serpent persuaded them and brought them knowledge and taught the man and the woman all of the knowledge of the mysteries above.

On account of the knowledge which he had revealed to humanity, the father, that is Ialdabaoth, was enraged and hurled him down out of heaven."[3]

While each myth tells the story differently, many place a high valuation on Eve and her ministry of revelation. Our purpose is not so much to spell out in detail all of the various stories about Eve as it is to delineate the kind of myth which we believe the writer of 1 Timothy was trying to refute. The Pauline author again and again repudiated the myths as a major part of the false teaching. Yet he mentions only two stories: that of Adam and Eve, and that of Jannes and Jambres, who tried to damage the credibility of Moses with the clever use of serpents. This may be significant, as certain groups of Gnostics in Asia Minor had a particular veneration for the serpent. One scholar noted that "the serpent's action marks the beginning of all 'gnosis' on to the world and its God, and indeed as a form of rebellion."[4]

In the myths of the Gnostics, the Adam and Eve story was frequently used to describe the spiritual experience of the individual in arriving at true gnosis (knowledge). In some, Eve represents the soul in its manifold struggles to arrive at the truth; but, as Elaine Pagels observes, "the majority of the known gnostic texts depict Adam (not Eve) as representing the psyche (soul), while Eve represents the higher principle, the spiritual self."[5] Often she was seen as the principle of spiritual awakening who brought enlightenment to the soul. Pagels continues: "And whereas the orthodox often blamed Eve for the fall and pointed to women's submission as appropriate punishment, gnostics often depicted Eve—or the feminine spiritual power she represented—as the source of spiritual awakening."[6]

Let us seek out those elements in the mythology of Eve against which a refutation appears to be formulated in 1 Timothy 2:13–14, concepts which appear to have been current at the time of the writing of First Timothy. It is unlikely that many of them existed precisely in the forms in which they are now known to us; and yet such ideas could not have been so widespread without a previous formulative period. To this preliminary period we assign the unorthodox mythology about Adam, Eve, and the snake.

First of all, the refutation declares (1 Tim. 2:13) that Adam was created first and then Eve. The Gnostic stories envisioned things quite differently, for Eve pre-existed Adam and was responsible for infusing him with life. We shall begin with the pre-existence of Eve, an Eve who is engaged in all sorts of exciting activities before the creation of Adam. As Zoe and Sophia, she was hailed among the Valentinians as a great creative power and primal parent.[7]

In another theology, Eve is associated with the serpent in the creation of the world, and the words of the first chapter of John are applied to her. Saint Hippolytus quotes with disgust from a book of the Peratae, who reverenced the serpent:

> The universal serpent is the wise word of Eve. . . . Concerning this one, he says, it is written, "in the beginning was the Word and the Word was with God, and the Word was God. This was in the beginning with God, all things were made by it, and without it was not one thing made. What was generated in him was life" (John 1:1–4). In him, it says, Eve was made, the Eve who is life. For she, it says is Eve, mother of all living (Gen. 3:20), a common nature, that is of gods, angels, immortals, mortals, irrational and rational beings. For, it says, the one who said "of all" meant "of all."[8]

For the Peratae, Eve has become the creative force of nature. Several traditions tell of a "heavenly Eve" who existed long before Adam. The earthly Eve was called the "image and symbol and seal" of a heavenly being.[9]

Before the episode in the Garden of Eden, Eve had many other vicissitudes. Irenaeus quotes a Gnostic source which declares, "However, others came and marvelled at her beauty and called her Eve and lusted after her and begat upon her sons, and they also say these are angels."[10] Eve becomes the mother of various sons by different fathers. Some myths taught that Ialdabaoth, the malignant god of the Old Testament, sires upon her Cain and Abel. One account describes how she gives birth to Yahweh and Elohim; thus she becomes the mother of the Supreme Deity of orthodox Christians and Jews. Another account tells of how she gives birth to one called "lord":

> And (δέ) the Hebrews (Ἑβραῖος) call its mother the Eve of Life (ζωή) which is the (female) instructor of life. But (δέ) her child is the progeny which is lord. Afterwards the powers (ἐξουσία) called him "the Beast" (θηρίον) in order that it might deceive (πλανᾶν) their molded creatures (πλάσμα). The interpretation (ἑρμηνεία) of the beast (θηρίον) is the (male) instructor. For (γάρ) they found him to

be wiser than (παρά) all of them. For Eve (Εὕα) is the first virgin, (παρθένος), the one who had no husband and yet gave birth. She is the one who acted as a physician-midwife to herself.[11]

The creation of Adam is described in various ways. Two accounts in particular will interest us. The first tells of how the created Adam lay on the ground, lifeless and inert, until Eve filled him with the spark of life:

> The spirit-filled (πνευματική) woman came to him and spoke with him, saying "Arise, Adam." And when he saw her, he said, "You are the one who has given me life. You will be called 'the mother of the living,' because she is my mother, she is the female healer, and the wife and the one who gave birth."[12]

Another tractate, On the Origin of the World, gives a similar account:

> After the day of rest (ἀνάπαυσις), Sophia (σοφία) sent Zoe (ζωή) her daughter, who is called Eve (Εὕα), as (ὡς) an instructor so that she should raise up Adam, who had no soul in him, so that those whom he would beget should become vessels (ἀγγεῖον) of the light. When Eve saw her co-likeness lying flat, she showed pity upon him and said, "Adam live! Rise up upon the earth." Straightaway her word became a deed (ἔργον). For (γάρ) when Adam had risen up, he immediately opened his eyes. When he saw her, he said "You will be called 'the mother of the living,' because you are the one who has given me life."[13]

Sophia Zoe (alias Eve) creates the psychic or animate Adam,[14] but later the fleshly Eve will be removed from the side of the earthly Adam.[15] The Reality of the Rulers also tells how Eve breathes the breath of life into Adam. As the female spiritual principle she now rests inside Adam to enlighten and empower him.[16] Later the rulers cut out the female part of Adam, who includes both male and female elements. This operation removes not only the fleshly Eve but also the female spiritual principle. The purpose of the archons is to extract and rape this female spiritual principle.[17] But the female spiritual principle escapes from their evil machinations and "returns precisely in the snake to teach the good news of liberation," as Bentley Layton puts it.[18] In this document, the heavenly Eve (or female spiritual principle) is inside the snake and addresses her revelation to the fleshly Eve.

Moreover, what we regard as the sin of Eve in eating the fruit and giving it to Adam receives a very different treatment from the Gnostics. One group declared "that when they had eaten, they recognized that Power which is above all, and they rebelled against those who had made them."[19] This information comes from Irenaeus, a native of Smyrna, not far from Ephesus. His testimony is useful in allowing us to see the traditions as they were circulating in Asia Minor.

The Deception of Adam

Most Gnostic accounts show Eve as pre-existing Adam; in one account she is actually the hermaphrodite from whom Adam is drawn. This material corresponds to the first point in the refutation (1 Tim. 2:13–14), in which the writer insists that Adam was created before Eve—and therefore in no way was she involved in giving him life. The second statement is that Adam was not deceived. Again, a significant tenet of Gnostic belief is that he had indeed been misled.

One story takes a most interesting turn as it tells us how the higher powers trick Adam into believing that he was actually made before Eve:

But (δέ) let us not tell Adam because he is not from among us but (ἀλλά) let us bring a sleep upon him, and let us teach him in his sleep as (ὡς) if she came into being from his rib so that the woman may be subject (ὑποτάσσειν) and he may be lord over her.[20]

Obviously the powers intended to trick both Adam and Eve. The myth demonstrates, however, the Gnostic assumption that Eve was actually made first, even if Adam had been deliberately deceived. If this sort of theory was circulating at Ephesus, it puts a different light upon our difficult section of Scripture.

Another area of purported deceit, as the Gnostic accounts tell us, was in Adam's supposition that the God who had made the material universe was the source of his spirituality and the high God whom he should worship. There were a number of variant accounts, but all feature Adam's lack of "knowledge":

And the archons brought him and set him in Paradise (Παράδεισος) and they said to him "Eat, that is in pleasure," for indeed (καὶ γάρ) their pleasure (τρυφή) is bitter and their beauty is without law (ἄνομος); and (δέ) their delight (τρυφή) is deceit (ἀπάτη) and their trees are impiety (ἀσεβής) and their fruit a poison which cannot be healed.[21]

A variant of the same treatise inserts the comment that the archons "intended to deceive him."[22] Although the text which survives is a Coptic translation of the original Greek document, the translator retained the Greek word *apate* for "deceit." The verbal form appears in 1 Timothy 2:14, which says that Adam was not deceived (*apatao*).

The Gnostics maintained that the beneficent serpent, through the instrumentality of Eve, undid the deceit perpetrated on Adam. Satan brought news of a spiritual world far higher than the material one, and of spiritual realities far grander than those provided to Adam by Ialdabaoth.

It is a fundamental platform of our belief that God created humanity and dealt with Adam and Eve truthfully and straightforwardly. They were told the truth but chose to believe a lie; and this constituted the original sin, which only the death of our Savior could overcome. Much of our theology falls apart if God was less than honest with Adam, and so we find in our target passage the assertion that "Adam was not deceived." The only true God and his righteous will had been revealed to him.

Both Hebrew and Septuagint versions of the Genesis story contain a phrase often missing from English translations. This phrase would have been known to the writer of the Pastorals, however. Eve gave the fruit to her husband "who was with her" (Gen. 3:6). Adam has been present all during the temptation! Here Paul is so anxious to refute the Gnostic versions that he glosses over the fact that Adam, who had received God's warning about the tree of knowledge, had sinned knowingly. (Logically and theologically which is worse—to sin knowingly or to be deceived?)

Eve as Enlightener

The next statement, "and Eve, being completely deceived, was in the transgression" (v. 14), concerns the total deception of Eve. The Gnostic notion of Eve as spiritual instructor with superior knowledge was solidly entrenched, and Paul categorically refutes it. Let us examine one of the statements about the truth revealed by Eve. In the Apocalypse of Adam, a book often "cited as evidence for First Century Gnosticism,"[23] Adam says:

> When (ὅταν) God created me out of the earth, together with your mother Eve, I used to walk with her in a glory which she had seen in the aeon (αἰών) from which we had our being. She instructed me with a word of knowledge (γνῶσις) of the eternal god. And we resembled the great eternal angels (ἄγγελος). For (γάρ) we were exalted above the god who had made us, and above the powers which were with him, whom we did not know.[24]

The crux of the matter, more than priority of creation, was the sort of activities in which Eve was supposed to have been engaged. We read that she consorted with the celestial powers, especially Satan. It will come as no surprise that in a number of traditions Eve and the serpent had sexual relations, either before or after the creation of Adam.[25] Johanan ben Zackai, a rabbi of the first century B.C.E., is quoted three times in his conviction that the serpent had copulated with Eve.[26] The belief grew as well because "to know" is sometimes used in the Hebrew Bible as a euphemism for sexual intercourse; and for Gnostics the important matter was the knowledge which passed between Eve and the serpent.

As we have seen, Eve is sent as an "instructor of Life" to rouse Adam from his sleep.[27] Often sleep represents spiritual ignorance and death; and from this spiritual deadness Adam was called by Eve. Another Gnostic tractate states that the woman made Adam wise, while the serpent had made Eve wise.[28]

Epiphanius speaks of a Gospel of Eve. It was, he says, named after her because she "discovered the food of *gnosis* [divine knowledge] through revelation spoken to her by the snake."[29] The wisdom of the snake was a major theme in Gnosticism. The Ophites, who took their name from the Greek word *ophis* (serpent), "ascribe all knowledge to this serpent, and say that it was the beginning of knowledge for humanity."[30]

The writer of the Pastorals repudiates the wisdom of the serpent and the wisdom passed on to Eve. Her superior knowledge was nothing of the sort. *Exapataō* (totally deceived), the word which is used to describe her erroneous viewpoint, is an intensification of the word which is applied to Adam. The idea is that she was absolutely hornswoggled. This same intensified word is also applied to Eve in 2 Corinthians 11:3–4:

> I am fearful lest somehow, just as the serpent (*ophis*) completely deceived (*exapataō*) Eve in his duplicity, your minds may be seduced away from the simplicity which is in Christ. For if one comes to you preaching another Jesus whom I have not proclaimed, or you accept a different spirit which you have not already accepted, or a different gospel which you have not previously received—you do well to hold it at arm's length.

Although the term *completely deceived* is usually viewed as a vehement condemnation of the benighted lady, we suggest that it might be instead an emphatic appeal to orthodoxy and the traditional biblical account. Eve did not bring enlighted knowledge but darkness and alienation from God. Any "knowledge" which she was supposed to bring must be rejected, for it had occasioned the transgression. Christian truth is based upon God's revelation through Jesus Christ and through the Word of God, not upon any secrets relayed by Eve.

How an Important Bible Story Was Turned Upside Down

The average reader of the Bible will be stunned by so shocking a distortion of the biblical account. What a terrible travesty of the first chapters of Genesis! This is precisely the complaint of the author of the pastoral Epistles: that stories out of the Jewish tradition are being told in a twisted form and that they are being heeded (1 Tim. 1:4; Titus 1:14). The tales, peddled about by old women, express opposition to God and turn many away from the truth (1 Tim. 4:7; 2 Tim. 4:4). It may seem ridiculous to us that the mere telling of stories could present a theological problem; but in the ancient world, theology often had to accommodate itself to myths that were already current. In the case of Gnosticism, it seems that the myths came first and that they were circulating by the first or second century B.C.E.

Quite clearly the distorted stories were a primary factor in causing their hearers to move in a different theological direction. This change of course in people's belief and behavior is noted in the Greek by verbs of turning. The myths and human mandates turned people away from the truth (*apostrepho*), according to Titus 1:14. As people turned away from the truth (*apostrepho*), they turned toward (*ektrepo*) the strange new mythology (2 Tim. 4:4). Those duped by the false teachers turned as well to foolish talk (1 Tim. 1:6), while younger widows turned to (*ektrepo*) Satan (1 Tim. 5:15).

In contrast, Timothy is told to turn away (*ektrepo*) from foolish babblings and oppositions to God, which are falsely called *gnōsis* (knowledge). (Those readers who have waded through the Gnostic myths in appendix 7 will know how difficult they are to follow in a rational fashion and how positive they are toward the enemy of the Hebrew God!)

If the stories told by old women were a pivotal part of the false teaching which the writer of the Pastorals opposed, we must inquire into the nature of both the stories and the storytellers. How, where, when, and why could such tales ever have developed? Who could have told them in so twisted a form? We believe that four major factors contributed to the development of the Gnostic portrayal of Eve:

1. The incredible literary creativity of western Asia Minor
2. The wholesale transformation of many older myths to convey new and sometimes startling theological concepts
3. The assimilation to Eve of many new elements within the Jewish tradition
4. The conflation with Eve of several mother goddesses

First, let us consider the extraordinary literary inventiveness of the inhabitants of Asia Minor.

Of Stories and Storytellers

In an age that knew neither movies, television, nor radio, there were other ways to provide spellbinding entertainment. The teller of stories was prized at many levels, whether that person was an old woman in the household, the storyteller in the village center, or the wandering singer of tales. It must have been professional minstrels in Asia Minor who fashioned the cycle of tales about ancient heroes into the epics known as the *Iliad* and the *Odyssey*. Here too the earliest Greek philosophical writings were composed.

Many of the most popular myths of the Greeks were placed in Asia Minor: Bellerophon and the chimaera, Arachne, Niobe, Jason and the Golden Fleece, the Trojan War, and Hercules and Omphale. We can be sure that these myths were told and retold on the eastern coast of the Aegean Sea as well as on the western coast. Dramatists too seized upon the rich mythic material told so freely in oral form. These stories were molded by Greek tragedians and in the process took on new details and meaning.

But the stories of the ancients were more often told in humbler settings. Children in particular loved to hear a member of the household spin a good yarn and must have been quite as insistent in demanding stories as their present-day counterparts. We cannot hear the tales as the women once told them, nor was there any way for illiterate crones to preserve them except in the minds of their hearers. We can only reconstruct their content from the written stories which men have left us.

Historiography

Storytelling took many forms in Asia Minor, where a new style of writing developed. Herodotus of Halicarnassus and Ctesias of Cnidus (ca. 400 B.C.E.) were the first to utilize this earliest Greek prose genre, historiography, or the writing of *historia*. While it was the precursor of modern history-writing, its subject matter was more inclusive. Travel descriptions, observations on folk culture, and local legends were important components. The reporting of actual historical events is interwoven with the recounting of myths. Tomas Hägg wrote, "Here popular story-telling has been taken up and cast in a literary mould. . . . It is no coincidence that so much of the story-telling in Herodotus and Xenophon deals with oriental themes. Ionia, the province on Asia Minor's west coast where *historia* was born, was a borderland between East and West."[1] We may be sure that the stories preserved by the historiographers had been told in the nursery by lamplight as well as in the more formal quarters of the men.

Fables

Another important genre which developed in Asia Minor was that of the fable. The slave Aesop entertained the court of King Croesus of Lydia with his tales of animals who displayed astonishingly human characteristics. In each case, the story is told to point out a moral. Sometimes the stories were made to serve political purposes, and their entertainment value made them popular as men sat around after dinner swapping stories. But most often they were utilized to delight and instruct children.

Ancient Novels

During the last two centuries before Christ, another new literary genre arose in Asia Minor. It was the romance, the prototype of our modern novel. The scenarios often looked back to the plays of Euripides and Menander; and they were written in prose, as earlier narratives of this kind may have been written in Egypt. The plots were of the "perils of Pauline" type, filled with star-crossed lovers, wanderings, shipwrecks, abductions by pirates or bandits, near-death experiences, and a happy ending.

For the first time, a literature was evolving which was of at least as much interest to women as it was to men. Indeed, there are indications that some of the authors may have been women.[2] In these tales, although there is much suffering, it is caused by evil men (bandits, pirates, slave dealers) rather than egocentric deities. The divinities who appealed especially to women are put in a positive light, often as savior goddesses.

Interestingly enough, Ephesus features prominently in these romances; and often there is a strange blending of Artemis of Ephesus with motifs of sex and death. The source of Shakespeare's *Romeo and Juliet* lies in Xenophon's *Ephesian Tale*, in which bridal chamber becomes tomb and tomb bridal chamber. In Xenophon's version, however, all ends happily ever after when the star-crossed lovers return to Ephesus.

Christian Romances

The genius for storytelling as displayed by the citizens of Asia Minor continued to develop. Numerous Christian tales began to circulate in the second century C.E. These stories related the missionary adventures of the apostles and their companions, frequently women. The stories seem to have been told and particularly enjoyed by members of the fair sex. Certain elements in the plots were borrowed from the contemporary novels which we have already discussed. The role of the women was strongly emphasized, and they are vigorous and effective proponents of the gospel.

Dennis MacDonald has suggested that the pastoral Epistles were written in part to refute these stories and the endorsement which they gave to the ministry of women.[3] This is a most interesting proposal, although the complaint in the Pastorals is that the stories were "Jewish myths" (Titus 1:14), perhaps a significant element in what are called "distortions" in Acts 20:30. We would do well to look for those stories that deal with specifically Jewish material which has been drastically distorted or altered.

Literary Adaptations in the Tales of Women

There are many literary allusions to the storytelling skill of women and to the tales which they told at night by lamplight.[4] Dio Chrysostom reminisced about how nurses told stories to children to comfort them after they had been punished.[5] Children learned their tales first in the nursery and then progressed to those of Aesop.[6] A pagan named Celsus observed that the Garden of Eden story, with Eve as heroine, drew women's special attention.

Female storytellers were fascinated by snakes[7] and included them in their tales.[8] Interestingly enough, the myths depicted in the ancient art around Ephesus feature a strange affinity between feminine figures and snakes. Medusa with snakes for hair is a favorite, as is Amphitrite, the wife of Poseidon, riding on a sea creature with the coils of a serpent. She gave birth to another sea deity, Triton, whose torso is that of a human male, but whose legs are serpents. Hygeia, the daughter of Asclepius, is frequently depicted with a snake, a symbol of knowledge and healing. Ancient inscriptions bear witness to the mingling of Jewish and pagan elements at Ephesus and its environs, and Ephesus was a fertile field for new renderings of the story of Eve and the serpent.

Philostratos knew that the stories told by women were full of the cruelties which the gods and heroes had inflicted on mortals (usually women), and that the nurses wept over Theseus' abandonment of Ariadne.[9] Seduction, rape, desertion, and vengeful wrath over an illegitimate pregnancy were standard fare. Apollonius of Tyana defended Aesop, whose fables were said to be fit only for children and old women, because Aesop knew better than to perpetuate slander against the gods![10] Even Euripides, who told the stories of many of the abused heroines, wrestled with the basic immorality of gods who by their own rash acts and subsequent irresponsibility left innocent mortals in such appalling predicaments. He concluded that human beings often had far higher standards than the gods.

Origen, a Christian, spoke of old women who told tales of the gods that ought to be repudiated.[11] He was not the first. Far earlier Plato had objected strenuously to the myths told by poets, mothers, and nurses because they put the gods in so bad a light. He specifically warned of the deleterious effect which the tales of old wives could produce on the young. He protested that mothers and nurses should have their bedtime stories censored so that they would not misrepresent the gods. Further, he said that some of the things of which they told should be revealed only in the deepest religious mysteries.[12] The remark indicates that the subject matter of these women's tales lay very close to the heart of mystery religion. Clement of Alexandria pointed out that in the Anatolian mysteries of Demeter women dramatized the mythological story of Persephone's rape in many different forms.[13]

Others viewed the tales more positively. Eratosthenes (ca. 274–194 B.C.E.) maintained that poets, as well as storytelling old women, had the right to shape their material in accord with what they deemed suitable.[14] The old women had a remarkable aptitude to adapt a story to fit a given situation, wrote Horace.[15] Theirs was no mere rote telling of a story—frequently they added their own inventions. Elegant Romans were fastidious in making sure that the Greek accent of their children's nurse was correct, but the stories which she told might be of her own devising.

Cicero confessed that the stories of the women dealt with important theological content, even if their religious aspect would scarcely appeal to intellectuals.[16] Philosophy was all very well for the philosophically minded, said Strabo, but for women and the lower classes of society religion must have myths with such ingredients as "tridents, torches, serpents." Indeed, he observed, all of ancient theology was myth.[17] Myth often precedes theology and shapes it, and Minucius Felix reported that the fables of old women had shaped religious opinion all too easily in the pagan past.[18] The old women had a remarkable aptitude to adapt a story to fit a given situation.[19]

Witnesses such as these make it apparent that women as well as men were at work in the radical revision of the myth. By the first century of the common era, the story of Eve was certainly included in the widespread transformation of story material.

12

New Stories for Old

Epiphanius wrote that every Greek sect revised Greek myths to suit its own purposes, and the story of Eve was by no means the only tale to undergo a radical transformation in the period preceding and following the New Testament era. In this chapter, we shall examine reinterpretations of some of the pagan myths and note the tendencies which are also apparent in the Eve mythology. The process seems to have involved the ingenuity of both men and women, and we shall follow the clues.

Spiritualizing the Traditional Heroines

Minucius Felix reported that the fables of old women had molded religious opinion all too easily in the pagan past.[1] As these stories were told, they began to change shape. By the first century C.E. the process of spiritualization of myths was widespread: Plutarch, for example, was said to convert myths reverently into "mystic theologies." Myths were being made to bear a message often quite at variance from the original purpose for which they were formed.

Quintilian (ca. C.E. 30–98) complained of the way in which storytellers, among them old women, encumbered basic stories with outrageous inventions and placed a new interpretation upon them.[2] Often, he said, the tales were so distorted that even the original author would not recognize them.[3] Furthermore, these strange embellishments provided impediments to learning.[4] Mythic material was most likely to suffer such manipulation,

135

which was sometimes carried to ludicrous or scandalous and shameful extremes. Indeed, a clever perpetrator could with impunity engage in outright lying.[5] Witnesses such as these make it apparent that women as well as men were at work in the radical revision of the myth. By the first century of the common era, the story of Eve was certainly included in the widespread transformation of story material.

One of the most important conservators of myth is the poet/playwright Euripides, whose works show a remarkable sympathy for women. Like the old nurses, he was fully aware of the pathos in the stories he told. There are many indications in his dramas that he was reworking materials which he had originally heard in the women's quarters. Although he repeated the stories, he was aware of their fundamental immorality and wrestled to give more positive interpretations to the injustices wreaked upon women.[6]

In the post-classical age, Euripides' stories came to be used as salvation motifs. A case in point is the great playwright's treatment of Alcestis, the heroic wife who gave her own life to spare that of her husband. She was rescued from the underworld by Hercules and restored to her grieving family. In subsequent religious thought Alcestis became a figure of salvation and immortality. The one remaining columnar drum from the famed temple of Artemis of Ephesus shows Euripides' heroine Alcestis being handed over by Hermes, the conductor of souls, to Death. She was frequently depicted on funerary vases, sarcophagi, and tomb walls as a symbol of consolation and an emblem of victory over death.

In this way a heroine whose story abounded in pathos was given redemptive meaning, and now she was a symbol of a happy afterlife. In subsequent generations, Euripides was called "the philosopher of the stage" who was able to "divine theological truth in a riddle."[7] The far-reaching influence which he exerted upon Greek religion caused his concepts to be enthusiastically promoted in many other situations. Thus his reworking of a traditional story so as to make its heroine a religious instructor was important in the developing spiritualization of feminine figures.

In the Archaeological Museum at Istanbul is a neo-Attic bas-relief from the first century C.E. It was discovered at Smyrna (modern Izmir), not far from Ephesus. This piece is particularly helpful because it labels the individuals depicted on it. In the center sits Euripides. Behind him is an archaic statue of the god Dionysos with a drinking vessel (perhaps in this case holding the wine of inspiration). Euripides' chair is turned away from the god, but at the back of the chair, on a small altar or perhaps mystic basket, is a theatrical mask facing Dionysos (receiving inspiration?). Euripides himself faces a female figure, to whom he holds out a tragic mask. The feminine figure is marked SKENE (scene or dramatic representation). The open mouth of the mask is facing her, with the back of the head toward Euripides. With one hand Skene receives the proffered mask, and under her other arm she holds a sword. A third mask, with the long curls of a heroine, rests at the feet of Skene, the back of its head toward the woman, and its face toward a somewhat indistinguishable entity, perhaps a snake. We interpret this bas-relief as the god giving inspiration and divine enlightenment to Euripides, who passes on the message through the medium of dramatic representation, especially in a feminine expression.

The Story of Melanippe

In the ancient world, and particularly in the area around Ephesus, certain myths were reinterpreted in a manner which gave a special importance to their heroines. Little by little in the constant retelling, the heroines—usually mortal women in some sort of dire predicament—grew to a stature quite outside of their role in the original story. They acquired a special religious significance, often revealed only to initiates of the so-called mystery cults. These cults offered secrets of salvation and immortality to their own adherents while excluding others from the promise of a happy afterlife. The secrets were conveyed through special mediators, often feminine ones.

The deities of these cults were for the most part feminine, and all had themselves been victims of direful experiences. Dionysos had been devoured by Titans, Demeter had her daughter stolen away by the king of the underworld, Isis wandered throughout the earth seeking the remains of her husband's dismembered body, and Cybele was consumed with grief at the death of her beloved Attis. Women flocked to deities and heroines who had known afflictions, mourning, death, and doom.

Disadvantaged and disenfranchised women must have identified with the cruelties heaped upon the hapless heroines of Greek mythology. Rape, mistreatment, slavery, compulsion to abandon newborn infants, and dehumanization were often the lot of those who told stories in the home. If they empathized with the unfortunate heroines, they could vest their tragedies with redemptive and spiritualized qualities that gave new hope to their own bleak lives. The prospect of a blessed hereafter mitigated the miseries of their present existence. The tragic stories were so transformed that they were painted on the walls of tombs and on funerary vessels as messages of consolation and promises of immortality.[8]

Eve, as represented in Gnostic texts, is raped by a celestial being in disguise, bears two children who are important progenitors, suffers outrageous abuse, is persecuted, and finally conveys the knowledge of good and evil to the human race. The story told in Gnostic texts bears a great similarity to other tales in which spiritually-endowed, often hieratic, heroines are raped and impregnated by superhuman beings (usually gods in disguise) and bear two children (usually sons). Often they were forcibly separated from their children at birth. The mothers endure toil, wandering, and various forms of persecution, repudiation by their families, deprivation, and dehumanizing suffering. Among these heroines are Melanippe, Antiope, Rhea Silvia (the mother of Romulus and Remus), Danae, Auge, Tyro, Io, Callisto, Creusa, and a host of others. Walter Burkert classifies tales of this sort as "the maiden's tragedy."[9] Those who told them first—Homer and Hesiod—emphasize the heroines' union with a god and the importance of the city or race which their sons founded.

In the end all of these heroines are vindicated, and those who have suffered the most have gained a mystic knowledge which they can impart to others. A case in point is Melanippe. As with many of the other tragic women whose stories he must have heard as a child in the women's quarters, Euripides empathized with her and devoted two plays to her. One is called *Melanippe the Prisoner* and tells of her plight during the many years of imprisonment which she suffered as a consequence of her illegitimate pregnancy. The second play is called *Melanippe the Wise* and tells of the spiritual insights which she gained.

Melanippe, in the treatment given her by the playwright, declares that in religion women have the chief part, that they alone may serve the Fates and Furies, that they alone may speak the will of the gods at the famed oracles of Delphi and Dodona.[10] Her speech constitutes a remarkable defense of women and of their effectiveness as religious intermediaries. In religious matters, she maintains, the role of women is dominant. Whatever griefs, dangers, and deprivations have assailed Melanippe, she is nevertheless self-confident in her knowledge of the religious power and legitimacy of women.

In the play, Melanippe also becomes an exponent of Orphic doctrine, and her exposition is still an important source for the study of the system of beliefs known as Orphism. It is made the more authentic by Melanippe's disclaimer, "This is not my saying, but that of my mother."[11] Thea, the mother of Melanippe, was a prophetess who had also known "the maiden's tragedy." Both mother and daughter gained their insights by their suffering.

Dionysius of Halicarnassus, a city almost directly south of Ephesus, wrote that in this cosmogonic statement Euripides affirmed an ancient doctrine through Melanippe.[12] She becomes a mouthpiece for significant doctrinal teaching. Melanippe's introduction, attributing the insight to her mother, was often quoted in antiquity to give particular emphasis to a pronouncement.[13] It was used by Plato and by others throughout the ancient world. This phrase, "not my word, but my mother's," declared that the insight was more profound than the speaker's own. At least in the case of Melanippe, Euripides seems to have claimed a special religious role for his heroine and her mother. He enlarged the basic lines of the old myth to include this concept of woman as religious mediator and conveyor of spiritual secrets. Women who had suffered, especially mothers, could communicate mystic *gnōsis* leading to salvation. Eve, the mother of all living, was to be no exception.

Antiope and Her Story

Another story in point is that of Antiope, the worst-treated of Zeus' rape victims. Violated by the king of the gods in the guise of a satyr, Antiope had to flee the wrath of her father when he discovered she was pregnant. She was seized by his soldiers and forced to abandon her twin sons upon Mount Cithairon, where they were found and reared by a kindly cowherd. Upon the death of her father, the vendetta against her was carried on by a vengeful uncle and his malignant wife, Dirce. Unlike other mythological rape victims, whose persecution lasted for a comparatively short time, Antiope endured twenty years of imprisonment, torture, toil, and degradation until she finally managed to escape.[14] In a vase painting of a scene from Euripides' play, the fate planned for Antiope is executed instead upon Dirce. Overwhelmed and terrified, the heroine cowers in the background while her sons prepare to extinguish the life of King Lycos, Dirce's husband. At the last moment, their hand is stayed by Hermes, who announces their true parentage and demands that they be given their position as rightful kings of Thebes. Antiope receives no rewards beyond her freedom and the restoration to her children. Other mythological rape victims are able to rear their own children and engage in subsequent happy marriages; some are even granted immortality.

The story of a woman who could win no forgiveness for an illicit pregnancy may well have struck a chord with those consigned to drudgery within the women's quarters for a similar offense. Perhaps as a result of frequent retelling in the home, the story of Antiope became an increasingly popular motif for writers and artists in Asia Minor. Coins at Thyatira and Akrasos,[15] a statue in the public meatmarket at Thyatira,[16] and a column in a temple at Cyzicus[17] depicted scenes from the story. Two sculptors, brothers from Tralles in southern Asia Minor, carved either the model or the actual Farnese Bull,[18] the largest piece of group statuary in the ancient world. The enormous sculpture stands today in the Naples Museum, an imposing sight as the bull rears up while Amphion and Zethos seek to control him. Dirce is begging for deliverance from her impending fate, and Antiope watches passively from the background.

By the early third century B.C.E., an elegist born at Colophon, fifteen miles from Ephesus, had a new interpretation of Antiope's story. Hermesianax described Antiope as the beloved of the prophet Musaeus and as a priestess who indoctrinated initiates into the mysteries of Eleusis. So great was her fame that she was known even in Hades, averred the poet.[19] Her power apparently extended to conferring blessings in the afterlife. This early account, hardly more than a century later than the production of Euripides' play, has transformed Antiope from woeful victim to a personage of religious power and authority. Her sufferings were closely paralleled by the ordeals known to have been part of mystery initiation and may have led to the perception that she could guide others through the rites.

By the time of Hadrian (early second century C.E.), Kephalion, a native of Asia Minor, described Antiope as a priestess and one who led others into the divine secrets of the god Dionysos.[20] She had been transformed into an adept in the mysteries. In a tomb painting from the third century C.E. on the Isola Sacra near Rome, she initiates the young Dionysos into his own rites. Instead of the cowering heroine of Euripides' play or the passive onlooker of the Farnese Bull group, Antiope now stands in the foreground, a picture of joyful assurance as she leads the youthful god to a knowledge of salvation as the pagans understood it. Beside her is a figure marked "Satur"—Zeus in disguise, giving her a new identity as the beloved of a god.[21]

The storytellers of the area told and retold the myth of this heroine of Euripides until she was no longer a mother who endured every sort of tribulation, but a woman with mystic insight which she could impart to others.[22] Her story would have had special relevance for the oppressed, especially women, who would find in it hopes of a better future. It may well have afforded consolation to victims of rape who were consigned to long years of punishment for bringing disgrace upon their families. Like Antiope, they must often have been deprived of their children and reduced to virtual slave status within the household. Her story had in it far more realism than the happy endings of other stories, and perhaps for that very reason held out more hope. It may have been in the women's quarters that the mystic aspects of Antiope were first developed.

In Asia Minor an amulet was recovered that bears another scene of initiation, in some ways similar to that of Antiope instructing Dionysos in his own mysteries. The amulet (illustration 11) shows Eve dispensing the knowledge (gnōsis) of good and evil to Adam. E. R. Goodenough identifies the amulet as Gnostic in view of the total lack of shame displayed—a marked contrast to Christian art.[23] The serpent twines around the tree and reaches out toward Eve with a kiss, perhaps indicative of their sexual union. Beside the tree are the Hebrew letters heth and daleth, which Birger Pearson suggests stand for life and knowledge: "the two trees of Genesis 2:9 understood gnostically as a single tree portrayed on the amulet."[24] Indeed, life and knowledge are the

Illustration 11. Amulet depicting Eve giving knowledge of good and evil to Adam.
Drawing by Louise Bauer

two blessings which Gnostic myth maintains Eve bestowed on Adam. In both the amulet and the tomb painting, female offers knowledge to male initiate; and in both scenes they are accompanied by the male sexual partner who made the revelation possible.

Cupid and Psyche

Another myth also serves as a prototype for the development of Eve's story. It is the tale of Cupid and Psyche. This myth appears to have circulated widely in the ancient world and is preserved for us in a novel by Apuleius. It is presented as a story told by an old woman to comfort a young bride who has been kidnaped by bandits.

In the story, Venus becomes jealous of a beautiful young woman whose name, Psyche, means "soul." She sends her son, Cupid, to wreak vengeance upon the hapless girl; but Cupid instead falls in love with her and manages to waft her away. He comes to her only at night and forbids her to see him. Her sisters are allowed to visit and, jealous of her beautiful surroundings, persuade Psyche to spy upon her mysterious lover. She lights a lamp and gazes upon the sleeping Cupid, but he awakes when she spills a drop of hot lamp oil upon him. Enraged, he leaves her; and in grief she wanders over the earth seeking him.

In despair Psyche turns to Venus, who commands her to perform formidable tasks. Like the other heroines she endures trials, ordeals, and dangers. Finally Venus sends her to Hades itself, where Persephone, goddess of the underworld, gives her a sealed jar supposedly containing beauty. Although she has been cautioned not to open it, Psyche breaks open the seal and is nearly overcome by a fatal sleep. But now Cupid, who at last regrets his hasty behavior, relents and begs Jupiter (Zeus) to sanction their marriage. The king of the gods assents, and Psyche is brought to heaven as the bride of Love. The plot clearly is developed along the lines of a mystery initiation.

Of all the myths of ancient heroines, this story most clearly describes the searching of the soul for salvation and union with the divine. Many of the vicissitudes of Sophia-Eve in Gnostic stories parallel those of Psyche. Scholars have noted the evidence of borrowing from the Cupid and Psyche story in certain Gnostic renderings of the Eve story.[25] Eve too is often allegorized as the Soul, and her story frequently includes a grievous fault committed, grief, wanderings, dangers, and trials. Her story had many antecedents.

Changing Perspectives on Eve

In each of these stories, a woman endured prolonged punishment for a misdeed, usually being unable to repel the seductive advances of a superhuman being. Even the feminine perpetrators of heinous crimes could be reinterpeted in a more kindly light. Classical mythology told the story of the fifty daughters of Danaus who had been forced to marry their cousins. The outraged sisters solved their problem by slaying their husbands and thereby earned for themselves in Hades the endless frustration of labor which could never be completed: carrying water in leaky jars. By the New Testament era, however, these same water-carrying women were thought to bring consolation and immortality to the dead. As we have seen, other women bearing other kinds of guilt were also transformed into figures of blessing.

No figure has been more consistently blamed and loaded with guilt than Eve. By the turn of the era, two widely divergent perspectives developed relating to Eve. The first viewed her as responsible for many of the tribulations and discomforts of being born a woman. Menstruation, labor pains, and subjugation were considered consequences of her primary role in the fall. This was true not only in Christian tradition but also in Jewish thought. In early Judaism women were required to walk before the corpse at a funeral because Eve had brought death into the world. They must light the Sabbath lamps because Eve had brought darkness. In further recompense, they must prepare the dough offering because Adam, the pure dough of the world, had been corrupted by his spouse.[26] These requirements served as constant reminders that women still bore the stigma of Eve's sin.

The earliest writer to lay at Eve's door the blame for the advent of sin and death into the world is Ben Sirach in the second century B.C.E. (Ecclus. 25:24). By the time of the New Testament, the pseudepigraphic versions of the Eve story bitterly denounce her for having been deceived by a celestial seducer. She must everlastingly bear the burden of guilt. In the first-century work known as Life of Adam and Eve, she cries, "Alas, alas, when I come to the day of resurrection, all who have sinned will curse me, saying that Eve did not keep the command of God."[27]

To the storytellers Eve may have presented a challenge. She too might be vindicated, as had others, and vested with mystic knowledge. If she had borne a universal opprobrium, she might also be the moderator who had brought life and enlightenment to the human race. In Gnostic circles another perspective developed on Eve. She came to symbolize blessing rather than blame, life rather than death, and light rather than darkness. Women intent on rehabilitation—or perhaps rebellion—could well champion her cause. This was one way to deal with the guilt of Eve.

We maintain that the apostle Paul offered a different view of Eve's status when he declared, "Nevertheless she shall be saved" (1 Tim. 2:15). Rather than consigning Eve to everlasting condemnation, he was pointing to the promise of Genesis 3:15, that the serpent should bruise the woman's child, but that the child would bruise the serpent's head. Through the defeat of Satan on the cross of Jesus Christ, her sin and guilt were wiped away. Eve was indeed redeemed through her blessed Offspring who brought salvation and forgiveness into the world. In a later chapter we shall suggest that the message of 1 Timothy 2:15 brings good news to womankind at another level.

13

Of Jewish and Gnostic Heroines

If the embellishment of myth can most clearly be traced in the beginning to the stories of Euripides, the process did not end there. Storytellers performed the same sort of operation with other materials. Myths could derive also from other sources which were deemed authoritative. One such authoritative source was the Hebrew Bible, and many reinterpretations of the basic stories emerged. An apparent favorite with old women was the Garden of Eden story, though the retelling process involved men as well as women.

A favorite technique was to vest an abstract quality (such as wisdom or life) with the characteristics of a human being, especially a woman. This trait was apparent in Alexandrian authors.[1] The writer of the Wisdom of Solomon (first century B.C.E.) declared that he embraced Wisdom (Sophia) and made her his bride (8:2). Wisdom herself initiated believers into the knowledge of God (8:4), brought with her mysteries (6:22), and was an instructor of those who sought her (6:17). She knew both past and future and understood the interpretation of dark sayings (8:8). In a similar fashion, a Jewish pseudepigraphic work, 4 Ezra (final redaction C.E. 100–135), describes the vision of a woman who imparts her instruction as a prophet. In time she is revealed as the heavenly Zion.

The Jewish community, both inside and outside of Ephesus, was not reluctant to vest women with unusual spiritual powers.

145

One of our sources for Hellenistic Jewish thought lies in the extensive writings of Philo of Alexandria, a contemporary of both Jesus and Paul. Philo, though a Jew, was profoundly influenced by Greek religious ideas and frequently tried to reinterpret Judaism in their light. He was especially fond of allegorizing Bible stories to convey Grecianized concepts.

Since sexual union was used in the pagan mysteries to heighten or portray religious experience, Philo draws on the same vein. For him, instruction in the mysteries was communicated by a feminine figure, whether a Bible character or an abstraction, such as Sophia (Wisdom). God, then, was the husband of Wisdom.[2] Philo carried the "feminine spiritual principle" one step further, however, and applied the image of enlightener to various Bible heroines. He allegorized the marriages of Abraham, Isaac, and Jacob as being the beginning of their spiritual maturity.[3] Their wives symbolized heavenly wisdom, and the consummation brought divine enlightenment.[4] Sarah, for instance, represents "virtue made perfect through teaching."[5] Rebecca's name is allegorized as Wisdom, the daughter of God, who is the first-born mother of all things.[6] Her function as drawer and carrier of water symbolizes carrying eternal wisdom of knowledge from the divine spring.[7] Philo conceived of Rebecca as instructor, "for the word was hers who was teaching, and the ears were his who received the teaching."[8] Like Sarah, she is a teacher of a man, and her mother's house is called "the maternal household of wisdom."[9] Rachel too brought enlightenment to her husband when he obeyed his father Isaac's command to take a wife who loved the wisdom of knowledge.[10] "Where else except from the house of wisdom shall he find a partner, blameless in judgment, with whom to remain always?"[11] Zipporah, the bride of Moses, symbolized soaring virtue which contemplated the divine, and Eve illuminated Adam.[12]

Jew though he was, Philo was far closer to mystery religion than Judaism when he declared that the union of Adam and Eve was the place where initiation must begin, and that the knowledge must extend only to those who shared the initiation secrets.[13] Most interesting of all, he allegorizes Adam as mind and Eve as sense perception. The scenario is truly astonishing: Eve, he maintained, "is represented as the one through whom animate beings receive life" (Gen. 3:20).[14] As Philo goes on, it is apparent that there is no meaningful life without her. It is Eve who brings Adam what he lacks.

This curious Alexandrian Jew explained that the mind, personified as Adam, was blind, not with an ordinary blindness, but totally deprived of all ability to perceive in any manner. It lacked all the sense organs. Adam (the mind) knew nothing of the outside world, "for that by which they could be made known, perception, did not exist." Without Eve he could not have knowledge. All material objects were wrapped in darkness. He could not even walk erect "without the staff of the sense organs with which to support his faltering steps." He was but half of a complete soul.

> God therefore, wishing to bestow upon him a grasp not only of immaterial but also of solid bodies, completed the whole soul, weaving together a second section which was counterpart to that already crafted. To this he gave the generic name of "woman" and the personal name of "Eve," intimating perception. As soon as she was created, through each of her parts, as if through orifices, she directed massed light toward the mind and dispersed the mist.

Eve caused the mind to see clearly the nature of things. Now Adam could perceive the reality which before had been unknown to him. Before the advent of Eve, he had no way of gaining knowledge. "Like one who is dazzled by a brilliant burst of sunshine in the middle of the night, or is roused from a deep sleep, or like a blind man who suddenly recovers his sight, the spirit encountered all the entire assemblage of those things which comprised the creation."[15]

These phrases are reminiscent of language and concepts used in mystery religion and Gnosticism. During the mysteries of Demeter at Eleusis and of Isis at Corinth there was said to be a brilliant light shining in the midst of the night. In Gnosticism, blindness and sleep were symbolic of ignorance which could be dispelled by true knowledge (gnōsis). In line with such traditions, the allegorical Eve is represented by Philo both as life-giver and light-bringer.

Here Philo is clearly allegorizing his interpretation of Eve, even though at other points he condemns her for causing Adam's death. He himself complains of those who distort the Genesis traditions. Yet if Philo can typify Eve as bringing light and understanding to Adam, how might the story be understood by his less orthodox contemporaries? If he can describe Eve, even symbolically, as the "one in whom the animate gains its life," it is not surprising that others revised the story to make her the source of human existence.

Philo utilizes the very theme which drew rebuttal by Paul: namely, Eve as the one who brings knowledge and meaningful life to Adam. His very treatment of the story indicates that he has had some contact with a more Gnostic point of view. He speaks of certain Alexandrian Jews who allegorized the Scriptures to the exclusion of their literal meaning.[16] Yet Philo himself was not beyond reproach. We have seen that by the early first century C.E. his allegorization had changed Eve from temptress to illuminator of Adam. He considered Genesis 2:21 to be "myth-like" rather than literal, and even the serpent is allegorized as a beneficent means of uniting mind and sense perception in order to give true comprehension.[17]

Birger Pearson suggests that at times Philo directed his polemic specifically against Gnostic doctrine.[18] It cannot be demonstrated with absolute certainty that Philo's opponents were Gnostic, but it can be demonstrated that there existed heretical elements in Alexandrian Judaism "which were co-terminous with the rise of Christianity."[19] The Jewish communities of Alexandria and Ephesus maintained strong commercial and religious ties. Apollos, a learned Jew from Alexandria, was welcome to teach in the synagogue at Ephesus (Acts 18:24–26). Others may have brought a less orthodox message.

Adaptations of the Eve Story

Gnosticism appears to be the work of heterodox Diaspora Jews.[20] The transition did not take place all at once or all in the same place. For our information about the process we are dependent upon the accounts of the church fathers, largely based upon religious conditions in Asia Minor. This knowledge has been greatly augmented by the discovery of a whole library of Gnostic writings at Nag Hammadi in Egypt. Before the discovery of the Nag Hammadi library, earlier scholars looked at the eclectic Jews of Asia Minor as the source of Gnostic thought. The Jews of Phrygia were notorious for their easy assimilation of pagan mores and beliefs. Everything in the society invited a blending of the religious culture.

Many different versions of the Adam and Eve story circulated in Jewish circles, and Josephus (first century C.E.) knew of some of the less orthodox renderings.[21] Josephus told of writers such as Apollonius Molon, Lysimachus, and others who maligned Moses as a cheat and a deceiver.[22] A repudiation and distortion of the biblical stories as told by Moses was certainly a major element in Gnostic myth. The phrase *not as Moses said* runs as a motif through some of the literature.[23]

In the Gnostic texts, we find that Cain is a hero instead of Abel, that Eve and the serpent are salvation figures, and that the God of the Old Testament is given extremely poor press. Indeed, one group taught that, since the Jewish God was evil, it was necessary to oppose him at every point. Since he commanded, "Thou shalt not commit adultery," the adherents were encouraged to commit adultery whenever possible! It is hard for us to conceive of an ethical system which is based upon a repudiation of the God of the Hebrew Bible. P. Van Baaren declared, "Gnosticism is a religion of revolt."

Epiphanius observed that the Gnostics discarded whatever they considered opposed to their own theology as having been spoken by "the spirit of the world." Whatever in Scripture advanced their cause was declared "spoken by the Spirit of Truth."[24] In this way they could effect a radical revision of biblical material.

Already it has become apparent that this is a very deviant sort of religious belief and that it is taking great liberties with the Genesis story. Celsus, a pagan, took the story of the serpent to be an old wives' tale and reported that Gnostics told Jewish stories of the Garden of Eden to old women. In point of fact, he said, these tales were so preposterous that they were fit only for old women.[25]

Haggadic, Mishnaic, and Septuagintal Elements

Gnostic writing reveals a usage of Haggadic traditions (the serpent, the tree, the creator God), some of which date back to the first century B.C.E. W. F. Albright wrote, "Gnosticism had already developed some of its most pronounced sects well before the Fall of Jerusalem [C.E. 70]," while Henry A. Green, in surveying the evidence, wrote, "What is certain is that by the end of the first century A.D. Jewish haggadic traditions had been employed by the

Gnostics."[26] Birger Pearson and others have traced the development of Midrashic and Septuagintal material, especially the tradition of Sophia, into the lore focused upon Eve.[27] Their insights are most helpful. Let us not forget, though, that as those versed in Jewish literary materials discussed those materials, servants would have been passing in and out of the room. Possibly they received a fragmentary impression if they were not privileged to hear the entire conversation. Associations of Eve with Zoe, Sophia, and the tree may have arisen in the minds of those who could only catch snatches of the topics under discussion.

Often those taken as slaves were transported far from home and brought their stories to new milieux. The Adam and Eve story, even in its canonical form, is one of the most eminently tellable stories. It is hardly to be wondered at that a tale told so often should be refashioned to fit preconceived frameworks harking back to pagan and classical sources rather than to the biblical one. As household storytellers, Gentile slaves in Jewish homes may have been required to tell stories of biblical characters, rather than those of classical mythology. It would be easy to pour the new wine of biblical figures into the old skins of a structure they already knew. Cultural exchange may have occurred far more readily in the women's quarters than elsewhere; and here young children of both sexes heard the tales which shaped their thought. Intelligent and embittered slave women may have deliberately twisted the story into one of rebellion against the God of the Jews. Certainly the mistreatment and abuse of Eve by the arrogant archons was a motif which they could well develop in accord with the pagan myths they already knew.

The Many Faces of Eve

The figure of Eve appears frequently in Gnostic writings. It is indeed a multiple image. There is both a heavenly and an earthly Eve,[28] the figure often moving interchangeably with that of Sophia (Wisdom) or Zoe (Life). The Hebrew word *Eve* literally means "Life," and in Genesis 3:20 she is called "the mother of all living." Often Eve becomes synonymous with Zoe. In the Septuagint version of Genesis 3:21, Adam names his wife not Eve but Zoe. This translation of the Hebrew Bible was widely read in the New Testament world and often was quoted by the apostle Paul. Using this Greek text, Philo wrote that Adam beheld the newly created Eve and "gave the name of Life (Zoe) to his own death."[29]

The Septuagint rendering of Proverbs 3:18 declares that Wisdom, Sophia, is a tree of life (Zoe) to all who lay hold upon her.[30] According to Philo, Sophia, the daughter of God, takes on the male role of father and both begets and generates.[31] Furthermore, the Septuagintal version of Proverbs 4:13 represents Sophia as instruction and cautions the reader to guard her as one's life (Zoe-Eve).[32] Thus Eve is identified in Jewish Hellenistic tradition with both Sophia and Zoe (wisdom and life), as well as with instruction.

The Aramaic roots for the words *life, serpent, instructor,* and *Eve* lay close together and became a play on words in both Jewish and Gnostic tradition.[33] The pun was picked up in a haggadah in Genesis Rabbah 20:11 as a commentary on Genesis 3:20, "The man called his wife's name Hawah (Eve)": "She was given to him for an adviser [or instructor] but she played the eavesdropper like the serpent: . . . He showed her how many generations she had destroyed."[34] Rabbi Aha's commentary took the form of an apostrophe to Eve, "The serpent was thy serpent, and thou art Adam's serpent."[35] This was an era when similarity in the sounds of words was often supposed to demonstrate other sorts of affinities. As Birger Pearson noted, "The teaching role of both the serpent and Eve is the subject of considerable speculation in Gnostic literature."[36] When Adam and Eve are still joined together as a being who is both male and female, they share a divine element, but lose it at their separation.[37] This divine element subsequently indwells the spiritual woman, Eve, who instructs the earthly Adam.[38] In some accounts, Eve has a power which she later loses.[39]

By the first century C.E., Eve had assumed a larger-than-life stature and had assumed the ability to communicate mystic knowledge. Like other literary heroines whom we have discussed, she was able to enlighten humanity. As we have seen, the Septuagint version created the impression that Eve was to be identified with Dame Wisdom, Sophia. Accordingly Eve sometimes appears in Gnostic literature as Zoe, sometimes as Sophia, sometimes as the Epinoia or Afterthought within Eve, and also as the female instructing principle. One account declared:

Because of this she was named "Zoe" (ζωή), that is the mother of
the living through the Forethought (Πρόνοια) of the Authentia
(Αὐθεντία) which is above. And through her they tasted the perfect
(τέλειος) knowledge (γνῶσις).[40]

It is the more confusing to discover that at some points there are
two Eves, one earthly and one spiritual, and that sometimes they
talk to each other! The heavenly Eve embodies a superior teaching principle and provides guidance for her earthly counterpart.

In each of the Gnostic accounts about the Garden of Eden
episode, the direction for Eve to partake of the fruit always comes
from a *feminine* cosmic source:[41] from Eve-Zoe, "the instructress
of life,"[42] from "the spiritual woman who is the instructor,"[43]
from the Epinoia of light.[44] Within the serpent, it is actually the
mother who is communicating;[45] and the serpent is itself Wisdom.[46] In our next chapter, we shall examine more closely the
identification of Eve with the mother goddesses.

The Great Goddesses and Eve

In order to understand how Eve could be viewed as a being powerful enough to bestow life on Adam, we must be aware of the identification that ancient people made between Eve and pagan goddesses. The process had begun by the second millennium B.C.E. A goddess bearing the Hurrianized form of the name *Eve* was worshiped widely in the ancient Near East, and E. A. Speiser maintains that the original Semitic name for "Eve" was transposed into the Hurrian name rather than vice versa. Hebat or (Hepat) was viewed as a mother goddess par excellence, and a Jebusite king of Jerusalem was named "Servant of Hepat" in the el Amarna letters (fourteenth century B.C.E.).[1] She was not unknown in Babylonian myth.[2] Borne along by spreading Hurrian influence, Hebat invaded the Hittite pantheon as the supreme female deity. She made her triumphal entry into Asia Minor by

Illustration 12. Queen Puduhepas offers a libation to Hebat (from a bas-relief at Fraktin).

Drawing by Louise Bauer

153

1250 B.C.E. Her cult appears to have been introduced by Queen Puduhepas, the Hurrian consort of King Hattusilis, herself a priestess of the goddess (see illustration 12).

In a bas-relief of the thirteenth century B.C.E. at Yazilikaya, near Bogazkeui in modern Turkey, we see Hebat as she leads a line of Mesopotamian and Hurrian goddesses to an encounter with Hittite gods (see illustration 13). Her name is inscribed in Luwian hieroglyphic. She rides upon a panther to meet and wed Teshub, the Hittite storm god. Her bridegroom and his attendants stand upon mountaintops (represented as men with pointed caps). The bride wears a high crown, similar to that worn by Cybele and Artemis of Ephesus, and a stiffly pleated skirt. Behind her follows the whole retinue of goddesses, as well as her son by Teshub, Sarruma, and her daughter Allanzu. She is attended by Dakita, "perhaps Semitic 'the little one', a servant of Hebat in the mythology."[3] Then follow Hutena and Hutellura, birth goddesses who were also the mythological creatresses of humanity. Under the impetus of Queen Puduhepas, her enthusiastic devotee, the new deity soon assimilated with the sun goddess of Arinna, the major goddess in the Hittite pantheon.[4] Hebat is also identified in the ancient texts as queen of heaven.[5]

Despite her majestic power, Hebat is also frail enough to encounter mishaps. One myth reveals that the powerful goddess can be dispossessed from her temple, be wronged by a diorite man, agonize over the fate of her consort, and suffer a near-death experience. Furthermore, she is in danger of being consigned to

Illustration 13. Depiction of Hebat, from a shrine at Yazilikaya.
Drawing by Louise Bauer

Illustration 14. Statue of Cybele.
Museum of Anatolian Civilization,
Ankara

the toil of grinding corn.[6] Here and elsewhere her association with the Babylonian Ishtar is explicit.[7]

The myths of Hebat were preserved largely in Hittite rituals used by feminine adherents known as "wise women" or "old women." The names of thirty-two such women still remain, as well as many of the actual rites over which they presided. Many of the rituals are specifically said to have women as their authors.[8] The names and language of these women are often Hurrian.[9]

The name of Hebat appears in Hittite and Hurrian texts, until new language groups invaded Asia Minor and Hebat became conflated with the Phrygian Cybele. Her development as a Phrygian goddess is harder to chart, as no Phrygian text has yet been discovered and Phrygian inscriptions are largely undecipherable. Illustration 14 shows Cybele with the tall headdress and stiff skirt worn by both Hebat and Artemis of Ephesus. As we shall see in the next chapter, Eve was venerated by two diverse Phrygian groups who may have been drawing on very old traditions.

Cybele

The mother goddess whose cult dominated Asia Minor was also linked with Eve. The iconography demonstrates that Cybele was worshiped at Çatal Hüyük as early as 5500 B.C.E. (see illustration 15). For thousands of years she maintained her identity as mother of gods and men. Many centuries later those who still celebrated her rites bestowed on Eve the attribution which the older goddess had borne for so long: "mother of all that live, universal in nature, of gods and angels, immortals and mortals, irrational of rational beings."

Cybele's cult became widespread, not only in Asia Minor but also throughout the Greek and Roman world. The legend of her origins and of her tragic love for Attis is told in many forms. Amid the varying details, the myths speak of her human birth, her persecution by her father when he discovered her pregnancy, her devotion to Attis, his betrayal of that love, and her grief over his death. The stories ascribe to her aspects both of human suffering and of divine omnipotence.

Illustration 15. Stele showing Cybele flanked by serpents.
Used courtesy of the Archaeological Exploration of Sardis. The stele is in Manisa Museum.

The multiplicity of Cybele legends indicates that women had been at their task as storytellers. The stories bear two images of Cybele, as at once human and a goddess who is both terrifying and beneficent, a characteristic which is clearly developed in the mythology of Eve. Ultimately, however, the dichotomy between the powerful Gnostic Eve as revealer and the sorrowful, very human Jewish heroine was stretched too far, and she split into a heavenly Eve and an earthly one. The opposing characteristics in Cybele's nature and myth were comprehended in a yearly cycle of rituals expressing her sorrow and mourning (the Day of Blood), followed by ecstasy and wild celebration (the *Hilaria*). This alternation of mood, necessitating in the worshipers enormous changes in response, may well have been one of the strengths of the cult.

Identification with Isis

In Egypt Eve was identified with Isis, an ancient goddess who was rejuvenated in the Hellenistic period. Her cult was popular all over the Mediterranean world, including Ephesus, as we have seen.[10] Her association with serpents was strong, as the vision of a devotee shows:

An intricately designed crown encircled her high forehead with many sorts of flowers. At the center of it, over her face, shone a flat disc like a mirror—or rather the white light of the moon. On the right and left were bound spirals of upraised vipers. . . . From her left hand hung a golden cup from whose handle, at a conspicuous point, there arose an asp, raising its head high, its throat puffed wide.[11]

At the behest of Ptolemy I, Isis was given a Hellenized interpretation by Timothy, a priest at Eleusis. Thereafter Isis developed a persona not unlike the Eleusinian Demeter, the earth mother who was raped by Zeus and bore a daughter who was subsequently stolen away by Hades, god of the underworld. The sorrowing mother searched throughout the world in grief until the girl was returned. Demeter's rites, like those of Isis, promised a blessed hereafter to those who were initiated. As faithful wife, Isis sought throughout the world for the remains of her slain husband.

Ultimately she rose to the status of savior and sovereign of the universe and promised to her devotees knowledge (*gnōsis*) of the One who is the First, a comprehension of true reality.[12]

Astounding claims were made on behalf of Isis. These claims were embedded in so-called aretologies in which Isis proclaimed her own virtues. Frequently the aretologies are couched in the "I am" (*ego eimi*) form that readers of the Bible will recognize as a formula employed repeatedly in the Gospel of John. The following list of virtues, found in Cyme in Asia Minor, is a copy of an earlier one. It reads in part:

> I am the eldest daughter of Kronos
> I am wife and sister of King Osiris
> I am she who finds fruit for humanity
> I am the mother of King Horus.
> I am she who commands the Dog Star.
> I am she who is called God among women . . .
> I am the mistress of battle . . .
> I am she who is called the law-giver.[13]

If Isis controlled the Dog Star, Eve was identified with Cassiopeia, one of the brightest constellations in the heavens.[14] As

Illustration 16. Isis Thermoutis depicted as a serpent.

Drawing by Louise Bauer

the mother of all, Isis is clearly conflated with Eve. This may have been especially true of an identification with Isis Thermoutis, who was worshiped in serpent form (see illustration 16). Her images sometimes showed her—even as a serpent—nursing her young son. Indeed, the affinity was not unobserved in the ancient world. Rabbi Judah particularly forbade the manufacture of idols in the form of Isis nursing her infant because "a woman giving suck alludes to Eve who suckled the whole world."[15] Ordinarily a prohibition implies that someone is actually engaged in such a practice.

The incorporation of the characteristics and in some places almost verbatim aretologies of the Egyptian goddess into Gnostic Eve-texts has been well noted. Rose Horman Arthur wrote, "The assimilation of Isis material within an account of Eve is a remarkable instance of the interweaving of Egyptian and Jewish material."[16] Eve material in Gnostic sources also sometimes takes the *ego eimi* (I am) form. Frequently, however, the *ego eimi* is posed in a baffling list of paradoxes:

> For I am the one who is the first and the last
> I am the one who is the honored one and the despised
> I am the one who is the harlot (πορνή) and the holy one (σεμνή)
> I am the one who is the wife and the virgin (παρθένος)
> . . . .
> I am the one who is mother of my father and the sister of my husband
> and he is the one to whom I gave birth.[17]

This quite clearly follows the formula of the Isis aretologies, a fact which is less surprising when we remember the importance of female deities in the ancient world.

In Thunder, Perfect Mind the heavenly Eve declares

> From the power was I sent forth,
> and to those who think upon me have I come
> And I was found in those who seek after me
> Behold me, you who think about me
> And you hearers, listen to me.
> You who await me, receive me to yourselves.[18]

For many are the delightful forms (εἶδος) that exist in manifold sins and incontinencies and passions (πάθος) and pleasures (ἡδονή) which last for (πρὸς) the night. People grasp onto these until they become sober (νήφειν) and flee up to their resting place. (κοιμητήριον). And they will find me in that place, and they shall live, and they will not return to death (i.e., not become reincarnate in a prisonlike body).[19]

Here Eve is portrayed as a savior sent into the world to free souls who have been entrapped in a body. To quote Bentley Layton, she descends "from another realm of power and rest, she suffers, recalls the soul to soberness and her proper home, and reascends, showing the way for those who will be saved."[20] Layton continues his commentary on this text:

> She is the savior of mankind; she saves by preaching, demanding a reorientation of mind and heart. She invites comparison with the authority of Isis and thence Dame Wisdom. She is an element within those to whom she is sent: the instrument of broadcasting and the instrument of reception are one and the same. She and they are in the same paradoxical situation, so that self-knowledge and knowledge of the savior may at least partly be the same. Finally, she and the saved have the same home.[21]

So it was that the figure of Eve developed from that of deceived sinner to that of a powerful spiritual being who could enlighten those in need of salvation. Her human frailty was replaced by the might of a goddess. The numerous variants of the story now projected the spiritual potency of Eve and had reshaped themselves into dangerous and destructive doctrines which the writer of the Pastorals repudiated.

15

The Veneration of the Serpent and Eve

Other than the stories is there any evidence for the existence of Ophite Gnosticism in Asia Minor by the time of the New Testament era? The literary traditions of Ephesus and its environs, the testimony of the Scriptures themselves, and the archaeological and art historic remains all demonstrate an emphasis on myth and cult exalting Eve and the serpent. An understanding of this background can radically change our interpretation of 1 Timothy 2:9–15.

The serpent was a religious symbol, widely venerated long before the first century. Philo of Byblos wrote that the serpent was the most "spiritual" (*pneumatikotaton*) of all reptiles.[1] Many temples had serpents as part of the cult, and frequently snakes in baskets were a prominent feature in mystery religion. Coins from the city of Ephesus reveal Artemis on one side and a basket with snakes on the other.

We have already mentioned the affinity of the goddesses Cybele and Isis for snakes (see illustration 15, p. 156). Sabazios, another popular god in Asia Minor, was often represented as a serpent. His female worshipers sometimes passed a live snake into their bosom and drew it out under their skirts. By 139 B.C.E., heterodox Jews in Pontus and Cappadocia identified their deity with Sabazios, this Thraco-Phrygian serpent god.[2] These worshipers invoked the name of the "Most High" in their cult and observed the Sabbath.[3] Thus a serpent veneration which was somehow related to Judaism predates the New Testament.

New Testament Evidence

There are indications within the New Testament itself that a nascent form of Ophitism was already present. The seven letters of the Apocalypse are written to churches which were beset by a Jewish heresy that venerated Satan. Two communities, Smyrna and Philadelphia, apparently displayed a blending of Jewish and heretical elements, for they were said to be "synagogues of Satan" (Rev. 2:9; 3:9). The writer complains, "They say they are Jews, but they are not" (Rev. 2:9; 3:9). Pergamum, a major cult center of the serpent god Asclepius, was identified as the location of "the throne of Satan" and "the place where Satan dwells" (Rev. 2:13). Here there is a specific identification of a pagan serpent deity as Satan. Indeed, Asclepius was also a Gnostic figure. Asclepius was frequently associated with women. His serpent form is often rep-

Illustration 17. Fresco of Hygeia, goddess of health, flanked by a serpent.
Photograph
by Fran Blanchard
Used by permission
of Ephesus Museum

resented in depictions of his daughter, Hygeia (see illustration 17).[4]

The church at Thyatira had within it a false prophetess named Jezebel who taught a doctrine containing "the deep things of Satan" (Rev. 2:20–24). The congregation is warned to eschew her instruction. The doctrine besetting these troubled Christian communities is said to be that of the Nicolaitans (Rev. 2:6, 15) and to involve unchastity and eating food which had been offered to idols (Rev. 2:14, 20). Both of these practices would have been repugnant to an orthodox Jewish community, and we have already noted the appeal of adultery to one Gnostic group. By contrast, the false teachers referred to in the Pastorals forbade marriage (though not necessarily sexual activity) and the eating of meat (1 Tim. 4:3).

In the Apocalypse, Ephesus is commended because it hates the deeds of the Nicolaitans (Rev. 2:6). This appears to be an indication that the church at Ephesus has, in one way or another, become acquainted with their teaching. We are reminded of the widows who have gone astray after Satan (1 Tim. 5:15) and of Hymenaeus and Alexander who have been given over to Satan (1 Tim. 1:20).

The Second Epistle to the Corinthians was written from Asia, probably from Ephesus (2 Cor. 1:1). It contained a detailed warning against Jewish missionaries who seem to have brought "another Jesus, another gospel, and another spirit" (2 Cor. 11:4). There was a danger that they would bring a message of deceit just as the serpent (ophis) had done to Eve (2 Cor. 11:3). Paul cautions believers against a message brought by disciples of Satan who masqueraded as disciples of Christ. Just as the false teachers of Ephesus were part of the Christian community, so those who threatened the doctrinal purity at Corinth were ostensibly servants of Christ:

> For such are false apostles, workers of deceit, transforming themselves into apostles of Christ. And no wonder, for even Satan disguises himself as an angel of light. It is no great thing, then, if his ministers masquerade as ministers of righteousness, whose end will be according to their works. [2 Cor. 11:13–15]

Although Gnostic myths were essentially distortions of the Hebrew Scriptures, there was an assimilation of certain Christian elements. The Ophites, among others, maintained that Christ was instrumental in bringing the message of the serpent. "For among them the snake says it is Christ."[5] The Ophites might deceive Christians just as the serpent (*ophis*) deceived Eve.

The Testimony of the Church Fathers

The church fathers attest that the glorification of Eve was widespread in Asia Minor by the second century C.E. We maintain that the process of such glorification must have begun at least by the first century. One indicator is that the lore of Eve as a powerful spiritual figure was accessible to two separate groups. It does not appear to be coincidence that the figure of Eve appears in two Phrygian cults whose origins hark back to a worship of the Great Mother of the gods, a goddess conflated with Hebat.

The first of these cults revived the Phrygian language and was very conscious of its Phrygian roots.[6] The Phrygian city of Pepuza was considered the new and spiritual Jerusalem. Montanus, founder of the cult, was said to have been a priest of Cybele, the goddess to whom male adherents must sacrifice their manhood. Thereafter they served as "she priests" garbed in feminine garments and referred to one another with feminine pronouns. Montanus, after his conversion, experienced within Christianity an onset of the same enthusiastic madness which had once led to his own demasculinization.[7]

Thus it was with a feminine identity that Montanus adapted Christianity to his/her own insights. The doctrines of the group seem to have been reasonably orthodox except for their insistence upon a superior revelation, higher than that given to the prophets or apostles.[8] This superior insight was received not only by the founder (man turned woman) but also by a series of prophetesses. One even had a direct revelation from Christ, whom she saw in a dream as a woman. She declared that the feminized Christ had put wisdom (*sophia*) into her.[9] Tertullian describes the illumination given to a woman Montanist regarding the soul.[10] Montanists unabashedly declared that "their instruction came from females."[11] Thus the Montanists, also known as the Cataphrygians, gained their ultimate truths from feminine instrumentality.

In a land where the foremost deities were maternal, it can well be understood that Eve, mother of all living, inspired reverence. It was a great honor, the women averred, that she should be the first to taste of the tree of knowledge (gnōsis);[12] and because of her women were ordained as bishops, elders, and priests.[13] For precedent, they told the stories of Deborah, Miriam, Hulda, Anna, and the prophesying daughters of Philip.[14] Although the non-Gnostic group is orthodox in its acceptance of Scripture,[15] its higher revelation points to Eve as revealer and a pattern for Christian leadership. Hippolytus observed that they preferred the myths and words of old women,[16] rather than a precise knowledge of the Scriptures. They thought they spoke correctly concerning the origin and creation of the universe,[17] and Theodoret maintained that "Montanus taught the same things we do concerning the creation of the world."[18] Yet above and beyond this orthodoxy lay the utterances of the prophetesses and the words and stories of the old women. The distortions of the Montanists centered on Eve as being given a special divine revelation, a view directly at variance with the biblical representation.

The Ophites and Naassenes

A second Phrygian group was undeniably Gnostic: the Naassenes and other Ophites who extol the serpent, the *Naas* (Heb.: serpent). At a sacramental meal the Ophites observed the Eucharist by having snakes squirm over the bread upon the table.[19] The Naassenes stressed the universal character of the serpent. Every other religion should be interpreted through the snake, they maintained, and the serpent was itself "a great symbol and mystery."[20]

A magnificent marble throne from the first century C.E. depicts a serpent rising high upon its back (see illustration 18, p. 166).[21] The snake encircles the bow of an archer god, while below on the seat lie a quiver of arrows and the headband of the deity. The headband appears more like a streamer of Artemis than of Apollo. The paraphernalia carved on the seat of this throne would have prevented it from being used as a seat for a human being, such as a ruler or priest. It is clearly a cult object.

This spectacular piece is from western Asia Minor, though its exact provenance is still a matter of debate.[22] On the front of the seat can be seen traces of a fleece, reminiscent of the fleece upon which initiates sat during initiation. The eagles of Rome perch

Illustration 18. Marble throne
(Roman, late first century c.e.) from
western Asia Minor.
Used by permission of Los Angeles
County Museum of Art, William
Randolph Hearst Collection

over the throne's front legs, while lion's paws, often associated with Cybele and Dionysos, adorn their lower ends. It is a remarkable illustration of what Saint Hippolytus says about the Naassenes: that they worshiped nothing except the serpent. Furthermore, they maintained that the serpent incorporated within itself all of the mysteries, rites, symbols, and attributes of other gods. Without the serpent, nothing could consist—nothing mortal nor immortal, animate nor inanimate.[23] As you can see, the serpent dominates, rising above the quiver and crown of Artemis and encompassing her bow. It brings to mind the statement about Pergamum, "where the throne of Satan is" (Rev. 2:13).

The Ophites repudiated the Genesis account of creation. The serpent was proclaimed as revealer and benefactor, communicating the precious *gnōsis* to Eve. Deriving from a pagan background, the Naassenes continued to celebrate the Phrygian mysteries of Cybele, the Great Mother, and to sing hymns to Attis, her paramour, who apparently was conflated with Adam.

There is considerable evidence that the Naassene cult developed from that of Attis and Cybele.[24] The Naassenes worshiped

Eve and Adam as Cybele and her consort, Attis, and observed in their honor the rites of Phrygian mystery religion. In the early part of this century, a German scholar, Wilhelm Bousset, pointed out that the figure of Eve resembled that of a mother goddess of Asia Minor far more than that of a frail victim of deception. He noted the transfer to her of the title borne by the Great Mother, "Mother of all living—of a common nature, that is (the nature) of gods, angels, immortals, mortals, irrational creatures, and rational ones."[25] Hippolytus quotes a Naassene writer who concurs with the account given in the Hypostasis of the Archons of the entrance of Eve into the snake. The universal serpent, says the Naassene, is the wise word of Eve, for Eve was formed in him as life; and by Eve within the serpent, all was created.[26] The Gnostic accounts relate that Eve, like Cybele, gave life to her own consort, a feat not usually ascribed to Isis.

Archaeological Evidence

At Ephesus a cult chamber from the first century C.E. shows three scenes of ritual meals with the participation of a serpent. This sanctuary for the worship of a serpent god was located in a private house.[27] Three bas-reliefs show a ritual meal, in each case with a serpent drinking from a libation cup offered to him by one of the participants in the meal (see illustration 19).[28] In one relief the serpent is actually coiled in a tree.[29] The three bas-reliefs are

Illustration 19. Stele of a serpent participating in a funerary meal.
Photograph by Dick Waters
Used by permission of Ephesus Museum

from the late Hellenistic or early Roman period and appear to have been installed in the shrine in the first century C.E. Originally they appear to have been designed as monuments displaying a "feast of the dead" in honor of a deceased hero or god—in this case probably Asclepius. Their removal from their original sites and subsequent grouping in the chamber signify that they were reinterpreted to suit a new religious purpose.

The room remained in use as a private shrine for several centuries. In the early third century C.E. a large red serpent, bearded, crested, and intricately decorated, was painted on a pillar in the shrine (see illustration 20).[30] H. Vetters comments that the snake indubitably has cultic significance.[31] Both the bas-reliefs and the picture had subsequently been painted over, perhaps to protect their sanctity when the room was no longer used for worship. The identification of the serpent deity remains a subject for debate. The representation of the serpent in a tree suggests the possibility that there may be an allusion to the Garden of Eden story in one form or another. A first century C.E. bas-relief similar to those at Ephesus was excavated at Smyrna and is now in the Archaeological Museum in Istanbul. It too reveals a ceremonial meal with a snake as participant.

Archaeological evidence from Ephesus demonstrates that serpent veneration was practiced at more than one site by the first

Illustration 20. Painting of a serpent, from a shrine at Ephesus.

Drawing by Louise Bauer

Illustration 21. Bronze serpent, used
as cult object in a home at Ephesus.
Photograph by Dick Waters
Used by permission of Ephesus Museum

century C.E. A handsome bronze serpent, originally covered with
gold plate, rises in coils nearly two and a half feet high (see illustration 21). The statue dates from the early first century C.E. and
was a cult object in a private house.[32] It was found in a niche
between busts of the emperor Tiberius and his mother, Livia. The
sculpture is so imposing that it does not appear to be merely a
household guardian, nor does its placement between the imperial
Roman busts bespeak a secondary cultic importance. Here was a
deity of major significance for the owner of the house.

These serpents tell their own tale of religious propensities at
Ephesus. When they are combined with testimony from the pastoral Epistles, the Book of Revelation, and from pagan, patristic,
and Gnostic sources, a picture develops of a group which endorsed
gnōsis (knowledge) falsely so called (1 Tim. 6:20) and distorted
biblical stories into vehicles which could divert the disciples of

Christ from the truth (Acts 20:30; 2 Tim. 4:4; Titus 1:14). A group in this setting, a group with heretical Jewish tendencies and preoccupied with genealogies (1 Tim. 1:3–4; Titus 3:9), could not escape a treatment of Eve, the source of life. The evidence points us to a Gnostic-like myth which claimed an existence for Eve prior to that of Adam and endowed her with a power of enlightenment that defied the God of truth who is revealed in the Bible.

Considerations
of Childbearing (2:15)

We have argued that 1 Timothy 2:13–14 should be considered an orthodox refutation of Gnostic-like mythology. The last verse of the passage (v. 15) is notoriously difficult and presents us with a new set of perplexities:

> Nevertheless she shall be saved through the childbearing if they continue in faith and love and holiness and good sense.

Now it is very good to see such excellent maternal qualities listed, and they are as needful in today's mothers as in those of the New Testament period. Nevertheless, there is a problem with the theology. Are women actually saved as a result of bringing children into the world and rearing them?

This is surely inconsistent with our evangelical view that people, women as well as men, are saved by faith and not by works (Eph. 2:8–9). Because of this problem, it has been suggested that the verse promises that the mother's life will be preserved during childbirth. Only within the last fifty years have most of the dangers associated with childbirth been overcome. Before then childbirth was sometimes a hazardous event in the lives of women; and many succumbed, Christians and non-Christians alike. In Jewish tradition, women were threatened with death in childbirth if they failed to observe certain religious obligations.[1] Is this promise intended to relieve Christian women of such a fear?

Alternatively, it has been suggested that the childbearing refers to the birth of Jesus Christ from the virgin Mary. This makes better sense theologically, but in the passage there has been no discussion of the mother of Jesus. The woman under discussion has been Eve. Verse 15 contains within it a switch from singular to plural: "*She* shall be saved . . . if *they* continue. . . ." Perhaps the first part speaks at one level of Eve, whom God involved in the first promise of the Savior's redemptive victory over Satan: "It [Eve's offspring] shall bruise your [Satan's] head, and you shall bruise its heel" (Gen. 3:15).

At another level, we believe that the directive in 1 Timothy 2:15 focuses on the women in the congregation. Thus it is appropriate to use the plural. As you recollect, some women had been victimized by false teachers who entered their homes and set them in the hopeless spiral of "ever learning and never able to come to the truth" (2 Tim. 3:6–7). By contrast, Paul asked that women be allowed to learn the truth and that they receive it as truly God's Word to them (1 Tim. 2:10). His opponents forbade marriage (1 Tim. 4:3),[2] while he asked that younger widows who might find their doctrines attractive "marry, bear children, rule the household, and give no opportunity for slander to the opponent" (1 Tim. 5:14). It appears that the call to childbearing has something to do with repudiating the false teachers. The Epistle to Titus also calls upon older women to encourage the younger ones in domestic virtues and responsibilities so that the Word of God would not be slandered (Titus 2:3–5).

Let us return to the heretics in the early church, especially those who venerated the serpent, and study their views on childbearing and the sexuality of women.

Gnostic Ideas of Salvation

Some Gnostic groups exalted the feminine principle as a divine, literary, or historical figure while they denigrated actual women. One saying describes a progression of evils: "The woman followed after the earth, and marriage (γάμος) followed the woman, and birth followed marriage (γάμος), and destruction followed after birth."[3] Childbearing is certainly a phenomenon unique to the female, and here we may see some of the misogyny and suspicion of feminine sexuality which so permeated Greek religion. (The

Greeks expressed a repugnance for the process of birth; and three of the twelve Great Gods had not been born from a woman.) Gnostics, however, had an even more negative view of women's sexuality.

In a work used by the Naassenes, the Gospel according to the Egyptians, Jesus announces, "I came to destroy the works of the female." Apparently in response to this statement, Salome asks him, "How long will death prevail?" Jesus replies, "As long as you women bear children." Salome comments, "Then I have done well in bearing no children."[4] Here we have a categorical condemnation of childbearing.

According to other texts, it is impossible to gain eternal life as a woman, one who is capable of bearing children. In the Gospel of Thomas, another work used by the Naassenes, we read, "Simon Peter said to them: 'Let Mary go out from among us, because women are not worthy of life.' Jesus said, 'Behold, I myself will draw her so that I shall make her into a male in order for (ἵνα) her to become (ὡς; as) a living spirit like you males, because every woman who will make herself male shall enter into the kingdom of heaven.'"[5] Another text declared, "That which is corruptible has [gone (χωρεῖν) up] to that which is incorruptible, and the nature of femininity has attained (κατανταν) to the nature of this masculinity."[6] In the Gospel of Mary, Mary declares, "But (δέ) rather (μᾶλλον) let us bless his greatness, for he has prepared us (and) made us into men."[7] A woman who retains her identity as woman, a being capable of bearing children, simply cannot be saved and has no part in the realm of light. Femaleness is often described as a defect.[8]

Gnostic texts indicate that salvation comes through masculinity, although some sayings from the Gospel of Thomas suggest an elimination of male sexuality as well as female:

> Jesus said to them, "When (ὅταν) you make the two into one, and when you make the inside as the outside and the outside as the inside and the above as the below, and when (ἵνα) you shall make the male and the female into one, so that the man is not male and the woman is not female . . . then you shall enter the kingdom."[9]

A similar phrase occurs in another work: "the Lord himself, when asked by someone when his kingdom would come, said: 'When two shall be one and the outside as the inside, and the male with the female neither male nor female.'"[10]

Gnostic Views of Procreation

To understand the Gnostics' aversion to childbearing, we must explain a bit more of their theology. We have already noted that most Gnostics viewed the material universe as evil and the result of mistaken activity. Light from the highest God had descended through lower powers, sometimes known as archons, who had entrapped the divine spark in human beings. The human soul was surrounded with a series of vestments which must be shed as one passed through the realms between earth and heaven. These realms were viewed as concentric rings, each controlled by an archon. In order to pass through the sphere guarded by a particular archon, one must know its name and the proper magic charm by which to gain passage through its domain. The objective was to return the divine light particles to their original Source, to restore completeness to the High God. Only then would the evil of the material universe come to an end.

For this reason one's physical body was also an evil, and the soul was entrapped within the body as a dead body lies within a tomb. Indeed, the Gospel of Thomas even stated that whoever had found the world had found a corpse.[11] Saint Hippolytus extends this by telling us that the Naassenes considered even the spiritual body a corpse.[12] Therefore the resurrection of the body did not appeal to Gnostics at all, a viewpoint shared by the people in 1 Corinthians 15:12 who said that the dead did not rise. They surely did not wish to be trapped again in any kind of a body. The Gospel of Thomas even declared that "the rest of the dead" has already taken place and has not been recognized. This sounds very much like the opponents (2 Tim. 2:18) who declare that the resurrection has already taken place.

As we have said, in many Gnostic systems human beings contain within them sparks of the highest deity and must seek to return these particles of the divine to the celestial realm. Only in this way could they restore the primal unity of spiritual essence. To procreate children is to scatter the divine particles still further and to entomb more human spirits in the flesh.

According to a Naassene writer, the priest who shouted aloud the news of a divine birth which was "holy, spiritual, heavenly and from above" had renounced all fleshly procreation.[13] Saint Epiphanius tells of one Gnostic group which he calls a successor to the Nicolaitans. We will recall that the church at Ephesus was said to hate the deeds of the Nicolaitans (Rev. 2:6). The surrounding churches were also having problems with the same group (Rev. 2:15). Epiphanius calls those who inherited the Nicolaitan tradition by many names, but they are best known as Phibionites. They rejected marriage and held their women in common. They possessed many books, one of which was called the Gospel of Eve, and they adhered to the "doctrine of the Serpent."

This group was vehemently opposed to childbearing.[14] When a departed soul left the body and began its ascent to heaven, it should say to each power above, "I have not sown children to the Archon, but have pulled his roots and I have collected the scattered members and I know who you are." But if the soul "is found to have procreated a son, it is kept beneath until it is able to take up its own children again and draw them back to itself."[15]

The group also told a story of the prophet Elijah. When he was taken up from earth, he was rejected and thrown back into the evil world. A daimon took hold of him and insisted that she had children from him, "and you cannot go up and leave your children here!" The holy man protested that this was impossible in view of his chaste and righteous life. The daimon replied, "Indeed, frequently when you had an emission in your dreams, I received the sperm from you and bore sons to you."[16] Thus it is that the procreation of children may keep even Elijah from entering into heaven. Though he was taken up in a chariot of fire, he was cast back because his purported children still anchored him to earth. To bring a child into the world was to create a serious spiritual impediment.

The Phibionites had an extreme solution to the problem. "While they have intercourse with each other they renounce the procreation of children." Although sexual activities made up a major part of their rites, they practiced coitus interruptus. This was in the main an effective means of birth control; but if a woman was found to be pregnant, she was forcibly aborted. The fetus was actually eaten in a ceremony so that its soul-particles might be assimilated. They prayed to God, "We were not tricked by the Archon of desire, but we have gathered up the misdeed of the brother."[17]

The Phibionites seem to be an isolated case, although their activities appear to have been known to several of the church fathers. Nevertheless, their negative attitudes toward marriage and childbearing were shared by a number of unorthodox groups. Such groups did their best to deny women a childbearing function. Paul spoke in 1 Timothy 4:3 of those who forbade marriage. By contrast, 1 Timothy 5:14 calls upon women of childbearing age to marry and have children.

1 Timothy 2:15 as an Affirmation of Femininity

If, as the Gospel according to the Egyptians says, Jesus came to do away with the works of the female, then bringing a child into the world was a malfeasance, one with serious spiritual repercussions. Can it be that the writer of the Pastorals affirms the preservation and validity of women within their role as childbearers? We have read of those Gnostics who deny to a woman her sexuality. She cannot find eternal life until first she surrenders her femaleness. One Gnostic writer even called upon believers to "flee from the bondage of femininity and to choose for themselves the salvation of masculinity."[18] Can Paul be stating that a woman may be saved while retaining the capacity to bear children?

The Greek preposition used in 1 Timothy 2:15 for "through childbearing" is *dia* with a genitive case. This does not primarily indicate "because of" or "on account of" as would be true of the accusative case. Rather it may have the sense of "during," "throughout," or "within an attendant circumstance."[19] It would be possible to translate, "she shall be saved within the childbearing function." Woman can be saved while she still possesses that distinctive which most decisively sets her apart from man. This constitutes both an affirmation of the spiritual wholeness of womanhood and a manifesto of women's God-given right to bear children.

With such an interpretation we would have a continued refutation of one or more false doctrines. First Paul attacks a highly unorthodox myth involving Adam, Eve, and the serpent; and then he turns to a defense of feminine functions. Salvation is available to the female as well as the male, and she need not surrender her gender. This sounds consistent with the apostle who wrote that in Christ there is neither male nor female and that as the woman came from man and man from woman, so neither is independent of each other in the Lord (1 Cor. 11:11–12; Gal. 3:28). Women are acceptable to God within their childbearing function and need not change their sexual identity to find salvation. Those who find the task of rearing children to be tedious and frustrating will find within the pastoral Epistles a strong affirmation of the essential validity of their often thankless ministry (1 Tim. 5:9–14; 2 Tim. 1:5; Titus 2:3–5). Paul extols for them the virtues of faith, love, and holiness with good sense. What splendid maternal attitudes! May God grant them to the entire body of Christ!

Epilogue

A brilliant and creative psychologist was employed by a very prestigious Minneapolis firm, and her research had gained national recognition. One day a friend introduced her to Christ; and she became a new person, born anew into the kingdom of God.

Soon she started attending a Bible-study group taught by an energetic and forceful leader. It was not long until he directed the attention of the group to 1 Timothy 2:11–15. He insisted vehemently that women should neither teach men nor be in a position of authority over them. The psychologist protested that she was the director of a research team and that she felt that it must have been God's providence which had led her to the position. He indicated that such employment was outside of the will of God and that to remain in her present job was a direct violation of a biblical command.

Each morning as she left the parking lot and entered her place of work, she seemed to feel a great weight descending upon her back. "Oh, God," she would pray, "why did you lead me to yourself and then deal me this blow?" What should she do? Was she to turn her back upon all the training, the hard work, and the implementation of her discoveries? Was that what God wanted for her life?

Instead of seeking to live Christ in the workplace, she was compelled to consider the legitimacy of her being there at all. It was hard to demonstrate a new respect, fairness, and kindness to those who reported to her, especially when she must keep asking herself whether it was right for them to be working under her supervision. Her concern for them became less than her concern over her own dilemma.

The feeling of bearing an enormous burden grew until it developed into full-fledged back trouble requiring a physician's care. As a psychologist, she was well aware that her medical problem had developed out of her response to the Bible-study leader's interpretation of 1 Timothy 2:11–15.

She began to study God's Word for herself, to seek out positive material, even to delve into the Greek. On the basis of Scripture, she became convinced of God's call to use all of her gifts and talents. In time she could walk from the parking lot into the building without feeling a burden on her back, confident that God had set her in that place so that she could demonstrate the love of Jesus Christ in a position of responsibility. Now she could seek to glorify God in all that she did.

A Call to Service

This book has been written for men and women alike, with the prayer that they may find God's purposes for their lives. First Timothy 2:9–15 is not meant to be a burden or a yoke of oppression. Rather it is a launching pad for service and study and the development of Christian character. It calls men and women alike to transforming and powerful prayer (1 Tim. 2:8–9), to godly and appropriate behavior (1 Tim. 2:9–10). Women are enjoined to make a profession of their faith (1 Tim. 2:10), just as Jesus insisted upon a public confession from the woman who had been healed of the issue of blood. Culture, tradition, and conditioning often make women reticent to tell of God's goodness and grace in their lives—yet this is Christ's call.

Verbal and theological commitment are essential, but women must implement their convictions by doing good (1 Tim. 2:10). Words and deeds are both required in a "profession of godliness." Whether at home, in the office or factory, at church or school, in the marketplace or in the farthest corners of the earth, women may bring the compassion and presence of Christ to each location and each situation. Living this out requires all of the energy, creativity, talent, time, and treasure which any of us possess.

A Knowledge of Truth

First Timothy 2:9–15 calls on us not only to make Christ known, but also to know him for ourselves. Jesus is himself the

Way, the Truth, and the Life (John 14:6); and in him are hidden all the treasures of wisdom and knowledge (Col. 2:2–3).

Verse 10 requires that women learn of him for themselves, with receptivity and responsivity (modern rephrasing of the ancient Greek). We salute the women who study the Word. We salute those with the courage to enter our colleges and seminaries, to engage in graduate studies, and to embark upon home Bible studies. We salute those who teach women, and those who learn from them. We commend those within the body of Jesus Christ who are entrusted with responsibility and administrative office.

Especially we hail those engaged in the tremendously important task of childbearing and childrearing. Above all, it is they who teach the next generation and win the little ones to Christ. Verse 15, for all its difficulties, affirms the significance of mothers in God's scheme. They are the primary evangelists in the Christian church, and from their homes will come the replacements for the leaders of this generation. Do not forget that it was Timothy's mother and grandmother who shared their faith with him (2 Tim. 1:5)!

In this book we have attempted to show that the passage called upon women to learn the truth and to refrain from teaching error. The writer presents an orthodox view of the seminal ideas in Genesis 1–3 in order to rectify distortions. The Word of God is always his antidote. His desire is to lead women away from victimization by false teachers toward a "knowledge of the truth" (2 Tim. 3:7; 2:25; 1 Tim. 2:4), to enable them to accept themselves as women and mothers and servants of Christ.

The Call to Christian Virtues

It is a shame that so much of the space in this book has been given to clarifying a matter of heresy rather than to discussing the qualities of character which the writer commended to women: faith and love and holiness with self-control.

Faith (*pistis*) as it is discussed in the Pastorals is directed towards God's faithfulness. "I know whom I have believed and am persuaded that he is able to keep that which I have committed unto him against that day" (2 Tim. 1:12). We are told that this saying is faithful: that Jesus Christ came into the world to save sinners (1 Tim. 1:15). Faithfulness also applies to God's servants, however;

and Paul thanks God that Christ judged him to be faithful and appointed him to the ministry (1 Tim. 1:12). May God grant us women who will also be adjudged faithful.

Love (*agape*) indicates not only the love which God bestowed upon us, but also the love which we return to our Creator, Redeemer, and Friend. It is this love which Christian women must shed abroad in every dimension of their lives by thought, word, and deed. This love cannot be stopped, nor must we allow it to be misdirected. God's love through us must pour out to all in need, whether that need is spiritual, emotional, physical, or social.

Holiness (*hagiasmos*) is that quality which separates us from the world and draws us to God. It implies both consecration and sanctification. We are not to be entrapped by the outward glitter of the world, but to make a deep commitment in our hearts. Katherine Bushnell observed that women who truly know the claim of God upon their lives will not be "given over to fashion and to folly." When the channel is unobstructed for their love and commitment, it will flow forth to all the world.

The last quality, self-control (*sophrosune*), implies not only good judgment, but also decency and chastity. All of these are characteristics which women need to apply in both private and public ministry. The Word of God exhorts them to guard their behavior against actions which are unwise, indiscreet, unchaste, undisciplined, or inappropriate. Framed in a more positive way, this final word calls women to use wisely and well their enormous power for Christian influence and example.

God has already raised up many women of power and prudence: Mother Teresa, Susanna Wesley, Florence Nightingale, Eleanor Roosevelt, Henrietta Mears, Lillian Dickson, Amy Carmichael, and Catherine Booth. Who follows in their train?

Appendices

1

Could Authentein *Mean Murder?*

Authentēs is applied on several occasions to those who perform ritual murder. The Septuagint uses the word of parents who participate in promiscuous mystery rites and sacrifice their children to pagan deities (Wis. of Sol. 12:6). Medea, a priestess of Artemis, engineers such an atrocity in the temple of the goddess. Her lover, who fells Absyrtes as "an ox for sacrifice," is called an *authentēs*.[1] The term *authentēs* is also applied to Agamemnon when his wife discusses his determination to sacrifice his daughter to Artemis.[2]

Human sacrifice and ritual murder were by no means unknown in the ancient world, nor were they totally unconnected with Ephesus. There are a number of ancient literary references to ritual murder in honor of Artemis, a practice which seems to have persisted at least until the second century C.E.[3] Symeon Metaphrastes spoke of Ephesians who thought the highest form of religious service was the slaughter of those who opposed Artemis.[4] The cult which was established at Ephesus by the man-slaying Amazons was that of the Taurian Artemis, who demanded human sacrifice. Euripides' *Iphigenia among the Taurians* preserved a tradition that a priestess of Artemis must be the one to consign the male victim to his death.[5] Indeed, at the lowest level under the Artemisium at Ephesus, there is a deposit of human bones, apparently of persons ritually sacrificed.[6]

Other shrines to which the cult of the Taurian Artemis was transported were said to have ceremonies that memorialized this tradition and offered substitutes for the ritual murder. At Sparta youths were flogged while the priestess stood by bearing the sacred image of Artemis, at Haloa a drop of blood was drawn from a man's throat, while at Brauron a goat was slaughtered. Later tradition spoke of an abhorrence of bloodshed in the Ephesian Artemisium.

We may recoil in horror from such a review of ancient religious practices. Nevertheless we must admit that such material does not allow us to rule out the possibility that 1 Timothy 2:12 prohibits cultic action involving actual or representational murder. The New Testament authors repeatedly called on their audiences to renounce the trappings, customs, and rituals of paganism and to adopt a new lifestyle in Jesus Christ (Rom. 13:13; 1 Cor. 8:10; 10:21; Gal. 5:21; Eph. 4:17–24).

185

The Simulation of Near-Death
and Murder in Mystery Initiations

More likely than actual murder is the "voluntary death" or sham murder which played a significant part in mystery initiations. The mysteries generally enacted a sort of death before the initiate's rebirth into immortality. The ceremony required that the initiate be viewed as one who had actually died.[7] Plutarch quotes Themistius, an ancient author, on the correspondence between death and initiation. When the time of death comes, "one suffers an experience like that of those who are being initiated into the great mysteries; therefore the words *teleutan* (die) and *teleisthai* (be initiated), and the actions are similar." Themistius next told of the wanderings, anxieties, and bewilderment which the initiate must endure. "Just before the end there are all kinds of terrors, with shivering, trembling, sweating, and utter amazement." At last the wanderer was admitted to green pastures, solemn dances, and sacred visions in the company of blessed spirits. "Now at last he is fully initiated and instructed and has become free and dedicated, walking about in the sacred revels, in the company of pure and holy men."[8]

Mystery rites were said to be dramatic enactments of the myths regarding certain deities, usually of those who had suffered a violent and often premeditated death. One of the church fathers complained: "And lastly, consider the sacred rites of the mysteries: you will find tragic deaths, dooms, funerals, mourning and lamentations of woebegone gods."[9] Clement of Alexandria charged that pagans "commemorated deeds of violence in their religious rites," and their mysteries "received the glory of funeral honors." The mysteries were, "to put it briefly, murders and burials."[10] In various cities women dramatized these sacred stories and thereby provided instruction in the violence inherent in the mysteries.[11] Such dramas were performed in Ephesus' great theater; one first-century philosopher found the city given over to the performance of wild pagan rites, overwhelmed by its preoccupation with elaborately choreographed pantomimes.[12]

These enactments of death were often produced with elaborate stage properties. Certain of the Egyptian temples contained coffins in which the devotee was actually entombed in the *mors voluntaria* (voluntary death) that was said to be part of the Isis initiation ceremony.[13] The indication of mummy-like bindings on some of the cult statues resembling that of Artemis of Ephesus has led certain scholars to suggest that they represent the shroud of the initiate. This appears more likely because of the strong affinity between Isis and Artemis of Ephesus. In the Ephesian temple of Osiris, the consort of Isis, Gunter Holbl finds evidence for a death and rebirth scenario. In such rites, the ritual slayer was also the instructor.

These murder scenes were enacted so realistically that the emperor Commodus once took advantage of an initiation actually to slay someone.[14] A Galatian priestess of Artemis seized a similar opportunity to dispose of her husband's murderer during a service in the goddess's temple. The Artemis ceremony, supposedly a wedding, contained within it elements which made it possible for a real murder to be accomplished.[15]

In Ephesus women assumed the role of the man-slaying Amazons who had founded the cult of Artemis of Ephesus. Each year women were required to dance as the Amazons had once danced, and a third-century B.C.E. poet issued a fearful warning against those who might shun the occasion.[16] The female dancers at the temple of the Ephesian Artemis clashed their arms, so lethal weapons were part of the priestesses' religious accoutrements. There are reasons to suspect that the dances may have contained a simulated attack on males, especially as they were performed with spears. To what other use these implements may have been put we cannot say. They would surely have inspired terror; and this, Strabo tells us, was one of the purposes of the dance.[17] These armed dances continued throughout the first century C.E.[18] The very epithet for the Amazons, "man-slayers" (as well as slayers of mothers and fathers), appears in a list of those who oppose sound doctrine (1 Tim. 1:5–6). The fact that women in Ephesus had a religious duty to impersonate the murderous Amazons should not pass unnoticed.

In Germany a cult center for mystery initiation yielded a trick sword which could be made to appear to be sticking in the front and out the back of a victim's chest.[19] In such situations, the instructor sometimes served also as would-be murderer. An ancient wall painting shows the initiate being inducted into the cult of Mithras.[20] He is blindfolded, bound, and kneeling, while the instructor approaches with a knife. At the last moment the knife will slash the bonds and free the initiate into a new life of salvation.[21] The role of slayer and instructor are merged.

The near-murders described by the ancient novelists, especially those glorifying Artemis of Ephesus, contain a motif similar to that of the Mithras cult. Achilles Tatius (second century C.E.) portrays his hero as strung up and ready to be slain before a special delegation arrives to consult Artemis of Ephesus. He is then cut down, as an execution may not take place when the goddess is being approached.[22]

The heroine of Xenophon's *Ephesian Tale* (ca. second century C.E.) is also strung up by brigands and is about to be offered as a human sacrifice to Ares or Mars, the god of war. She is saved by the arrival of the local soldiers, who cut her down.[23] The hero of the same novel is at another point tied to a cross which, in answer to his prayer, topples into the River Nile and floats along until he is rescued. In each of these cases, the victim is tied in the manner of one consigned to death. He is then delivered at the last moment. These episodes are thought to contain hints of actual rituals in mystery religions.[24]

The representation of initiation scenes of various sorts was common in the graves of southern Italy. One vase painting shows a group of women with drawn swords who threaten the life of a man sitting as a suppliant upon an altar.[25] The man himself has a naked sword and is trying to defend himself. One of his assailants even wears the fawnskin characteristic of devotees of Dionysos. Others appear to be holding a thyrsos, also an accoutrement of worshipers of Dionysos. Ephesian women on occasion played the role of maddened followers of Dionysos.[26] Although such women were supposed to have performed actual murders in their wild rites, nothing of the sort is happening in this vase painting.

Careful examination shows that the women in this scene are involved in a pretense of murder. The two women closest to the man brandish swords which are still in their sheaths, although the two further away—and less likely to inflict damage—have unsheathed theirs. This precaution shows that they have no intention of actually killing the man, but certainly their aspect is menacing. The vase painting depicts some sort of sham murder with strongly religious overtones, as the altar and the Dionysiac attributes show. The scene may be indicative of an initiation ordeal which the deceased endured during his lifetime in order to gain a happy hereafter.

Gnostic Simulations of Death

Gnostics too participated in the dramatic spectacles.[27] Those who distorted the Garden of Eden story and venerated the serpent appear to have retained a rite similar to those of the Hellenistic mysteries.[28] One of the Gnostic snake-revering groups, the Naassenes, celebrated the Phrygian rites in which an initiate was called "a man about to die."[29] These so-called Phrygian mysteries of Attis and Cybele are of interest to us because they were a powerful influence in Asia Minor. Artemis of Ephesus was essentially a Phrygian goddess and closely related to Cybele. A Naassene initiation hymn speaks of the soul as it succumbs to death, mourns, and dies.[30] After death, the soul is led into true *gnōsis* by Jesus. Since the soul was called a "corpse" buried in the tomb of the body,[31] Naassene mysteries doubtless portrayed some sort of death.

The pagan Celsus had many complaints to bring against the Christians. His treatise may have been written as early as C.E. 120, though modern scholarship generally assigns it a date around C.E. 178. The Christian apologist, Origen, recognized some features in Celsus' polemic against Christianity and was able to identify them as belonging to the snake-revering Ophites. The outrageous allegations must be laid at the door of the Gnostic Ophites rather than that of Christians. Celsus likened their rites to those of the Mithraic mysteries, a valuable observation since in the religion of Mithras there was sham murder. He also accused Christians (i.e., Gnostics) of employing in their cult phantoms and objects of terror as did the Bacchic mysteries.[32]

An inveterate detractor of Christianity, Celsus described the "unhallowed mysteries" that he had encountered in an apparently Gnostic type of mystery ritual where sun, moon, and many men were said to be slaughtered in order that they might live. He was told of "a power flowing from one Prunicos, a virgin and a living soul; and a heaven slain in order to live, and an earth slaughtered by the sword, and many put to death that they may live, and death ceasing in the world, when the sin of the world is dead."[33]

It does not behoove us to dismiss too quickly Celsus' charge that many were slain. This does not necessarily mean that individuals were actually murdered. One cannot, after all, literally kill the sun or moon. It may have happened only in pantomime as a sham murder in the same fashion as in the Mithraic and other mysteries. The repetition of the theological justification formula, "that they may live," suggests that it may have been a phrase from a liturgy. Celsus may actually have heard of both a rite and its rationale.

It is at least possible that some sort of ritual murder, probably of a simulated nature, could be involved.

2

A Lesson in Greek Grammar

If we were to read 1 Timothy 2:12 as "I do not allow a woman to teach nor to proclaim herself author of man," we can understand the *content* of the forbidden teaching as being the notion that woman was responsible for the creation of man. We recall that a preoccupation with controversial genealogies, the matter of origins, was one of the principal characteristics of opponents to sound teaching. In this case, we would understand *oude* as linking together two connected ideas.

There is another manner in which *oude* might be used here, though it would not change the sense appreciably. The following section is offered for those who desire to review certain technicalities of language. It is important for readers to understand, however, that it is possible to translate this difficult verse in more than one way, and that the Greek construction lends itself to more than one interpretation. We need to bear in mind that one of the distinctives of the Pastorals is the use of expressions which may be construed variously.

Further Considerations in Greek Grammar

Double Negatives

The *ouk . . . oude* pattern naturally leads us to expect a "neither . . . nor" construction. It is possible, though, that the negatives are employed here for another purpose. *Ouk* can also convey a sense of "not" or "not even." The negative in Greek may be used somewhat differently from the English. With us, a double negative makes a positive; but that is often not so in Greek. There a double negative may simply serve to intensify the negation.[1] When the second negative is a compound (such as *oude*) it serves to strengthen the first (*ou* or *ouk*).[2] Examples occur at Luke 4:2; 20:40; and Romans 13:8.

In the story of the two men who went up to the temple to pray, we read that the sinner did not even wish to raise his eyes toward heaven (Luke 18:13). Here the text uses *ouk . . . oude*, which must be translated "indeed he did not. . . ."

189

or "he did not even. . . . " It is possible that *oude* in 1 Timothy 2:12 should be understood as simply intensifying the point rather than as conveying a double prohibition. In that case, we should translate the clause "I absolutely do *not* permit a woman. . . ."

Indirect Discourse

In English we also use infinitives of indirect discouse, such as "Aspasia, a native of Asia Minor and the mistress of Pericles, was said to be the second most powerful person in Athens" or "The pilot is reported to have parachuted safely to earth." We may also use such an infinitive with the verb *to teach:* for instance, "During World War I a University of Minnesota professor was fired for teaching English to be a low Germanic language." It is not a very comfortable way of expressing things in English but it was used quite freely in Greek and Latin. Verbs of saying or thinking often took the infinitive.

We find an example in 2 Timothy 2:18, where Hymenaeus and Philetus say that the resurrection is already past. The statement of the heretics is put into indirect discourse with the verb in the infinitive. The statement of a heretic reputed to be the first Gnostic (note the infinitive!) also involves the same construction: Simon Magus asserts himself to be someone great (Acts 8:9). Other examples of erroneous statements or opinions which use the infinitive of indirect discourse may be found at Acts 14:19; 28:6; Romans 1:22; 2:19; Mark 12:18; James 1:26; and Luke 11:18; 20:6, 27. Indirect discourse is also used in many other situations in the New Testament.[3]

It is generally assumed that 1 Timothy 2:12 omits the main verb: "I do not permit a woman to teach nor [do I permit her] *authentein* but [I do permit her] to be in silence." A question might be raised, however. *Authentein* is in the infinitive, as are *didaskein* (to teach) and *einai* (to be in silence or harmony). It is assumed that all three infinitives are dependent upon *epitrepo* (I permit). Conceivably *authentein* may be an infinitive of indirect discourse, dependent upon *didaskein*.

In classical Greek, *ou* (*ouk* before vowels) or a compound such as *oude* was the negative generally used before infinitives of indirect discourse while *me* commonly preceded other sorts of infinitives. Although by the time of the New Testament *me* was ordinarily employed with infinitives of indirect discourse, sometimes the *ou* still persisted.[4] The older usage of *ou* with an infinitive of indirect discourse remains in Acts 26:26 and 1 Corinthians 2:2.[5] Examples of *me* before an infinitive may be found in the pastoral Epistles at 1 Timothy 1:3–4 and 2 Timothy 2:14. In the first, Timothy is supposed to charge certain individuals neither to teach a different doctrine nor to give heed to myths and genealogies. In 2 Timothy 2:14 he is not to squabble over words with his opponents. Why did the writer of the Pastorals use *oude* here rather than *me* or *mede* as at 1 Timothy 1:3–4 and 2 Timothy 2:14? We must ponder, then, whether *oude* may be an indication of indirect discourse. This would allow a translation very nearly the same as the one in chapter 8, although upon a different grammatical basis.

The subject of an infinitival clause (as in indirect discourse) need not be given in the clause itself if it is the same as the subject of the verb on which that clause depends. An example of this occurs at Luke 2:26 (It is revealed to Simeon not to see death [i.e., that he should not see death] until he had seen the Lord's Christ.). Further instances may be found in Luke 24:23; Acts 8:9; Romans 1:22; Philippians 1:17; Hebrews 11:4; and James 1:26.

A Second Alternative Rendering

Bearing in mind that *oude* can introduce an infinitive of indirect discourse and that the subject need not be repeated, perhaps we should translate, "I do not allow a woman to teach that she is the originator of man." If this is so, then we would be dealing with a definition of what it is that a woman should not teach. The actual content of the objectionable instruction is spelled out here. If this is indeed an infinitive of indirect discourse, then it would be possible to translate: "I do not permit a woman to teach that she is the originator of man but she is to be in conformity [with the Scriptures][or that she keeps it a secret]. For Adam was created first, then Eve."

Another Alternate Translation

The word *didaskein* (to teach) is frequently accompanied by an infinitive which defines what was taught.[6] For instance, the disciples said, "Lord, teach (*didaskein*) us to pray" (Luke 11:1).[7] Later Jesus commanded them to go into all the world and make disciples of all nations, "teaching (*didaskein*) them to observe all things" (Matt. 28:20). In Revelation 2:14, John calls to memory Balaam who taught (*didaskein*) Balak to throw a stumbling block before the children of Israel, to eat meat offered to idols, and to fornicate. (You may recall that Balaam, when he discovered that he was unable to curse the children of Israel, arranged to have Moabite women seduce them into the worship of Baal-Peor [Num. 25; 31:16].) Revelation 2:20 records of Jezebel, the prophetess of Thyatira, that she "teaches (*didaskein*) my servants . . . to fornicate and to eat meat offered to idols." The same construction (*didaskein* followed by an infinitive) occurs in 1 Timothy 2:12. We could appropriately translate, "I absolutely do not allow a woman to teach [someone] to maintain that she is the author of a man."

The verb *didaskein* requires that the direct object be placed in the accusative case.[8] "I do not allow a woman to teach a man" would be *ouk epitrepo gynaiki didaskein andron*. In 1 Timothy 2:12 the word for "man" is not in the accusative case as it should be if it is governed by *didaskein*. Rather it is in the genitive case and is governed by *authentein*. It is normal for verbs signifying to rule or to begin to be followed by a genitive. Six Greek words separate "to teach" from "a man," and it is usually assumed that the object ("man") is put in the genitive because it is the direct object of *authentein*.

Can it be that the object of "to teach" is not expressed in this verse? Although such a construction would be difficult in English, *didaskein* can be used in Greek without a direct object.[9] If we look back to verse 11, we find that the subject under discussion is the right of women to learn receptively and accurately, in contradistinction to the false teachers who cause women to become confused and estranged from "a knowledge of the truth" (2 Tim. 2:6–7). Can *didaskein* in 1 Timothy 2:12 refer to what a woman should not teach to those who desire to learn? We remember that some of the widows were going about from house to house, telling women "what they ought not" (1 Tim. 5:13), and the false teachers in Crete were upsetting whole households as they taught "what they should not" (Titus 1:11). Obviously the content of the teaching was wreaking havoc among women. As an antidote, the older women are asked to teach the younger ones and to guide them into a life of positive actions and attitudes (Titus 2:3). With this understanding, it would be appropriate to render the verse, "I categorically forbid a woman to teach [anyone] to maintain that she is responsible for the origin of man. Rather let her be in harmony [with the Scriptures]."

Although we have reviewed several possibilities, we consider the strongest to be the rendering given in chapter 8: "I do not allow a woman to teach or proclaim herself author of man."

3

Sex Reversal
and Female Dominance

An early Amazon queen, Lysippe, decreed that women should go forth to battle and govern while the men were to stay at home and do the household work. "To the men she assigned the spinning of wool and the household tasks of women. She introduced laws by which she led forth the women to battle, but she hung humiliation and servitude upon the men."[1] Her daughter succeeded her as queen and both established the worship of Artemis Tauropolus and built temples to her.[2] A later queen, Hippo, brought the image of the Tauropolian Artemis to Ephesus, set it in an oak tree, and instituted the cult. Attendants of this Amazon queen danced at the shrine of Artemis of Ephesus first with shields and later with rattling quivers. A hymn to Artemis recollects:

> For you, too, the Amazons, who are always zealous for war, at Ephesus beside the sea set up a wooden image beneath the base of an oak tree, and Hippo performed for you a holy rite (instituted a mystery?). They themselves, O Lady Upis, executed an armed dance around the image—first in armor wielding shields and then again positioned in a circle as a broad choir. And the clear-voiced pipes made a delicate accompaniment, so that they might dance to the beat of music. For [to make flutes] they did not yet bore through the bones of the fawn, an evil for the deer, Athena's work. And the echo rang all the way to Sardis and to the Berecynthian territory. And their feet stamped briskly while their quivers rattled.[3]

The Amazons were famed for their military prowess, their hostility to males, and the dominance which they exerted over men.[4] In the lands of Asia Minor which they had conquered, the tradition of the rule of female over male continued at least as a fiction if not a reality.[5] William M. Ramsay held that the matriarchy of which the ancient authors wrote was not an ingredient of the workaday world but still prevailed within the temple systems and especially in the mysteries.[6] Modern scholarship tends to find that female dominance is not attested in the civil affairs of western Asia Minor, and that matriarchy can be found with

193

certainty only in the religious realm of Bronze Age Crete.[7] Nevertheless the tradition of a religiously-based rule of men by women is incontestable.

Strabo commented that stories of the military organization and conquests of the Amazons were still in circulation in Asia Minor and were still regarded as historically true. He complained that it was the same as saying "that the men of those times were women and that the women were men."[8]

The Lycians were said to have been ruled by women from ancient times. They claimed descent through their mothers, honored women more than men, and bestowed the inheritance on daughters rather than sons.[9]

"It was the custom that [Carian] women should rule equally with men."[10] The ascendancy of women among the Carians is probably best demonstrated by the brilliant naval leadership of Queen Artemisia at the Battle of Salamis.[11] Xerxes commented, "My men have turned into women, and my women into men,"[12] while the Greeks bore for centuries the humiliation of having been bested by a woman.[13]

The Tradition of Hercules and Omphale

Those women most closely connected to the Ephesian Artemis, the Lydians, were also said to dominate their menfolk.[14] "The[ir] men are subject to female domination."[15] The tradition harked back to the time when Hercules served the Lydian queen Omphale as her slave in order to gain purification from a homicide which he had committed.[16] He had already tried to find absolution at the hands of males, but without success. The oracle of Apollo commanded his servitude, and so the mighty Hercules consented to be ruled by a woman. Omphale dressed him as a serving maid and compelled him to do women's work while she paraded about with his lion's skin and club.[17] A Pompeian wall painting shows a treatment of this popular theme. There has been a clothing exchange, and Hercules sports the jewelry and silken attire of his mistress.

Though famed for his mighty labors, Hercules must now ply the shuttle and the distaff. The women of Lydia were famous for their skill in spinning and weaving, and Hercules did not measure up to their standards. When his clumsiness spoiled the weaving, Omphale paddled him with her golden sandal.[18] A famous sculpture in the Naples Museum shows him spinning, with spindle and distaff, under the tutelage of Omphale; and there is also a small bronze statue in the Walters Art Gallery in Baltimore.[19] His occupation in wool-working may have earned for him religious authority, *auctoritatem religiosam* as Pliny puts it.[20]

The citizens of Ephesus maintained that it was during this period of subjection and role reversal that he augmented the rites of their great Artemis.[21] In the myth, Hercules' acceptance of servitude to a woman brings purification after the masculine rites administered by Deiphobus have failed. There have been scholarly suggestions that Omphale was in fact a goddess or a Lydian priestess who dispensed a matriarchal form of religion and that Hercules was undergoing some sort of primitive ritual.[22] At any rate, the great hero made his contribution to the rites of Ephesus only after he had experienced female dominance. Through subjection to a woman, Hercules, the symbol of machismo, gains both forgiveness and "religious authority."

Once the ordeal was over, Hercules was enormously resentful at having been compelled to serve a woman (even though it was the will of Zeus). As retaliation, he utterly demolished the city of the culprit whom he considered to be responsible at the human level for the outrage.[23] In other stories, Hercules slew the man-slaying, man-ruling Amazons and would not countenance the rule of women in any nation.[24] The Omphale episode represents a radical reversal of his normal pattern. Such a reversal constituted a significant feature in some of the mystery religions; and Hercules himself was a prominent figure in several of the mystic cults.

Subjugation to female dominance was a humiliating and temporary phase in his life, much akin to the toils, terrors, and degradations experienced during initiation into these religions.[25] In rites of Hercules at other locations, sex reversal is well established, especially the assuming of female garb on the part of the priests. At Tarsus his priests donned purple robes reminiscent of Omphale. Their behavior appears to indicate cult actions of sex reversal involving clothing exchange and submission to a female figure. Paul, a native of Tarsus, surely could not have been unaware of the tradition.

One group of serpent-revering Gnostics also employed the motif of Hercules and Omphale in their myth. The Book of Baruch told of the Good One's efforts to communicate with humanity and of the messengers who failed. At last Hercules was sent as a prophet. He was an important figure in Greek mystery religion because he had descended to Hades and returned to the upper world. For this reason, he was considered a prophet of secret things and especially of the key to survival in the afterlife. He completes his mighty labors but is enticed by the seductress Omphale, who "strips him of his power" (obedience to the commands of Baruch) and takes on his attributes herself. She "envelops him in her own peculiar robe, that is in the power of Edem, who is the power below." Thus Hercules, even though he was sent as a prophet, never completes his mission.[26] Rather he is overcome by a woman.

Religiously Inspired Female Dominance and Reversal of Gender Roles in the Cult of Isis

It was said that religion also inspired such a sex reversal among the Egyptians and that the men of Egypt did the weaving while their wives conducted business in the marketplace.[27] In the cult of Isis, an Egyptian goddess specifically identified with Artemis of Ephesus and sometimes indistinguishable from her, there is both reversal of gender roles and domination by women. A hymn declares that Isis vests women with power equal to that of men.[28]

In the first century B.C.E., Diodorus of Sicily told the story of Isis and Osiris. The latter deity, before he left to disseminate throughout the world the blessings of agriculture, bestowed upon his wife Isis supreme power over everything in Egypt. The god Hermes served as her counselor and Hercules as her general. After the death of her husband Osiris, she avenged his murder and continued to rule with all due respect for the law. Diodorus declared that by her reign she became the source of more and greater blessings to humanity than any other deity. For this reason, queens were more honored than kings, and wives had authority over their husbands.The husband was required to vow obedience to his spouse in the marriage contract.[29]

It is important to note that this ascendancy of female over male is specifically a religious act of devotion to a great mother goddess whose dominance had brought far greater blessing than that of any male god. Extant Egyptian marriage contracts in no way bear out Diodorus's assertion that husbands promised to obey wives. What he says must apply to religious rather than secular life.

At Ephesus Isis enjoyed a strong following. Not only was there a shrine to her within the Artemisium, but there was as well a separate temple well-equipped for the celebration of the mysteries. The strong affinities between the Isis and the Artemis cults, together with the tradition of the subservient Hercules who embellished the rites of the Ephesian goddess, point to a religiously oriented dominance by women at Ephesus. During the period when Hercules made his contribution to the ritual, he not only was subjugated to a woman but also was clothed in the vestments of a woman and compelled to do women's work. The inclusion of castrated priests and hermaphrodites in the official retinue of the Ephesian Artemis further suggests the presence of sex reversal.[30] The assumption of ultimate power in the cult by a high priestess rather than a high priest again indicates that the primary religious power lay with women by the first century C.E.

4

Sex and Death in Ancient Novels

The earliest novels were written in the last century before Christ and in the first centuries of the common era. A curious feature of them is the frequency with which Ephesus is mingled with features of sex and death. The cult of the Ephesian Artemis is also prominent. Death, both apparent and actual, is often intertwined with sexual union; and in no fewer than four of these novels, Ephesus becomes the place of consummation and of happy marriage.

Xenophon's *Ephesian Tale*

The *Ephesian Tale* by Xenophon begins with a magnificent procession in honor of Artemis of Ephesus. Both the hero, Habrocomes, and the heroine, Anthia, take part in the celebration, and here the young people first see each other and fall in love. The lovely Anthia, already a priestess of Artemis, and the handsome cadet, Habrocomes, pine for each other but dare not confess their love. They refuse nourishment, weep, and sigh until the two sets of distraught parents send to a nearby oracle to inquire how to cure the malady of their children. The oracle sends back identical responses which foretell that a bridal chamber will serve for both of them as a tomb. The parents decide to marry them to one another and subsequently to send them on a sea voyage in order to escape the predictions of the oracle.

The name of Ephesus occurs on nearly every page of this charming romance but much of the action occurs in faraway places. Soon an attack by pirates and a shipwreck separate the happy bridal couple. The story is full of wanderings, ordeals, and hairbreadth experiences. Each of the lovers believes the other to be dead. Each is tested in his or her fidelity to the other.

At one point, Anthia is compelled to agree to marry a man who has bought her as a slave. In hopes that she can devise a way of escape, she obtains from him a promise that the nuptials will be deferred for thirty days. At the end of the time she importunes an Ephesian physician to give her a fatal potion. In return she promises to give him the wherewithal to return to his native Ephesus. The physican finally consents but actually gives her a sleeping draught instead. One can already discern the outlines from which William Shakespeare drew his idea for the sleeping Juliet.

On the morning appointed for the wedding, Anthia is found as though dead in the bridal chamber by her master, the would-be bridegroom. He laments that she shall be brought to a tomb instead of a bridal chamber. After the burial, robbers find her in the tomb and carry her forth to many more adventures. At one point she slays with a sword a robber who seeks to rape her. As punishment she is placed by the other robbers in a pit in the ground, there to await death.

Here we see the bride who slays a man in order to preserve herself for her husband and finds herself in a tomb-like enclosure. Reinhold Merkelbach, one of the world's greatest scholars of Greek mystery religion, holds that the ancient novels contained scenarios of initiation rites. He maintains that this act of murder is the beginning of Anthia's initiation trial and calls attention to the similar action of another heroine, Sinonis, in slaying a would-be rapist with a sword.[1]

Meantime Habrocomes, in his wanderings, has encountered an old fisherman who has mummified the body of his dead wife and still sleeps with her in his bed. Bridal chamber again serves as tomb. Frustrated at every turn in his search for Anthia, Habrocomes decides to kill himself. His friend advises him to wait until he has returned to Ephesus and built a tomb for his dead wife and observed proper lamentations. On his homeward journey he stops at Rhodes, where he is reunited with Anthia.

The happy couple continue on to Ephesus to thank the goddess who has served as guardian, protectress, and savior. At the Artemisium they dedicate to her an inscription bearing an account of all that they had suffered and done. The temple dedication of the story of their adventures is an indication that the entire saga may have a sacred significance. It may well, as Merkelbach maintains, follow the scenario of a religious ceremony.

Petronius's *Widow of Ephesus*

A vignette in a longer novel picks up the theme of tomb as bridal chamber in Ephesus. The tale is told by Petronius in his *Satyricon*, a piece concerned with Roman mores and manners. The vignette, told at a dinner party, concerns an Ephesian matron, a woman famed for her chastity and marital devotion, who suddenly finds herself a widow. She is inconsolable and insists upon remaining in the tomb with her dead husband.

Nearby is a soldier who has been appointed to guard the corpses of some thieves who have lately been crucified. He finds his patrol duty tedious and enters the tomb out of curiosity. He finds there the woman and her serving girl, who cannot prevail upon her mistress either to leave or to take nourishment. He plies the girl with food until the widow also eats, and then he lays siege to her heart. The maid joins in pleading his case, and the woman yields to him on three successive nights in the tomb.

A seventeenth-century English author, Walter Charleton, in his retelling of this ancient story, declares that they performed the rites of Venus and used the dead husband's coffin as an altar upon which to perform their service.[2] Petronius's version lacks this detail, but the reader is conscious of the presence of the dead husband. The soldier is so preoccupied with the widow's charms that the family of one of the thieves steals the crucified body and buries it—a situation which will surely result in a death sentence for the negligent guard. He informs his ladylove of his plight and bids her adieu. She insists that he hang the body of her husband upon the cross, for she would rather "hang the dead than kill the living."[3] Thus Ephesus serves to host a happy consummation in a strange mingling of life and death: the dead husband and the crucified thieves, the bereaved widow about to die from her refusal to eat, and the soldier who will be consigned to death if his misdemeanor is discovered.

Apollonius, King of Tyre

Ephesus, and especially the temple of Artemis, serves as the place of the happy consummation of marriage in other ancient novels as well. The cult and shrine of Artemis form a basic part of the plot in a work entitled *Apollonius, King of Tyre*. Apollonius goes on a voyage and takes along his wife who is late in her pregnancy. She is delivered of a daughter but is unable to deliver the afterbirth and so expires. The grieving husband sets her afloat in a coffin which is washed up on the shores of Ephesus close to the house of a physician. In the city of Artemis, protectress of childbirth, a clever medical student discovers that life still clings to the mother. He turns to the physician and reports that the woman supposed to be dead is actually alive.[4] As we have already seen, the theme of apparent death is a common one in these novels.

As she wishes to retain her chastity, the wife of Apollonius is sent to the temple of Artemis, where she eventually becomes high priestess. Her beauty and commitment to chastity make her most fit for that environment. Apollonius continues through many adventures and is at last reunited with his daughter, whom he had thought was also dead. An angel tells him to recount his troubles in the presence of Artemis of Ephesus. In obedience to the goddess, he travels to the sanctuary and relates his woes before her image.

During his recitation, he declares that he had wished only for death until the goddess restored his life by leading him to his long-lost child. The wife, present in her function as high priestess, recognizes her husband and daughter; and all of Ephesus rejoices in the glorious reunion of their high priestess with her family. Apollonius is restored to the wife whom he thought was dead and reenters the marriage. She sails away with him after she has appointed a new high priestess.

Just as in the account of Anthia and Habrocomes, a copy of all Apollonius's adventures is placed in the temple at Ephesus. Artemis has again wrought a happy ending in her own temple and city. The temple-based dedication of the story itself suggests that it is intended as some sort of sacred myth, containing within it a religious import.

Achilles Tatius's *Adventures of Leucippe and Clitophon*

> Behold, we have sailed across the sea; and behold Ephesus, the city fore-appointed
> of the marriages.[5]

So spoke an Ephesian matron, designated by Achilles Tatius as "one of the most
prominent Ephesian women, mad with love" for the hero.[6] The woman is a
wealthy young widow "so beautiful that you might think her a statue; an Ephesian by race, named Melite."[7] She succeeded in contracting a marriage with the
reluctant hero, Clitophon, who consented in desperation.

Clitophon had languished in Alexandria six months while he mourned the
supposed death of his beloved, Leucippe. At the beginning of the novel, the
lovers had embarked upon a journey, hoping to be wed when they came to Ephesus. In the manner typical of the literary genre, they were separated and threatened with death. In truth, Leucippe had suffered a whole series of apparent
deaths, each more hair-raising than the last. No sooner would the hero catch a
glimpse of Leucippe than he would behold another form of destruction wreaked
upon her. Grief and bewilderment contributed to his straitened circumstances
until at last he was forced to accept the unwelcome marriage to Melite. "After
death comes a wedding, and after the dirge the marriage hymn," he complained.[8]

Clitophon consented to marry the importunate widow provided she would
promise not to insist upon a consummation until they reached Ephesus. The
woman, whose husband had been lost at sea, happily agreed to the arrangement;
and the couple exchanged their vows in the temple of Isis. There Clitophon
promised that consummation would take place once they reached Ephesus. During the wedding feast, Melite made a macabre joke:

> I seem to be undergoing a unique experience of the sort which I have seen when an
> empty tomb honors those whose bodies cannot be found, but I have never before
> seen a vacant marriage-bed.[9]

The fusion of sex and death in an Ephesus-oriented context continues. During
the sea voyage back to Ephesus, Melite attempted to make the marriage a reality
and asked why she must wait until they arrive in Ephesus. Clitophon replied
that they could not consummate the marriage because they are sailing over the
watery grave of his beloved, Leucippe. Here again is an intimation of bedchamber as tomb and tomb as bedchamber, and a connection with Ephesus. Melite,
the wretched but persistent bride, continued throughout the sea voyage to beg
for consummation. Her terms became those of a priestess instructing an initiate
in the secrets of a mystery religion:

> My dearest, let us be initiated into the mysteries of Aphrodite . . . Every place is a
> marriage chamber for lovers, and there is no place which the god may not enter.
> What place could be more hospitable than the sea for the mysteries of Eros and
> Aphrodite?[10]

She urged Clitophon to propitiate Aphrodite and to honor Hera by their marriage, but the reluctant bridegroom assured her that ships were themselves

sacred and should not host the rites of love. Melite objected that Clitophon did not respect Love's mysteries and that she herself felt no shame to speak forthrightly of "Love's mysteries."[11] The author repeatedly speaks of sexual communion in technical terms which refer specifically to mystery religion. One cannot be sure whether Achilles Tatius was merely utilizing a literary convention in speaking of the physical union as a rite, or whether the anticipated consummation at Ephesus is to be viewed by the reader as a "sacred marriage"—an integral part of many mystery rituals.

When they arrive in Ephesus, Melite demands the consummation of the marriage and reminds Clitophon of the oaths which he swore before the altar of Isis. She charges that he will fail in piety toward the goddess if he does not fulfill his vow. But, in the extravagant tradition of the novel, both Melite's husband and the beloved Leucippe turn up alive in Ephesus. Clitophon is captured by Melite's husband, and Melite promises that she will secure his release and restore Leucippe to him if he will yield but once to her demand. She represents to him that she conveys the command of the god Love. She is to induct him into the sacred rites, for her flame comes from Eros himself. Though Clitophon has been obdurate against the pleas of Melite, he heeds the divine summons. The hero, still a virgin, yields lest he anger the god of love. Close to the Artemisium, he is initiated by a woman who claims that the fire of Aphrodite belongs to her as well as to the goddess.[12]

It can be no coincidence that the name of this instructress is *Melite* (bee). Earlier in the novel, the bee had been introduced as an erotic symbol at the point of Clitophon and Leucippe's first kiss. Bee imagery was an important component of the cult of Artemis of Ephesus. Artemis herself, with the attenuated form, was queen bee. Her priests were called drones, and priestesses served as honeybees (*melissai*). All but three of the cult statues which have been recovered display carvings of bees.[13] The bee priestesses themselves appear on some of the statues, with wings attached to their backs, their naked torsos seeming to emerge from flowers (see illustration 6, p. 71). A woman named Melite who demanded to serve as mystagogue (one who inducted an initiate into the mysteries) in Ephesus surely stood in a long tradition.

Melite also stands in the tradition of the mature woman who provides erotic instruction to the hero of the ancient novel. Lykainion thus instructs young Daphnis in Longus's *Daphnis and Chloe*. She tells him that the nymphs have bidden her to *save* him by teaching him the ways of love.[14] Daphnis is described as a disciple (*mathētēs*) who offers to pay for his education in a great matter which has been sent by the god.[15] Lykainion's instruction is referred to by the word *paideuein* six times and by *didaskein* four times.[16] Through this initiation he is "saved" so that he may enter into marriage with Chloe, as Clitophon was promised the salvation of Leucippe if he would submit to Melite's initiation.

The theme of murder by a female devotee of Artemis is found on several occasions in the ancient novels.[17] If Melite appears in the priestly office of mystagogue, she is also specifically called a murderess (*androphonos*),[18] the very epithet used of the Amazons and also of the false teachers at Ephesus (1 Tim. 1:3). The Amazons were reputed to have established the shrine of Artemis at Ephesus. Four great statues of Amazons stood in the Artemisium, and Amazonian dances were performed in honor of Artemis at Ephesus into late antiquity.[19] Tradition held that Amazons must first kill a man in battle before they were allowed to mate.[20] The great scholar William M. Ramsay pointed out in connection with the cult of *Artemis Ephesia* that the queen bee kills the male who mates with her.[21] Although Melite commits no actual murder in *Clitophon and Leucippe*, her association with Clitophon causes him nearly to be slain. He has actually been strung up as a sacrificial victim before the arrival of a sacred embassy requires that he be set free.

The conclusion of the novel takes place in the actual precinct of Artemis of Ephesus, amid great confusion as to whether an actual murder has been committed and whether there has been sexual infidelity. The plot is resolved through divine intervention, the innocent justifed, and the virtuous rewarded.

To the very end sex and death, together with an emphasis on mystery initiation, are the dominant themes in this very Ephesian novel. So persistent a tradition strongly suggests a religious basis in the secret rites practiced at Ephesus. While these could not be openly divulged, they might be hinted at in a romance. A hidden meaning or scenario may have been one of the attractions of this type of novel.

We know that mysteries, as well as mystic rites, were celebrated in the cult of the Ephesian Artemis. We read of a priestess who "renewed all the mysteries of the goddess and established them in their ancient form" in the early third century C.E.[22] This implies that the mysteries of the famed Ephesian Artemis had a long tradition. Since mysteries usually dealt with sex and death (either real or simulated), there is reason to believe that these themes had major theological importance in Ephesus.

5

The Curse Tablets of Cnidus

The city of Cnidus, lying to the south of Ephesus along the coast of western Asia Minor, is mentioned in Acts 27:7. A discovery there affords us an interesting perspective into women's use of magic and the frequency with which they might be accused of trying to kill men. Both aspects are of interest to us: some widows are called "workers of magic" (1 Tim. 5), and Gnostics practiced astrology and magic on a major scale. Furthermore, 1 Timothy 2:12 may be translated "I forbid a woman to slay a man." Curiously enough, this crime seems to have been feared in Cnidus.

Although the city was famed for a marvelous statue of Aphrodite by Praxiteles, the cult of Demeter had a long history at Cnidus. Demeter, also worshiped in Ephesus, was the earth mother whose daughter Kore (or Persephone) was queen of the underworld. In 1858 Sir Charles T. Newton excavated at Cnidus the remains of a small sanctuary sacred to Demeter, her daughter Kore, Hades, and other infernal deities. It had been dedicated about 350 B.C.E. by Chrysina and appeared to be the private sanctuary of one family. The statuary seems to have been produced in the latter half of the fourth century. Some of the pieces were very fine, and Newton noted one female head, probably Aphrodite, of excellent workmanship though badly mutilated.[1]

There was much of interest in the sanctuary of Demeter and her daughter Kore. There were lamps in abundance, some of quite extraordinary intricacy.[2] There were terra-cotta statuettes and larger-than-life statues of Demeter. Reproductions of pigs, calves, and human breasts were found in substantial numbers. Another sort of votive offering exposed a new aspect of sanctuary life. Along with statuary and lamps lay a series of rolled-up lead sheets inscribed with lively *dirae* (curses) which had originally been tacked to the altar.

Magic spells, charms, enchantments, and curses were widely employed in the ancient world; many still survive. Magic could be used for many purposes—for healing, love charms, fertility, averting of malignant forces, and so forth. Curses were used to deter persons from certain courses of action, such as desecrating a grave or moving a boundary stone. A whole community might even be called upon to execute vengeance upon an offender who violated the prescriptions of the curse.

The *defixio*, such as those found at Cnidus, differed from ordinary curses in that it was always addressed to infernal deities, while other types of curses might call upon human beings, either living or dead, and other deities to work on behalf of the imprecator. A *defixio* was essentially a dedication of a miscreant to the gods of the underworld, so that the object of the curse might be carried off by them or experience some other unpleasant fate. Only proper behavior might free the individual from the claims of these deities. A *defixio* was motivated by hatred or jealousy of a feared or an unpopular individual, and the purpose was either to hinder her or him from a certain course of action or to dispose of the individual permanently.[3] There is reason to believe that the underworld deities made a powerful impact, especially in Caria. The cult of Hecate, a chthonic deity and patroness of witches, was enormously popular there. In the sanctuary of Demeter and "the gods beneath the earth" there was a place for Hecate. Carian women appear to have been strongly imbued with a sensitivity to the world of the dead.[4]

The cult of Demeter and Kore appears to have been important both in the swearing of an oath of innocence and in the cursing of the guilty. If an oath was the binding of oneself to a chthonic deity, then a curse was a *katadesmos* (binding down, as the Latin *defigo* and *defixio* also imply) of another. The person cursed or bound down was in some sense a gift or a sacrifice to the gods of cursing, the underworld gods. Curses of this type were known in Greek as *katadesmos, katadesis,* and in the verb form as *katadein. Devotio* (devotion), when used in connection with a chthonic deity, also constituted a curse. The *defixio* was in point of fact often nailed (i.e., bound down) to the wall or the altar of a sanctuary, and the nail holes are still visible in the tablets from Cnidus. At other times a special knot was used. Thus there was an immediate fastening of the curse tablet, as well as the magical binding. Plato condemned both the magic knot, *katadesis,* and binding of an individual to the infernal deity, the *katadesmos,* and spoke disparagingly of the charlatans who prepared such curses for the general public.[5]

Presumably many of the individuals desiring to make curses, especially the women, would have been unable to write. Professionals well versed in the correct formulae and in the lore of the nether world may have hawked their services in Cnidus as well as at Athens. This may also explain the presence of two different curses, one on each side of the same lead tablet. The services may have been rendered at the same time for more than one client, and the same sheet of lead could be used for both.

Lead was by far the preferred writing material, although occasionally gold, bronze, potsherds, or even a seashell might be used. There is a scholarly debate as to whether lead was used because of its magical power or because of its economy, durability, and malleability.

To be successful, a curse must command the attention of an infernal deity or dead person. David Jordan writes:

The only places that we so far know to have been magically appropriate for depositing *defixiones* at this period were chthonic sanctuaries and graves of persons dead before their appointed hour (*aoroi* or *biaiothanatoi*), whose ghosts were believed to linger on earth until the time originally allotted for their owners' mortal lives had elapsed.[6]

The Curse Tablets of Cnidus in Translation

(not available elsewhere in English)

Three of the texts mention that a woman has been accused of trying to poison a man. In the first curse, the mention of a woman who might be summoned to the temple and engaged to do away with Asclapiades is most interesting. We are not told whether the temple woman also was suspected of using poison, but it appears a natural supposition.

If the lady who protests her innocence so loudly had in fact carried on nefarious negotiations with a would-be assassin, it would have had to be at a temple other than the sanctuary of Demeter and Kore. The goddesses could hardly be expected to ignore what had happened in their own sacred precincts. The suggestion that the temple woman might be produced, as well as the mention of a specific price for her services, leads the reader to suspect that there was something afoot which Demeter and Kore would do well not to overlook.

1. Antigone makes a votive offering to Demeter, Kore, Pluto, and to all the gods and goddesses with Demeter. If I have either given poison to Asclapiades or if I have contemplated within my soul to do him any evil or if I have summoned a woman to the temple and given her three half-minas so that she would remove him from among the living, may Antigone go up, sold[7] from among her fellow slaves to Demeter and may she not find favor with Demeter but rather may she be tormented with great afflictions. But if anyone speaks against me to Asclapiades or produces the woman who has been bribed with copper coins to testify against me

[Here there is a break in the text. The remainder of the curse continues on the back of the tablet.]

and may it be lawful for me to go in to the bath and to enter under the same roof and to come to the same table.[8]

Plutarch twice told a story of Camilla, the Galatian priestess of Artemis, who slew her husband's murderer in Artemis's temple.[9] She accomplished her purpose during a wedding rite by administering a fatal potion from a chalice, an act which William M. Ramsay considered "an old Anatolian ritual."[10] There is also the remark of Tatian that "Artemis is a poisoner."[11] In any event, a cult of Artemis Hyakinthotropos existed at Cnidus and was served by a priest who held office for life.[12] The possibility that a plan for poisoning could be hatched by a woman in Artemis's sanctuary is a tantalizing one.

2. Artemeis invokes the wrath of Demeter, Kore, of all the deities who are with Demeter upon whoever did not return to me upon demand the

cloth, garments, and short tunic which I left with him/her. Let him/her make compensation to Demeter and if anything . . . [here occurs a break in the text] Let him be sold from among . . . And may it be lawful for me freely . . . to drink and eat together and to enter under the same roof. May Hades and Demeter requite his iniquity.[13]

Augustus Audollent, who reexamined the tablets some fifty years after Newton, emends the text to read, "If anyone else has my property, let him be burned with fever until he makes confession" and ends with "May I be avenged by the Lady Demeter." Like the preceding tablet, there is writing on both sides. In this case, there is visible in the middle of the margin a nail hole by which the tablet had been affixed to the shrine.

The items of clothing may include the type of tunic which Carian women were said to have adopted and passed on to Athens. Herodotus records a savage attack by the women of Athens on the single survivor of an expedition against Aegina. When he returned home, the women attacked him with the brooch pins with which they fastened their dresses. The men were so horrified that they decreed that henceforth women must wear tunics of the Ionian type which required no brooches. Herodotus pointed out that this style of dress was not originally Ionian but belonged to the women of Caria.[14] The women of mainland Greece had originally worn the Dorian dress which required pins. While Athenian women were henceforth forbidden pins, the women of Aegina and Argos now adopted ever-longer brooch pins, and gave them as dedicatory gifts to Demeter.

3.   Nanas consigns those who took . . . Nanas invokes the wrath of Demeter and Kore and of the gods who are with Demeter and Kore upon those who took from Diocles a deposit entrusted to them and did not give it back but instead withheld it. May it be blessed for those who pay it back, and may those be accursed who fail to do so and to make compensation . . . To Demeter and Kore [are consigned] those punished by Demeter and Kore because she is unfavorably disposed toward one who defrauds. [Audollent offers a textual revision: "After they have been chastised by those in the company of Demeter and Kore, may they make restitution to Demeter and Kore."[15]]

On the reverse is another dedication of the offenders to the deities of the underworld:

Nanas invokes the wrath of Demeter and Kore and the gods who are with Demeter and Kore upon Emphanes and Rhodos, because they took a deposit from Diocles and failed to return it but purloined it instead. May it be blessed for me, but a curse for those who do not pay it back, but if they say anything more against me.[16]

Although the imprecation breaks off in the middle, there are no further signs of any writing on the tablet. Apparently it was not necessary to complete the sentence in order for the curse to be effective.

The next woman has been accused of trying to poison her husband.

4. I dedicate to Demeter and Kore the person who accused me of making
    a deadly potion for my own husband. May he be sold by Demeter with
    those of his . . . May he when he has made confession be sold to Deme-
    ter with all that is his. May he not obtain favorable treatment from
    Demeter and Kore nor from the gods who are with Demeter, but may it
    be blessed to be freely housed under the same roof and to have inter-
    course in any fashion. I invoke a curse upon the one who made an accu-
    sation against me in writing or directed another to accuse me. May he
    not find favor with Demeter nor Kore nor with the gods who are with
    Demeter, but may he go up to be sold to Demeter with all his posses-
    sions.[17]

*The imprecator, almost certainly a woman, is nettled over a number of difficul-
ties and uses a single tablet to vent her spleen about several concerns. A theft,
a questionable business deal, and domestic tranquility all lay within the
purview of the goddesses. On the reverse is written:*

I dedicate to Demeter and Kore and all the gods and goddesses the one
who secretly cut off the bracelet which I lost in the . . . of Rhodokles.
May it be lawful and permissible for the one who gives it back to
receive a reward for the return of the lost property, and to the woman
who restores it and to the man who gives it back to me. May the one
who does not give it back become slave to Demeter and Kore and all
the gods who are with Demeter and Kore. If that one be already sold,
may Demeter and Kore take care of her or him! I also consign to Demeter and Kore Despoina, the Mistress, anyone who may have over-
charged me if I have paid more than was due for the weight which I
requested. Further I dedicate . . . the one who has done this destructive
thing [?], both him now and all of his kin and offspring hereafter. But
may it be lawful and permissible for me in every way.[18]

The name Despoina *used in connection with Kore is a point of particular interest.[19] To invoke a goddess by a special name gave one particular power in
obtaining one's wish.*

*This curse of a jealous wife was perhaps one of the few recourses open to a
woman facing a very old problem. The difficulty appears not to be the husband's casual relationship with a courtesan but that he has left Prosodion for
another woman. The abandoned state of the children is stressed, perhaps to
gain the pity of Demeter, who was a mother par excellence.*

5. Prosodion invokes the curse of Demeter and Kore and the gods who are
    with Demeter upon whoever has taken Nakon, the husband of Proso-
    dion, away from the children. May she not experience any kindness
    from Demeter nor from the gods who are with Demeter. If she receives
    the messengers of Nakon to the detriment of Prosodion, may it be law-

ful for Prosodion herself and the children in every particular. And if any woman receives Nakon, the husband of Prosodion, to the hurt of Prosodion, may Demeter and the gods with Demeter be unfavorable to them, but may there be blessing for Prosodion and the children in every particular.[20]

Desertion by a husband threatened the wife not only with loneliness and humiliation but also with severe economic peril. The presence of children would further strain the earning power of a mother who sought to provide for a household. Unless a woman had some special skill such as midwifery, only prostitution or the manufacture of textiles held the hope of financial gain.[21] It is to be hoped that a curse which would frighten another woman into refusing to receive Nakon was an expeditious way of settling the matter.

Perhaps because of the urgency of the request, this tablet is more carefully inscribed than the preceding ones. Lines and margins have been incised so that the lettering may be better arranged within their confines.

The following deals with a problem which has plagued us all.

6. I have sent to Demeter and Kore the garment which I lost. And to the one who brings it back, may it be propitious for him, but if he does not give it back to give it as an offering to Demeter and Kore, let him be sold and may the goddesses not be gracious to him until . . . [22]

The next curse, written on the opposite side of the same tablet, is essentially the same as the last:

And I have sent the *himation* which I lost. To the one who gives it back, may there be blessing. I have sent a curse upon him and all that is his and if he does not bring it back as an offering, may he be sold by Demeter and Kore and may he not find them propitious.[23]

This tablet is bady eroded around the edges, and the next one even more so.

7. I dedicate to Demeter and Kore and all the gods who are with Demeter also a boy just reaching maturity, Philosthenes who dishonors my great love. And Trophimos the son of Trophimos . . . and whoever . . . Trophimus to me . . . and other women . . . from Zeus . . . cut . . . be initiated . . . and the one who is initiated to eat . . . he was vowed . . . the vow fulfilled

The reverse side apparently continues the same curse:

May it be wholly blessed for me either to take or . . . and to enter under the same roof and to come to the same table and . . . all that is mine.[24]

Newton surmised that the object of the preceding curse is a young boy who has spurned a pederastic attachment with an older man.

The next tablet is too mutilated to be certain as to its purpose, though it may also deal with unrequited love.

8. I dedicate to Demeter and Kore and all the gods with Demeter both the child Telesia and Philosthenes who . . . from love . . . shamefully . . . and that Trophimos the son of Trophimos to me . . . and other women . . . from Zeus. . . And Telesia . . . and the one who sanctifies me I would say at the . . . completed [or initiated] . . . together with and unlawful . . . but lawful for me . . . sold . . . of Demeter.[25]

The next tablet deals with poisoning, but much of it is effaced. Clearly the gentleman has his suspicions about the murderous intentions of a woman.

9. of poison
    . . . . . . [someone] makes
    . . . . from me and
    . . . and of Muroidos
    . . . . . to children
    . . . these wrongs. . .
    . . . . . may it be, but . . .
    . . . . . on her
    . . . . of the garment which is mine
    . . . . . if I am avenged. . .
    . . . . lords, may s/he not find favorable
    . . . . . spirits[?]
    May the woman who is not purified not find
    thee propitious if she has made for me poison
    either as a drink or ointment or some strange poison
    imported from another country. . .
    . . . our Mistress Despoina, and not . . .
    let not that one enter under the same roof,
    but let that person encounter vengeance; but
    for me may it be lawful. . .
    I, Mistress Despoina[?], . . .
    I am wronged by you . . .
    . . . . but to have worked a hardship upon me . . .
    all punishment, but to me may it be lawful
    to eat together and to pass under the same
    roof with her.[26]

There is the possibility that the poison was ineffective and that suspicions were aroused when someone became violently ill. We have again the mention of a woman who seeks to harm someone by the use of poison. This time, however, the curse is not made by one who protests her innocence but by one who fears that a specific woman may poison him. A prayer for safety as the imprecator eats at the same table with the suspect and enters under the same roof is surely most appropriate. The categories of poison are informative: a drink, an ointment, or some substance of foreign import. It might be questioned whether a severe paranoia had afflicted the citizens of Cnidus, whether this represented a general superstition as in the witchhunts of later times, or whether there was some basis in fact.

To women who had little power to control their own destinies, poison may on rare occasions have afforded an attractive option. Even a woman as powerful as the empress Livia used poison for her own purposes, if we are to believe the ancient historians. A woman, even one who was continually sequestered in her own home, might well find occasion to season the food or drink according to her own predisposition. Such a method would require no violence or bloodshed, and guilt might be very hard to substantiate. The women of Asia Minor enjoyed a far greater freedom than those of Athens; but, judging from these tablets, their lives were not free from frustration. If they lacked power over their own lives, they might at least control the death of another.

10.   . . . concerning the little child of Menekleas [?] whether concerning or . . . concerning deeds . . . to offer to Demeter and Kore and all the gods and goddesses who are with Demeter, and may it be lawful and permissible for me to eat and drink together with . . . and to enter under the same roof . . . with him who has.[27]

The first part is badly mutilated, and we cannot tell whether a woman has been accused of killing a child, or whether she might be invoking its dead spirit to help in the curse.

This tablet appears to be the execration of a woman disappointed in love and vengeful toward her rival.

11.   To Demeter and Kore and all the other gods I dedicate Dorothea who has my man . . . to Demeter.[28]

These two tablets seem to refer to the return of stolen or lost property.

12.   May it be blessed for the one who gives it back and cursed for one who refuses to return it.[29]

13.   I invoke the curse of Demeter and Kore and the gods with Demeter on the one who lost the . . . horns. May it be lawful and permissible to the one who brings it back, but to the one who took . . . because of . . . May he not find favor with Demeter nor with Kore.

and on the reverse

with Demeter [?].[30]

Theft was not the only crime which could be committed to the goddesses. It seems that Demeter and Kore may also assume the role of policeman and magistrate in cases of assault and battery.

14. I dedicate to Demeter and Kore and the gods with Demeter those who assaulted and scourged and bound me and those who brought a charge . . . but to me it is pure.[31]

The lead tablets of Cnidus enable us to view the fears, hostilities, and beliefs of ordinary citizens. We are confronted with some of the more sordid aspects of their lives. These defigents are far removed from the lofty precepts of Plato, and they appear to have known little of those qualities which Cicero said so ennobled the religion of Eleusis. The men and women who offered these curses nevertheless made pragmatic use of the same deities and the same cult. Although they do not appear to have found a spiritual uplift, they have nevertheless found an acceptable outlet for their pent-up emotions. It is possible that their action in preparing a curse, by the threats which it conveyed, brought refractory opponents into line.

It is significant that these tablets deal largely with women. The victim of every curse tablet found in the sanctuary of Demeter at Corinth was a woman.[32] One of these women, a garland-maker, was actually the object of three imprecations! These curses afford us a glimpse into the thoughts and attitudes of the world of women. Often we must view ancient women through the eyes of male authors, but here the women, even though they use formulae, speak for themselves. Their anger, frustration, and hurt show through the conventional phrases of the cult professional.

Euripides' Phaedra asked what trick a woman possessed to unloose the knot of her fate. In Cnidus, one of the answers was the use of lead curse tablets. In the coming of Jesus Christ, women would be afforded a better solution.

6

Gnostic Use of Sex

In certain Gnostic traditions, sex was very much a part of the sacrament. The Gospel of Philip, a Gnostic document which seems to represent a transitional stage between mystery religions and later Gnosticism, emphasizes the necessity of entering the bridal chamber. One could not be part of the believing community or achieve salvation without the rite of the bridal chamber.

The Phrygians, whose cult practices were followed by the serpent-revering Gnostics known as Naassenes, engaged in "inferior mysteries" which related to "carnal generation." These inferior mysteries dealt with Persephone, queen of the underworld, and had to do with death. Yet they were said to lead to "highly-honoured Aphrodite's grove."[1] The way of death led somehow to sex. After a person had been thus initiated into the "lower mysteries," the greater or "heavenly mysteries" were open to him. Now the initiates became "bridegrooms, emasculated through the virginal spirit." Henceforward they renounced sexual activity, "despising all carnal generation," and held that intercourse with a woman was the work of swine and dogs. Nevertheless, the way to their highest mysteries led first through sex and death.[2]

The Phibionites too communicated spiritual grace through sex. Women imparted "knowledge" to men through the sex act (we must bear in mind that the Bible uses "to know" as a euphemism for sex). Men introduced women to the many celestial beings by teaching them one name of a divinity at each act of intercourse. It was essential for the soul to know the name of each archon and to address him properly in order to pass safely through his sphere after death. When 730 sexual conjunctions had been accomplished, one consecrated to each archon in both ascending and descending order respectively, the man said, "I am the Christ since I have descended through the names of the 365 archons."[3]

The Cainites, who taught that Cain was descended from a Power known as "Authentia," believed that such intercourse brought them "perfect knowledge." They were said to dedicate their acts of immorality to the name of an angel and to declare, "O thou Power, I accomplish thy operation."[4]

The sexual union of the celestial beings constituted a basic part of Gnostic cosmology and geneaology.[5] The recurring theme in the literature compelled Hippolytus to complain that some Gnostics found it inconceivable that a male

213

deity could produce anything by himself without copulation.[6] Sexual activity was required of certain Gnostic adherents as a reenactment of the unions of the celestial beings: "For some of them prepare a nuptial couch and perform a sort of mystic rite (pronouncing certain expressions) with those who are being initiated, and affirm that it is a spiritual marriage which is celebrated by them, after the likeness of the conjunctions above."[7]

Marcus, another prominent Gnostic, would withdraw into his bedchamber with a woman whom he found attractive. Then he would declare that she had received grace to prophecy. Thereafter she had a privileged status in the community. His male followers also bestowed their sexual and spiritual favors upon women. Irenaeus complained that they

> have deceived many silly women and defiled them. They proclaim themselves as being "perfected", so that no one can be compared to them with respect to the immensity of their knowledge, not even were you to mention Peter or Paul or any other of the apostles. They assert that they themselves know more than all others, and that they alone have imbibed the greatness of the knowledge of the power which is unspeakable. They also maintain that they have attained to a height above all power, and that therefore they are free in every respect to act as they please, having no one to fear in anything.[8]

Some biblical scholars have found a similarity between this behavior and that described in 2 Timothy 3:6–7, where the heretical teachers led forth as captives silly women laden with sins who were ever learning and never able to come to the truth.

7

Alternative Versions of the Creation Story

The following will not necessarily make easy reading, but it will allow interested readers an opportunity to examine actual texts for themselves. The translations represent an attempt to stay as close as possible to the original documents rather than to render the versions smooth or graceful. This may present some obstacles, especially since Gnostic literature was often intended to befuddle the uninitiated reader. Do not be discouraged if you have to read through several times in order to make sense of these strange treatises.

The first account is written in Greek by Philo of Alexandria (d. C.E. 45), a contemporary of Jesus and Paul. He had a wide influence among Greek-speaking Jews and was fond of allegorizing biblical stories. Philo considered himself an orthodox Jew but did not hesitate to distort the role of Eve rather drastically. He was not a Gnostic, but he worked with some of the same concepts of Eve which appeared in later Gnostic writings. The account is interesting because it demonstrates that people were already taking these liberties before any of the New Testament books were written.

From Philo of Alexandria's *On the Cherubim*

Whenever the mind in us (let it be called Adam) encountering sense perception, the agency by which all animate things appear to live (and it is called Eve)—whenever it draws near to her (aroused by desire for mutual intercourse), she seizes, as though with a fishing or hunting net, upon what may be perceived externally: color through the eyes, voice with the ears, scent through the nostrils, flavor by the organs of taste, through those of touch the entire body. She conceives and immediately goes into labor and gives birth to the greatest of the evils of the soul, presumption. It supposed that every created thing was its own possession, whatever it saw, whatever it heard, tasted, smelled, and touched; and it considered itself discoverer and maker of everything.

This did not happen without a reason. There was a time when the mind had no communication with perception, nor was it possessed of perception itself. It was like a lone, solitary animal living far from mate and herd.

Then, proving to be in a class by itself, it had no contact with any body, for the mind did not have an organ of perception about it, whereby it might hunt out that which was external to itself. It was blind and helpless, but not in the way which many people describe the condition when they see someone disabled by the lack of vision. For being deprived of only one sense, that person has full use of all the others. Rather, the mind was cut off from the power of all its senses, being powerless and only half of a complete soul, stripped of the ability by which it might naturally be enabled to comprehend bodies. It was a cut-off section of itself, deprived of its natural complement, miserable. It was its lot to exist without the staff of the sense organs with which to support his faltering steps. For this reason a great darkness was poured down on all the bodies, while none of them was able to be seen. For that by which they could be made known, perception, did not exist.

God, therefore, wishing to bestow upon him a grasp not only of immaterial but also of solid bodies, completed the whole soul, weaving together a second section which was fellow to that already crafted. To this he gave the generic name of "woman" and the personal name of "Eve," intimating perception.

As soon as she was created, through each of her parts, as if through orifices, she directed massed light toward the mind and dispersed the mist. She rendered the mind capable of seeing distinctly and with the utmost clarity the nature of the bodies, as now being a master. Like one who is dazzled by a brilliant burst of sunshine, or rises up from a deep sleep, or like a blind man who suddenly recovers his sight, the spirit encountered all the entire assemblage of those things which comprised the creation: heaven, earth, water, air, plants, animals, along with their distinctives, qualities, faculties, habits, composition, movements, activities, actions, changes, degeneration. He saw them and heard them and tasted them and smelled them and touched them. He inclined toward those which worked pleasure and turned away from those that wrought pain.[1]

Three Gnostic Texts

In these three differing Gnostic treatments of the material about Eve, there are both differences and remarkable similarities in the distortions of the Genesis account. The first two, The Hypostasis of the Archons and On the Origin of the World, contain so much of the same material that it seems very likely that both drew on an earlier Greek text and adopted various changes to suit the views of the individual editors. Probably all three documents were originally written in Greek, though they survived only in Coptic. Where Greek words still remain in the text, they are noted. This is intended as a help to those who know Greek; English readers need not trouble themselves over this parenthetical material, as it does not add any new words to the text.

In some of these accounts you will see that there is more than one Adam and more than one Eve. Frequently it is hard to keep all the characters straight. Gnostics believed that the most spiritual people were pneumatic, while those with less spiritual insight were psychic, *and those with no spiritual perception were* hylic *(i.e., wooden).*

The Hypostasis of the Archons

They opened his rib in the fashion of a living woman, and they built up out of his rib a flesh (σάρξ) in her place, and Adam became wholly psychic (ψυχικός). And the pneumatic (πνευματική) woman came to him. She spoke with him, saying, "Arise Adam." And when he saw her, he said, "You are the one who has given me life. You will be called the mother of the living, because she is my mother, she is the physician, and the woman and the one who gave birth."

And (δέ) the Authorities (ἐξουσία) came into their Adam when they saw his co-likeness speaking with him. They were disturbed with a great agitation, and they fell in love with her. They said to one another, "Come, let us cast our seed (σπέρμα) down upon her." They pursued (διώκειν) her, and she laughed at them on account of their stupidity, and their blindness; and she became a tree.[2] . . . She put her reflection like herself before them. . . .

And (δέ) the female spiritual principle (πνευματική) entered into the snake, the Teacher. And he instructed them, saying, "What was it that he said to you? Was it 'From every tree in the Garden (Παράδεισος) you shall eat of it, but (δέ) do not eat from the tree of the knowledge of evil and good'?"

The fleshly (σαρκική) woman said, "Not only (οὐ μόνον) did he say 'do not eat' but (ἀλλά) also 'you shall not touch it because in the day that you eat of it, you shall die.'"

And the snake, the Instructor, said, "By death you shall not die. For (γάρ) when he spoke these things to you, he was jealous (φθονεῖν). Rather (μᾶλλον) your eyes will be opened, and you will be like gods who know the evil and the good." And the feminine instructor[3] was taken out of the snake. And she left behind only a creature of the earth. (89.3–90.12)

In the next account, sometimes Sophia (Wisdom) becomes interchangeable with Eve. Since Eve's name means "life," she is also equated with Zoe (Gk.: life).

On the Origin of the World

And when Sabaoth had taken the place (τόπος) of rest (ἀνάπαυσις) in exchange for his repentance (μετάνοια), still (ἔτι) Pistis (Faith—πίστις) gave to him her daughter Zoe (ζωή), along with great authority (ἐξουσία) so that she might teach him about all the things which are in the eighth heaven. (104.28–35)

And he sits upon a throne (θρόνος) of light in a great cloud which shelters (σκεπάζειν) him. And no one is with him in the cloud except (εἰ μήτι) for Sophia (σοφία), daughter of Pistis (πίστις), who was teaching him all the things which are in the eighth heaven so that there might be created likenesses of those things in order that his kingdom might remain until the consummation (συντέλεια) of the heavens of chaos (χάος) with their powers (δύναμις). Then Pistis (πίστις) Sophia (σοφία) separated him from the darkness and summoned him to her right hand, but the original parent she put on her left. (106.3–13)

The woman followed after the earth, and marriage (γάμος) followed the woman, and birth followed marriage (γάμος), and destruction followed after birth. (109.22)

The Wisdom (Σοφία) which is in the lower heaven, when she wished it, received power (ἐξουσία) from Faith (Πίστις). She made great light banners and all the stars. She set them in the sky so that they would shine upon the earth, and they designate signs (σημεῖον) of the time (χρόνος), and of seasons (καιρός), and of years, and months, and days, and nights and moments, and all other time. And in this fashion, the entire area was adorned (κόσμειν) upon the sky.

And when the Adam of light wished to go into his light—that is to say, the eighth [heaven], he could not find the strength on account of the destitution which had mingled with his light. Then he made for himself a great aeon (αἰών); and in that aeon (αἰών) he made six aeons (αἰών) with their embellishments (κόσμος), being six in number, seven times better than the skies of Chaos (χάος) and their embellishments (κόσμος).

And all these aeons (αἰών), and their embellishment (κόσμος), are in the infinite, which is between the eighth [heaven] and the Chaos (χάος) beneath it, being reckoned with the world which pertains to destitution. If you wish to understand the placement of these, you will find it recorded in the *Seventh World* (κόσμος) *of the Prophet* (Προφήτης) Hieralias.

Before the Adam of light withdrew (ἀναχώρειν) into the Chaos (χάος), the Authorities (ἐξουσία) saw him and made fun of the original parent (ἀρχιγενέτωρ), because he had told a lie in saying, "I am God. There is no one before me." When they came to him, they said, "Is not this the god who destroyed our work (ἔργον)?"

He answered and said, "Yes. If you want him not to have the power to destroy our work (ἔργον), come let us make a man out of the earth according (κατά) to the image (εἰκών) of our body (σῶμα) and according (κατά) to the likeness of this one.[4] He[5] will worship us so that if he sees his likeness, he will fall in love with it. He will no longer (οὐκ ἔτι) destroy our work (ἔργον). But (ἀλλά) those who will be born out of the light we will make our servants in all the time (χρόνος) of this aeon (αἰών)."

And (δέ) all of these things came about according to (κατά) the forethought (πρόνοια) of Faith (πίστις) so that (ἵνα) the man should appear after his likeness and should condemn (κατακρίνειν) them as a result of their molded being (πλάσμα); and the molded being (πλάσμα) became a hedge of light. Then the Authorities (ἐξουσία) received the knowledge (γνῶσις) so that they might create the man. Sophia (Σοφία) Zoe (Ζωή) had a start on them, she who is with Sabaoth, and she made fun of their plan (γνώμη), because they are blind; in their ignorance they created him for themselves alone. And (δέ) they do not realize what it is that they were going to make.

Because of this (διά τοῦτο) she acted pre-emptively and made her own man first so that (ἵνα) he might teach their molded creature (πλάσμα) in what manner to scorn (καταφρόνειν) them and in this way to be safe from them. And (δέ) the birth of the Instructor happened in this way. When Sophia (σοφία) cast down a drop of light, it flowed upon the water. At once a man appeared who was both male and female.

She made that drop first in the pattern (τύπος) of the body of a woman. Afterwards she made in the body a pattern (τύπος) of the likeness of the mother which had appeared. She completed it (feminine) within twelve months. A human being was born who was both male and female, which the Greeks (Ἕλληνες) call hermaphrodite (ἑρμαφρόδιτης). And (δέ) the Hebrews (Ἑβραῖος) call its mother the Eve of Life (ζωή), which is the female instructor of life.

But (δέ) her child is the progeny which is lord. Afterwards the Authorities (ἐξουσία) called him "the Beast" (Θηρίον) in order that it might deceive (πλανᾶν) their molded creatures (πλάσμα). The interpretation (ἑρμηνεία) of the beast (Θηρίον) is the Instructor. For (γάρ) he was found to be wiser than (παρά) all of them.

For Eve (Εὕα) is the first virgin (παρθένος), the one who had no husband and yet gave birth. She is the one who acted as a physician-midwife to herself. Because of this (διὰ τοῦτο), she is said to have proclaimed, "I am the portion (μέρος) of my mother, and I am the mother. I am the wife. I am she who is the virgin (παρθένος). I am she who has conceived. I am she who is the midwife. I am she who is the consoler during labor pains. My husband is the one who bore me, and I am she who is his mother. And it is he who is my father and my lord. It is he who is my strength. That which he wishes he says with good reason (εὐλόγως). I am coming into being. Yet (ἀλλά) I have given birth to a man who is lord."

But (δέ) these things, in the will [break in the text] The souls who were about to go into the molded bodies (πλάσμα) of the Authorities (ἐξουσία) were revealed to Sabaoth and his Christ (Χριστός). And concerning these ones, the holy voice spoke, "Become many and be good. Become lord over all created things." And these are the ones who were made captives according to their lot (κατὰ κλῆρος) by the original parent (ἀρχιγενέτωρ). And in this way they were enclosed within the prison of their molded bodies (πλάσμα), or in the consummation (συντέλεια) of the aeon (αἰών).

And (δέ) in that time, then the primal parent (ἀρχιγενέτωρ) gave a plan (γνώμη) concerning the man to those who were with him. Then (τότε) one by one, each of them cast his seed into the midst of the navel of the earth. Ever since that day, the seven archons (ἄρχων) have fashioned (πλάσσειν) the man with his body (σῶμα) being on the one hand like their body, and on the other hand with his likeness similar to that of the man who appeared to them. His molding proceeded one by one (κατὰ μέρος). And (δέ) their Greatest One created the brain (ἐγκέφαλος) and the marrow.

Afterwards he was revealed as (ὡς) antecedent to him. He became a psychic (ψυχικός) man, and they called him Adam, which is "father" according (κατά) to the name of the one who is antecedent to him. And (δέ) when they had completed Adam, he left him as a vessel (σκεῦος) because he had taken shape (μορφή) in the manner of a miscarried fetus, lacking a spirit (πνεῦμα) within him. Concerning this matter, when the Greatest One of the archons (ἄρχων) remembered the saying of Pistis (Πιστις), he was afraid lest (μήπως) the true man should go into his molded body and become lord over it.

Because of this he left his molded body for forty days without a soul (ψυχή). And he withdrew (ἀναχώρειν) and left it. But (δέ) on the fortieth day the Sophia (σοφία) of Life (ζωή) sent her breath into Adam, who had no soul. He began (ἄρχειν) to move on the ground. And he did not have the strength to rise up. But (δέ) when the seven archons (ἄρχων) came, they saw him, and they were enormously disturbed. They advanced upon him. They seized him, and he said to the breath which was within him, "Who are you? And whence did you come here?" It answered and said, "I have come out of the power (δύναμις) of the man on account of the destruction of your work (ἔργον)." When they heard, they gave him glory because he gave them rest from the fear and the concern which was in them. Then (τότε) they called that day Rest (ἀνάπαυσις), because they rested from their labor.

And (δέ) when they saw that Adam was unable to rise up, they rejoiced. They took him and put him in the garden (παράδεισος). And they went back (ἀναχώρειν) up to their heavens. After the day of rest (ἀνάπαυσις), Sophia (σοφία) sent Zoe (ζωή) her daughter, who is called Eve (Εὕα) as (ὡς) instructor so that she should raise up Adam, who had no soul in him, so that those whom he would beget should become vessels (ἀγγεῖον) of the light.

When Eve saw her co-likeness lying flat, she showed pity upon him and said, "Adam live! Rise up upon the earth." Straightway her word became a deed (ἔργον). For (γάρ) when Adam had risen up, he immediately opened his eyes. When he saw her, he said "You will be called 'the mother of the living,' because you are the one who has given me life."

Then (τότε) the Authorities (ἐξουσία) received the news that their formed creature was alive, and that he had risen up. They were highly disturbed. They sent seven archangels (ἀρχάγγελος) to see what had happened. They came to Adam. When they saw Eve (Εὕα) speaking with him, they said to one another, "What is this (feminine) person of light? For truly (καὶ γάρ) she is like the similitude which appeared to us in the light. Come now, let us seize her and cast our seed (σπέρμα) into her in order that when she is in a state of defilement, she will be unable to go up into her light. But (ἀλλά) those whom she will bear will be made subject (ὑποτάσσειν) to us.

"But (δέ) let us not tell Adam because he is not from among us, but (ἀλλά) let us bring a sleep upon him, and let us teach him in his sleep as (ὡς) if she came into being from his rib so that the woman may be subject (ὑποτάσσειν) and he may be lord over her." Then (τότε) Eve (Εὕα), since she was a power (δύναμις), laughed at their plan (γνώμη). She cast mist into their eyes. Stealthily she set her likeness beside Adam.

She went into the tree of knowledge (γνῶσις) and stayed there. And (δέ) they followed after her. She showed them that she had gone into the tree and had become a tree. And (δέ) when the blind [archons] were in a great fright, they fled away.

Afterwards, when they had sobered up (νήφειν) from their oblivious sleep, they came back to Adam; and when they saw the likeness of this woman with him, they were very upset, thinking that this was the true (ἀληθινή) Eve (Εὕα). And they behaved arrogantly (τολμᾶν). They came to her and seized her and cast their seed (σπέρμα) upon her. They did it in duplicity (πανοῦργος), not only (οὐ μόνον) defiling her naturally (φυσικῶς) but (ἀλλά) in ways that are polluted, as they first defiled the seal (σφραγίς) of her voice, with which she had spoken to them, saying, "Who is the one who exists before you?"—so that they might defile the ones who would say that they were begotten by the word from the true (ἀληθινός) man at the consummation (συντέλεια). And they were in error (πλάνη) because they did not understand that they had defiled their own body. The likeness was that which the Authorities (ἐξουσία) along with their angels (ἄγγελος) defiled in every aspect.

First she conceived Abel by the first of the archons (ἄρχων), and the rest of the children which she bore were sired by the seven Authorities (ἐξουσία) and their angels (ἄγγελος). And all of this happened according to (κατά) the forethought (πρόνοια) of the original parent (ἀρχιγενέτωρ) so that the first mother might give birth from within herself to every seed which is mingled and suited (ἀρμόζειν) to the destiny (εἱμαρμένη) of the world (κόσμος) and of its aspects (σχῆμα) and to righteousness (δικαιοσύνη).

An arrangement (οἰκονομία) was devised concerning Eve (Εὕα) so that the molded bodies (πλάσμα) of the powers (ἐξουσία) might become containers of the light. Then (τότε) it [the light] would judge (κατακρίνειν) them by means of their molded bodies (πλάσμα). Therefore the first Adam of the light is pneumatic (πνευματικός). He appeared on the first day. The second Adam is a psychic (ψυχικός). He was revealed on the sixth day, which is also (δέ) called Aphrodite (Ἀφροδίτη). The third Adam is earthly (χοικός), that is to say, a doer of the law (νόμος), who appeared on the eighth day. (112.1–117.36)

The last account shows a greater dissimilarity from the other two Gnostic versions but still features Eve as prime mover in the creation and enlightenment of Adam.

The Apocryphon of John

But (δέ) when the Mother wanted to take the power which she had given to the first archon (ἄρχων), she asked the Mother-father (μητροπάτωρ) of the All whose mercy is great. He sent five luminaries (φωστήρ) by means of the holy plan down upon the place (τόπος) of the angels of the primal archon (πρωτάρχων). They counseled him that (ὥστε) he should bring out the power of the mother; and they said to Ialtabaoth, "Breathe upon his face some of your spirit (πνεῦμα), and his body (σῶμα) will arise." And he breathed upon him of his spirit (πνεῦμα) which is the power of the Mother. He did not understand this because he was in ignorance. And the power (δύναμις) of the Mother went out from Ialtabaoth into a psychic (ψυχικός) body which they had formed for him according (κατά) to the likeness of the one who had existed from the beginning. The body (σῶμα) moved and received strength and shone.

Then the other powers (δύναμις) became jealous for (γάρ) he had come into existence through the instrumentality of all of them, and they had given their power to the man, and his wisdom caused him to be superior to those who had made him and to the first archon (ἄρχων). But (δέ) when they understood that he was light and thought more ably than they did and was devoid of evil (κακία), they took him and threw him into the lowest section (μέρος) of all matter (ὕλη). But (δέ) the blessed Mother-father (μητροπάτωρ), the compassionate benefactor, took pity upon the power (δύναμις) of the mother which was taken out of the primal archon (Πρωτάρχων), and took pity because they might get power over the psychic (ψυχικός) and the sensory (αἰσθητός) body (σῶμα). And he sent forth from his spirit, beneficent and abundant in his mercy, a helper (βοηθός) for Adam, an Epinoia (Ἐπίνοια) of light which is from within him. And they named it Zoe (ζωή), and (δέ) she renders assistance (ὑπουργεῖν) to the whole creature (κτίσις), works with him, and sets him to right in his fulfillment (πλήρωμα), and teaches him about the descent of his seed (σπέρμα). She teaches him about the road to go up and the road which he came down from there.

And the Epinoia ('Επίνοια) of light is hidden in Adam so that the archons (ἄρχων) should not understand but (ἀλλά) that the Epinoia ('Επίνοια) may be a setting right of the mother's deficiency. And the man was revealed because of the shadow of light which was within him, and his intellect was higher than (παρά) those who had made him. When they stared up at the sky, they saw that his thought was exalted, and they took counsel with the entire archontic (ἀρχοντικός) and angelic (ἀγγελικός) host. They took fire with earth and water. They mixed them together with each other and with four winds of fire and joined them to one another and made a great disturbance and they brought him [Adam] into the shadow of death so that they might again form him (πλάσσειν) from the earth and water and fire and the spirit (πνεῦμα), which issues from matter (ὕλη), that is of the ignorance of darkness and desire (ἐπιθυμία) and their substituted spirit (πνεῦμα). That is the sepulchre (σπήλαιον) of the new creation (ἀνάπλασις) which the robbers (λῃστής) bestowed upon the man, the shackle of forgetfulness. And this one became a man subject to death. That is the one who first came down and the first separation. But (δέ) the Epinoia ('Επίνοια) of light who was within him, she is the one who would awaken his thought.

And the archons (ἄρχων) brought him and set him in Paradise (Παράδεισος). And they said to him, "Eat, that is in pleasure," for indeed (καὶ γάρ) their pleasure (τρυφή) is bitter, and their beauty is lawless (ἄνομος), and (δέ) their delight (τρυφή) is deceit (ἀπάτη) and their trees are impiety (ἀσεβής) and their fruit a poison which cannot be healed. . . .

Then (τότε) the Epinoia ('Επίνοια) of light hid within him [Adam], and the primal Archon (πρωτάρχων) wished to bring her out of his side. But (δέ) the Epinoia ('Επίνοια) of light is unattainable. When the darkness pursued her, it did not apprehend her. And it brought forth just a part (μέρος) of his power out of him, and it formed another creature (πλάσις) in the form (μορφή) of a woman, according to (κατά) the likeness of the Epinoia ('Επίνοια) which had appeared to him. And it brought the part which it had taken from the power of the man into the creature (πλάσμα) of femininity, and not in the manner (κατά) which Moses spoke "his rib." And he looked upon the woman beside him, and (δέ) in that moment the Epinoia ('Επίνοια) of light appeared as she uncovered the veil (κάλυμμα) which was upon his mind.

And he became sober from the drunkenness of darkness; and he recognized his image; and he said, "This now is bone out of my bone and flesh (σάρξ) out of my flesh (σάρξ) . . . And (δέ) our sister Wisdom (Sophia—Σοφία) is she who came down in innocence (ἄκακος) so that she might rectify the deficiency. Because of this she was named Zoe (ζωή), that is, the mother of the living through the Forethought (Πρόνοια) of the Authentia (Αὐθεντία) which is above. And through her they tasted the perfect (τέλειος) knowledge (γνῶσις). (The Apocryphon of John BG 67–71)

Endnotes

Preface

1. *The Northwestern Lutheran*, September 15, 1990, 316.
2. *The Northwestern Lutheran*, January 15, 1991, 35.
3. We are grateful to Professor David Scholer for first pointing this out to us.
4. Charlotte Brontë, *Shirley* (1849; reprint ed., London: Harper, 1899), 2:17.

Introduction: *Problems with a Traditional Interpretation*

1. His mother, his sister, the midwives, Pharaoh's daughter and her ladies-in-waiting all conspired to save his life.
2. Thomas R. Edgar, "Contextualized Interpretations of 1 Timothy 2:12: An Analysis," unpublished paper presented at the national meeting of the Evangelical Theological Society in Wheaton, Illinois, 1988.
3. Ibid.
4. Tertullian *De cultu feminarum* 1.1.1–2.

Chapter 1: Approaching the Bible with Faith

1. For a list of the exegetical problems in the so-called difficult passages on women, see the appendix by Sanford G. Hull in *Equal to Serve*, ed. Gretchen Gaebelein Hull (Old Tappan, N.J.: Revell, 1987).

Chapter 2: The Pastoral Epistles:
Who Wrote Them and Why

1. A. T. Hanson, *The Living Utterances of God: The New Testament Exegesis of the Old* (London: Darton, Longman, and Todd, 1983), 134.
2. Helmut Koester, *Introduction to the New Testament*, vol. 2, *History and Literature of Early Christianity* (Philadelphia: Fortress, 1982), 304.
3. See also C. F. D. Moule, "The Problem of the Pastoral Epistles: A Reappraisal," *Bulletin of the John Rylands Library* 47 (1964–65): 430–52; August Strobel, "Schreiben des Lukas? Zum sprachlichen Problem der Pastoralbriefe," *New Testament Studies* 15

(1968–69): 191–210; and Stephen G. Wilson, *Luke and the Pastoral Epistles* (London: SPCK, 1979).

4. A number of similar concerns prompt both the writer of Acts and the writer of the pastoral Epistles: the need for correction at Ephesus, especially on the matter of heresy; the interest in medical conditions; the familiarity with the coterie of Paul. The writer also shares certain grammatical propensities with Luke.

5. See, for instance, Helmut Koester, *Introduction to the New Testament*, vol. 1, *History, Culture, and Religion of the Hellenistic Age* (Philadelphia: Fortress, 1982), 298–300. For the suggestion that Polycarp of Smyrna may have been the author, see 305–8.

6. At Ancyra (modern Ankara), Apollonia in Pisidia, and Antioch in Pisidia.

7. See J. L. Houlden, *The Pastoral Epistles*, Pelican New Testament Commentary (London: SCM, 1976), 24–26; John A. T. Robinson, *Redating the New Testament* (London: SCM, 1979), 84.

8. There are some indications of the influence of the Pastorals in the writings of Ignatius and Polycarp and also in 1 Clement.

Chapter 3: Destination: Ephesus

1. Flavius Philostratus *The Life of Apollonius of Tyana* 7.7.

2. "All Asia was the possession of the Persian king, and all Ephesians became the spoils of war. They are unaccustomed to true freedom, that is to rule. Now they are likely to obey when they are given commands, or to wail aloud if they do not obey." Pseudo-Heraclitus of Ephesus *Epistle* 8.

3. τοῖς ἐν Σάρδεσιν · αἰτίαν ἔχετε τὴν πάτριον θεὰν σέβειν τε καὶ τιμᾶν. ἢ δὴ μήτηρ ὀνομάζεται παρ' οἷς μὲν θεῶν, παρ' οἷς δὲ καὶ ἀνθρώπων, παρὰ πᾶσι δὲ καὶ καρπῶν· ἡ δὲ μία κοινή τε καὶ πάντων. εἶτα πῶς μόνων ὑμῶν ἐχθρὰ τὰ γένη νόμῳ καὶ φύσει κὰ ἔθει, τῶν Δήμτρος ἰδίων. . . . In Robert J. Penella, "Apollonius of Tyana to the Sardians," *Harvard Studies in Classical Philology* (1975), vol. 79, 308. For Demeter as a goddess of Sardis, see 309–10.

4. Pausanias 4.31.8.

5. G. H. R. Horsley, *New Documents Illustrating Early Christianity. A Review of the Greek Inscriptions and Papyri* (North Ryde, N.S.W: The Ancient History Documentary Research Centre, Macquarie University, 1987), 19.

6. Diodorus of Sicily 5.77.3–8.

7. Strabo *Geography* 10.3.7.

8. A. Boeckh, *Corpus Inscriptionum Graecarum* (Berlin: G. Riemas, 1828–77), n. 6797.

9. Solinus 11.8.

10. Aelian *Varia historia* 3.26.

11. William M. Ramsay, "The Worship of the Virgin Mary at Ephesus," in *Pauline and Other Studies in Early Christian History* (London: Hodder and Stoughton, 1906), 125–59.

12. Josephus *Jewish Antiquities* 12.125–28; 14.223–31; 16.27–64.

13. Thomas A. Robinson, *The Bauer Thesis Examined: The Geography of Heresy in the Early Christian Church*, Studies in the Bible and Early Christianity 11 (Lewiston, N.Y.: Edwin Mellen, 1988), 114.

14. A. T. Kraabel, "Judaism of Asia Minor under the Roman Empire," unpublished Th.D. thesis, Harvard University, 1968, especially 51–59.

15. Marclay V. Head, *Catalogue of the Greek Coins of Phrygia* (London: Trustees of the British Museum, 1906), plate 1: Apameia; Sammlung V. Aulock, *Sylloge Nummorum Graecorum Deutschland* (Berlin: Mann, 1962), *Phyrgien*, Heft 9, nos. 3506, 3510, 3513, plate 114.

16. Flavius Philostratus *The Life of Apollonius of Tyana* 4.2; *Epistles* of Apollonius 27.65. See also the *Epistles* (9.12–19) of Pseudo-Heraclitus of Ephesus. As to whether or not the writer was a Jew, see Harold W. Attridge, *First Century Cynicism in the Epistles of Heraclitus*, Harvard Theological Studies 29 (Missoula, Mont.: Scholars, 1976).

Chapter 4: Identifying the Problem:
Evidence from the Pastorals

1. See Patricia Miller, "In Praise of Nonsense," in *Classical Mediterranean Spirituality: Egyptian, Greek, Roman*, ed. A. H. Armstrong, World Spirituality Series (New York: Crossroad, 1986).

2. Gordon D. Fee, "Issues in Evangelical Hermeneutics, Part 3: The Great Watershed—Intentionality and Particularity/Eternality: 1 Timothy 2:8–15 as a Test Case," *Crux* 26, 4 (December 1990): 32.

3. Ibid., 37 n. 11.

4. Menander *The Charioteer* frag. 202 Kock.

5. Pliny the Elder *Natural History* 30.2.11.

6. For an extended list of ancient references to women as storytellers, see Dennis Ronald MacDonald, *The Legend and the Apostle: The Battle for Paul in Story and Canon* (Philadelphia: Westminster, 1983), 13–14, 105 n. 4.

7. "The 'old woman' enacted a wide range of roles and was the most prominent magic-religious specialist in Anatolia. . . . Although many of her incantations are in Hurrian and are therefore very difficult to decipher, enough is known about their content to conclude that the 'old woman' was one of the primary transmitters of mythic tradition in Anatolian society." Michael S. Moore, *The Balaam Traditions: Their Character and Development*, SBL Dissertation Series 113 (Atlanta: Scholars, 1990), 21–22.

8. See in particular Henry A. Green, *The Economic and Social Origins of Gnosticism*, SBL Dissertation Series 77 (Atlanta: Scholars, 1985).

9. Philo *On the Cherubim* 57–60.

10. Philo *On the Migration of Abraham* 89ff.

11 Irenaeus *Against Heresies* 3.3.4; Eusebius *Ecclesiastical History* 4.14.6.

Chapter 5: An Examination of 1 Timothy 1:3–2:11

1. E. R. Dodds, *Pagan and Christian in an Age of Anxiety: Some Aspects of Religious Experience from Marcus Aurelius to Constantine* (1965; reprint ed., New York: Norton, 1970), 38.

2. Plutarch *Moralia* 415A.

3. Plutarch *De Iside et Osiride* 372; see also *Moralia* 1014D, 1015D, and 1023A; Plato *Timaeus* 49A, 51A.

4. Epiphanius *Panarion* 33.7.2.

5. Strabo *Geography* 14.1.23.

6. Autocrates 1 as quoted by Aelian *De natura animalium* 12.9.

7. Aristophanes *Clouds* 599–600.

8. F. Sokolowski, *Lois Sacreés de l'Asie Mineure* (Paris: E. de Boccard, 1955), 48.19–20; M. P. Nilson, *The Dionysiac Mysteries of the Hellenistic and Roman Age* (Lund: Gleerup, 1957), 6–7.

9. Joscelyn Godwin, *Mystery Religions in the Ancient World* (San Francisco: Harper and Row, 1981), 141.

10. Strabo *Geography* 7.3.3.

11. τὰ δ' ἐν θεοῖς αὖ· πρῶτα γὰρ κρίνω τάδε· μέρος μέγιστον ἔχομεν. ἐν Φοίβου τε γὰρ δόμοις προφητεύσουσι Λοξίου φρένα γυναῖκες, ἀμφὶ δ' ἀγνὰ Δωδώνης βάθρα φηγῷ παρ' ἱερα θῆλυ τᾶς Διὸς φρένας γένος πορεύει τοῖς θέλουσιν Ἑλλάδος. ἃ δ' εἴς τε Μοίρας τάς τ' ἀνωνύμους θεὰς ἱερὰ τελεῖται, ταῦτ' ἐν ἀνδράσιν μὲν οὐ ὅσια καθέστηκ', ἐν γυναιξὶ δ' αὔξεται ἅπαντα. ταύτῃ τ'αν θεοῖς ἔχει δίκης θήλεια. *Tragicorum Graecorum Fragmenta Papyracea Nuper Reperta*, ed. Arthur S. Hunt (Oxford: Clarendon, 1912), 6 Εὐριπίδου Μελανίππη lines 1–22. Nauck frag. 499 contains the first three lines.

12. Juvenal *Satires* 6.540–47.

13. For the suggestion that she was the priestess of a syncretistic Judeo-Phrygian cult, see Richard Reitzenstein, *Hellenistic Mystery-Religions: Their Basic Ideas and Significance*, trans. John E. Steely (Pittsburgh: Pickwick, 1978), 176–77. See also Franz Cumont, *Oriental Religions in Roman Paganism* (New York: Dover, 1978), 62ff.

14. Shepherd of Hermas.

15. Many of the documents now available only in Coptic were first written in Greek. When the translation is from Coptic, the original Greek words will be reproduced.

16. The Gospel of Mary 10.1–8, Papyrus Berolinensis 8502.1.

17. Origen *Against Celsus* 5.62.

18. See Origen *Against Celsus* 5.62. Mentioned in Mark 16:1, Salome is one of the Lord's apostles in the Gospel of Thomas and Pistis Sophia. Clement of Alexandria mentions her in connection with the Gospel according to the Egyptians (*Miscellanies* 3.45.63, 66, 92).

19. Hippolytus *Refutation of All Heresies* 5.7.1; 10.9.3; Origen *Against Celsus* 5.62.

20. Irenaeus *Against Heresies* 1.23.2.

21. See also Tertullian *De anima* 34; Hippolytus *Refutation of All Heresies* 6.19; Origen *Against Celsus* 5.62. See Wilhelm Bousset, *Die Hauptprobleme der Gnosis* (1907; reprint ed., Göttingen: Vandenhoeck und Ruprecht, 1973), 78ff. for the tradition about Helen.

22. Epiphanius *Panarion* 34.4.2 (Migne *PG* 41.589).

23. Trimorphic Protennoia NHC 13.1. 42. 9–14, 17–18.

24. Irenaeus *Against Heresies* 1.25.6 (Migne *PG* 7.685); Epiphanius *Panarion* 27.6.1 (Migne *PG* 41.372).

25. b. Hullin 89a, as quoted by Aida Besançon Spenser. For an extensive listing of rabbinic sayings on silence see Spenser, *Beyond the Curse: Women Called to Ministry* (Nashville: Nelson, 1985), 77–80.

Chapter 6: A Closer Look at Our Target Verse

1. Martin Dibelius and Hans Conzelmann, *The Pastoral Epistles*, ed. Helmut Koester, trans. Philip Buttolph and Adela Yarbro (Philadelphia: Fortress, 1972), 55, 77.

2. See *TDNT* 2:164.

3. See *TDNT* 2:162, sect. 3.

4. *TDNT* 2:164.

5. Jerome Quinn, *The Letter to Titus*, Anchor Bible (Garden City, N.Y.: Doubleday, 1990), 81–82. See also 92–97.

6. See John Toews, "Women in Church Leadership: 1 Timothy 2:11–15, A Reconsideration," in *The Bible and the Church: Essays in Honor of Dr. David Ewert*, ed. A. J. Dueck, H. J. Giesbrecht, and V. G. Shillington (Hillsboro, Kans.: Kindred, 1983), 84. We do not find the use of *epitrepo* necessarily to be a limited one in 4 Macc. 5:26, however.

7. From an unpublished paper which Dr. Payne presented to the national meeting of the Evangelical Theological Society in Atlanta, Georgia, 1986.

8. Euripides *Andromache* 614–15.

9. This definition is found in Sophocles *Electra* 272–75.

10. μήτε θυγατρὶ τῇ σῇ μήτε αὐτῷ σοὶ εἴην αὐθέντης. Herodotus 1.117.12.

11. Antiphon *Tetralogy* 2.3.4.

12. Ibid., 2.3.11.

13. Euripides *Andromache* 615; scholion on Aeschylus *Eumenides* 212; see also Robert Parker, *Miasma: Pollution and Purification in Early Greek Religion* (Oxford: Clarendon, 1983), 122–23, 351.

14. Aeschylus *Agamemnon* 1573; *Eumenides* 212; Euripides *The Madness of Hercules* 839, 1359.

15. Philo *Quod deterius potiori insidiari soleat* 78.7; Appian *Bellum civile* 4.17.134.

16. Scholion on Aeschylus *Eumenides* 42.

17. "Ce qui rendrait parfaitement compte des deux références suivantes au premier couple humain: la femme est dépendente de l'homme et c'est une meutrière qui l'a induit à pêcher." Ceslaus Spicq, *Les Épîtres Pastorales*, 2 vols. (Paris: Gabalda, 1947), 1:380.

Chapter 7: That Strange Greek Verb *Authentein*

1. Friedrich Preisigke, *Worterbuch der griechischen Papyrusurkunden mit einschluss der grieschichen inschriften, auschriften, ostraka, mumienschilder usw., aus Agypten* (Berlin: Selbstverlag der Erben, 1925–27), s.v.

2. H. I. Bell, *Greek Papyri in the British Museum*, 8 vols. (London: Trustees of the British Museum, 1917), 5:119. London Papyrus 1708.

3. Jean Maspero, *Papyrus Grecs d'Époque Byzantine, Catalogue Général des Antiquités Égyptiennnes du musée du Caire*, 3 vols. (Cairo: Imp. de l'institut françois d'archéologie orientale, 1911–16), vol. 2, no. 67151.

4. Professor George Sheets kindly pointed out to us that in both these documents *authentein* seems to function as a Greek equivalent of the Latin legal term *vindico*—to appropriate, lay claim to, or claim as one's own, including the right of deriving income from a property.

5. *Forschung in Ephesos* 3 (1923), no. 44.

6. *Phrynichi Sophistae praeparatio Sophistica*, ed. I. de Borries (Liepzig: B. G. Teubner, 1911), 24.

7. Scholion on Thucydides 3.58.4.

8. David Kovacs, "Tyrants and Demagogues in Tragic Interpolation," *Greek, Roman, and Byzantine Studies* 23 (1982): 37. See also Louis Gernet, *Droit et société dans la Grèce ancienne* (Paris: Receuil Sirey, 1955), 29–38.

9. Moeridis Atticistae, *Lexicon Atticum*, ed. J. Pierson (reprint ed., Hildesheim, N. Y.: G. Olms, 1969), 58; Thomas Magister, *Grammaticus*, ed. F. Ritschl (reprint ed., Hildesheim, N. Y.: G. Olms, 1970), 128.

10. John of Damascus *Epistola ad Theophilim Imperatorem* 3 (Migne *PG* 95.248).

11. Eusebius *Commentary on Isaiah* 40:10 (Migne *PG* 24.369).

12. Eusebius opp. Part 2 - *Apologetica* (Migne *PG* 22.48B).

13. John Chrysostom *Homily on the Gospel of St. Matthew* 44.1 (Migne *PG* 7.467C).

14. John Chrysostom *Homily on the Gospel of St. John* 66.2 (Migne *PG* 8.396D).

15. John Chrysostom *Homily on Colossians* 10.1; 11.2 (Migne *PG* 11.396C; 11.406E).

16. In about C.E. 112 two Christian female leaders known as ministers (deacons) were interrogated in Asia Minor by Roman officials. Pliny the Younger *Letter to Trajan* 10.96.

17. Justin Martyr *First Apology* 65.

18. Katherine Bushnell, *God's Word to Women: One Hundred Bible Studies on Women's Place in the Divine Economy* (Oakland: Katherine Bushnell, 1930); Russell C.

Prohl, *Woman in the Church: A Restudy of Woman's Place in Building the Kingdom* (Grand Rapids: Eerdmans, 1957).

19. Diodorus of Sicily 2.45.1–3; 3.53.1–3.

20. William M. Ramsay, *Cities and Bishoprics of Phrygia* (Oxford: Clarendon, 1895), 134.

21. Ibid., 7.

22. James Donaldson, *Woman: Her Position and Influence in Ancient Greece and Rome, and Among Early Christians* (London: Longman, Green, and Co., 1907), 124.

23. Michel Glycas *Annalium* 2.143.

24. Bardesanes, trans. from Syriac by B. P. Pratten, *Ante-Nicene Fathers*, 8:726–27; Clementine *Recognitions* 9.22–23; Caesarius *Dialogue* 2.109–10; Eusebius *Preparation for the Gospel* 6.10; Cedrenus 126–27.

25. Ambroiaster *Questions on the New Testament* 115.18.10–13; 113.7.7–12 Souter; Augustine *The City of God* 6.8, 14–21.

26. Firmicus Maternus *De errore profundo* 4.2. 29–30.

27. Ambroiaster *Questions on the Old and New Testament* 113.11.8–11 Souter.

28. Pseudo-Heraclitus of Ephesus *Epistle* 9.

29. Euripides *Trojan Women* 660.

30. Euripides *Andromache* 170 ff.

31. Sophocles *Electra* 271–74.

32. Euripides frag. 645.

33. *e paisin authentaisin koinone domon*, line 4.

34. Euripides *Suppliant Women* 442ff. Professors Jeffrey Henderson and Michael Poliakoff kindly pointed out to us the sexual nature of this allusion.

35. ὅτε δὲ αὐτὸς αὐθεντὶ ἐπέλθῃ σοι, χρείαν σοι ποιήσει. Pseudo-Callisthenes *Historia Alexandri Magni* 2.1.6, 3.6.6.

36. Philodemus *Volumina rhetorica* 2, ed. S. Sudhaus (Leipzig: B. G. Teubner, 1896), 133.

37. μετὰ τὴν φθορὰλν δὲ τοῦ γάμου τῆς ἁρπαγῆς
ἐκάλεσε πλῆθος εἰς τὸν αὐθέντην γάμον
ἀνδρῶν χορευτῶν καὶ γυναικῶν ἀθλίων. *Anthologia Palatina* 15.19.3.

38. Aeschylus *Eumenides* 212.

39. Emily Townsend Vermeule, *Aspects of Death in Early Greek Art and Poetry*, Sather Classical Lectures, vol. 46 (Berkeley: University of California Press, 1979), 101.

40. Pindar frag. 139 Bergk.

41. Homer *Odyssey* 6.121.

42. *Clementine Homilies* 13.19 (Migne *PG* 2. 314). This document was compiled in the fourth century but is based on an earlier work and contained much earlier materials.

43. Pollux *Onomasticon* 3.38.

44. Firmicus Maternus *De errore profundo* 7.5.

45. For the blending of marriage, death, and initiation into mystery rites, see H. R. W. Smith, *Funerary Symbolism in Apulian Vase Paintings*, ed. H. K. Anderson, Publications in Classical Studies Series 12 (Berkeley: University of California Press, 1976), and the review by Eva C. Keuls, *American Journal of Archaeology* 81 (1977): 575–76.

46. *Orphic Hymn to Artemis* 36.13–14.

47. Artemidorus of Daldiensis *Oneirocritus* 1.80; 2.65.

48. Ibid., 1.80; 2.49.

Chapter 8: Is Another Translation Possible?

1. Pierre Chantraine, "Encore *Authentes*," in *Aphieroma ste mneme tou M. Triantaphyllidis* (Salonica: Institution Neohellanikon Spadōn, 1960), 89, 93. Besides the work of Chantraine, modern scholarly inquiry includes Louis Gernet, "Authentes," *Revue des*

études grecques 22 (1909): 13–32; M. Pischari, "Efendi," in *Mélanges de philologie et de linguistique offerts á M. L-Havet* (Paris: Hachette, 1908); Paul Kretschmer, "Authentes," *Glotta* 3 (1912): 289–93; A. Dihle, "Authentes," *Glotta* 39 (1960): 77–83; A. J. Festugiere, *La revelation d'Hermes Trisgimeste*, 4 vols. (Paris: Lecoffre, 1953), 3:1677 n. 4; Bentley Layton, "The Hypostasis of the Archons," *Harvard Theological Review* 69 (1976): 71 n. 158; Walter Scott, *Hermetica*, 2 vols. (Oxford: Oxford University Press, 1925), 1.2, 13.15 note; Friedrich Zucker, "Authentes und Ableitungen," *Sitzungsberichte der Sachsischen Akademie der Wissenschaften zu Liepzig*, Philologisch-historiche Klasse, Band 107, Heft 4 (1962), 3–27. For an early inquiry into the sexual elements of the term, see Catherine Clark Kroeger, "Ancient Heresies and a Strange Greek Verb," *Reformed Journal* 29, 3 (March 1979): 12–15. For views not supportive of women's full participation in ministry, see George W. Knight III, "ΑΥΘΕΝΤΕΩ in Reference to Women in 1 Timothy 1:12," *New Testament Studies* 30 (1984): 143–57; C. D. Osburn, "ΑΥΘΕΝΤΕΩ (1 Timothy 2:12)" *Restoration Quarterly* 25 (1982): 1–12; A. J. Panning, "ΑΥΘΕΝΤΕΙΝ—A Word Study," *Wisconsin Lutheran Quarterly* 178 (1981): 185–91. For a more complete bibliography, see D. M. Scholer, "I Timothy 2:9–15 and the Place of Women in the Church's Ministry," in *Women, Authority and the Bible*, ed. Alvera Mickelson (Downers Grove, Ill.: InterVarsity, 1986), 194 nn. 3, 4.

2. Polybius 12.14.3; 22.14.2.

3. Josephus *Wars* 1.582; Diodorus of Sicily 16.61; 17.5; 35.25; Appian *Mithridates* 90.1.

4. M. Pischari, "Efendi," in *Mélanges de philologie et de linguistique offerts á M. L-Havet* (Paris: Hachette, 1908), 426.

5. Alexander Rhetor *On the Origins of Rhetoric*, 3 vols., ed. L. Spengel, *Rhetores Graeci* (Leipzig: B. G. Teubner, 1856), 3:2.1–7.

6. Similitudes of Hermas 9.5.6.

7. *Clementine Homilies* 12, *Ante-Nicene Fathers*.

8. Eusebius *De ecclesiastica theologia* 3.5 (Migne *PG* 24.0103A). αὐθέντης καὶ εἰσηγητὴς νέας καὶ σωτηρίου πᾶσιν ἀνθρώποις καταστὰς νομοθεσίας (the author and introducer of a new legislation salvific for all people) *Demonstratio evangelica* 1.7.1.4; Τὸν μὲν οὖν Χριστὸν ἐν πρώτοις αὐθέντην καὶ ἀρχηγὸν ἔσεσθαι τῆς εὐαγγελικῆς πραγματείας (That Christ should in the first place be the originator and prime mover of gospel activity) *Demonstratio evangelica* 3.1.3.5; κατέστη διδάσκαλος φοιτητῶν καὶ τοιούτων νόμων καὶ λόγων αὐθέντης (What teacher of so many students has arisen, the author of such laws and words) *Demonstratio evangelica* 3.6.29. See also A. Dihle, "Authentes," *Glotta* 39 (1960): 82 n. 2, 83 n. 1.

9. *Sybilline Oracles* 7.69.

10. Clement of Rome *Homilies* 18.12.1.4.

11. Eusebius *De ecclesiastica theologica* 1.20 (Migne *PG* 24.865).

12. Hermes Trismegistes *Poimandres* 1.2, 6, 8.

13. Leiden Magical Papyrus W., ed. A. Dietrich (Leipzig: B. G. Teubner, 1891), 14.25, 21; *Papyri Graecae Magicae*, ed. Karl Preisendanz (Leipzig: B. G. Teubner, 1931), 1.36; 9.13.

14. Leiden W. 6.45; Preisendanz 13.2.38.

15. Preisendanz 13.141, 351, 388, 446.

16. 2 Clement 14:3.

17. "In der ersten Bedeutung ist *authentia* mit *exousia* synonym, die zweite leitet zur Bedeutung *authentikos* 'urschriftlich' uber." Dihle, "Authentes," 83.

18. Hippolytus *Refutation of All Heresies* 7.21.

19. *Aegiptische Urkunden aus den Museen zu Berlin: Griechische Urkunden* (Leipzig: J. C. Hinrichs, 1912), 5: no. 1208. Preisigke offers the translation *fest auftreten* (stood firm) in his *Wörterbuch der griechischen Papyruskunden*, 3 vols. (Berlin: Selbstverlag der Erben, 1925).

20. *Sammelbuch Griechischer Urkunden aus Ägypten*, ed. Friedrich Preisigke and Friedrich Bilabel, 2 vols. (Gottingen: Hubert, 1952), no. 10205, p. 257. See also N. Lewis,

"Leitourgia Papyri," *Transactions of the American Philological Society* n.s. 53, 9 (1963): 26–27.

21. Johannes Laurentius Lydus *de Magistratibus populi Romani*, ed. R. Wuensch (Leipzig: B. G. Teubner, 1903), 3:131.

22. αὐτὸν αὐθεντῆσαι περὶ τὸ πρᾶγμα, ἐκλεξάμενον ἄνδρας ἱκανοὺς μὲν ὁδοιπροπίας πόνους διενεγκεῖν (to take the initiative concerning the matter in choosing suitable men to endure the difficulties of the journey). Basil *Letter* 69.1, 3.

23. *Griechische Urkunden* 103.

24. Ὁ Πατὴρ νομοθετεῖ· ὁ Υἱος· κελεύει· Τὸ Πνεῦμα αὐθεντεῖ (The Father ordains, the Son commands, the Spirit brings into being). Athanasius *Testimonia e scriptura (de communi essentia patris et filii et spiritus sancti)* [Migne *PG* 28.41.41]; ὡς τοῦ υἱοῦ τὰ πάντα ποιοῦντος καὶ αὐθεντοῦντος (The son who made and originated all things). Epiphanius *Panarion* 37.2; 69.75.

25. Πρῶτος τοῦ πράγματος αὐθεντεῖ (He is in the first instance responsible for the deed). John Chrysostom *Homily on Acts* 3.3 (Migne *PG* 9.26D).

26. τοῖς δὲ μὴ αὐθεντοῦσι μὲν τῆς ἀσεβείας, παρασυρεῖσι δὲ δι' ἀνάγκην καὶ βίαν (To those not being responsible for instigating the impiety but drawn in by necessity and force). Athanasius *Epistle to Rufinus* (Migne *PG* 26.1180C).

27. Ait hoc vocabulu olim tantu significasse ton *autocheira*. Postea vero et supra mille annos *authenteo* Graece hoc significare coepisse quod apud Latinos actor significat. Guillaume Budé, *Commentarii linguae Graecae* (Paris: Jodocus Badius Ascensius, 1529), 814–15.

28. George Dunbar, *A Greek-English Lexicon*, 3d ed. (Edinburgh: MacLachlan and Stewart, 1850); Benjamin Hederich, *Graecum Lexicon Manuale* (London: Wilks and Taylor; 1803); T. Morrell, *Lexicon Graeco-Prosodiacum* (Cambridge: J. Smith, 1815); John Pickering, *Greek Lexicon* (Boston: Wilkins, Carter, and Co., 1847); Johann Scapula (fl.1580), *Lexicon Graeco-Latinum* (Oxford: Clarendon, 1653); Cornelis Schrevel, *Lexicon Manuale Graeco-Latinum et Latino-Graecum* (Edinburgh: Bell and Bradfute, 1823); *The Greek Lexicon of Schrevelius Translated into English with Many Additions* (Boston: Cummings, Hilliard and Co., 1826); Stephanus, *Thesaurus Graecae Linguae*, ed. W. and L. Dindorf (Paris: Didot, 1831–65).

29. This value disappeared from classical dictionaries about the time when the translation of 1 Timothy 2:12 was being challenged by feminists, in the mid-nineteenth century.

30. Basil *Epistle* 51.1 (Migne *PG* 32.389A).

31. τῆς . . . κρίσεως αὐθεντεῖ ὁ ὕψιστος θεός. Eusebius *Life of Constantine* 2.48 (Migne *PG* 20.1025C).

32. Leo the Great *Epistle* 30 (Migne *PL* 54.788A).

33. Pseudo-Chion *Letters* 13.1; 14.5; 16.5–8. See also Plutarch *Moralia* 53B; 798E–F; Dio Chrysostom *Orations* 34.52; 47.2; Epictetus *Dissertations* 1.10.2.

34. Plutarch *Moralia* 472B.

Chapter 9: The Feminine as Primal Source

1. We are indebted to Dr. Giglia Parker of the obstetrical faculty at Brown University Medical School for pointing this out to us.

2. Forstenpointner, Scherrer, Schultz and Sattman, "Archäologisch-paläoanatomische Untersuchungen an einer hellenistischen Brunnenlage in Ephesos, Turkei," *Wien Tieräril Monatschrift* 80 (1993), 216–24.

3. See G. M. A. Hanfmann, "Excavations at Sardis, 1958," *Bulletin of the American Schools of Oriental Research* 154 (1959): 32 n. 69; G. M. A. Hanfmann and Jane C. Waldbaum, "Kybebe and Artemis: Two Anatolian Goddesses at Sardis," *Archaeology* 22 (1969):

265–67; J. and L. Robert, "Bulletin Épigraphique," *Revue des études grecques* 84 (1971): 520.

4. See R. E. Witt, *Isis in the Greco-Roman World* (Ithaca, N.Y.: Cornell University Press, 1971), 141–51.

5. *Oxyrhyrchus Papyri* 11.1380.

6. Apuleius *Metamorphoses* 11.2.

7. Ibid., 11.5.

8. τὸ τῆς φύσεως θῆλυ καὶ δεκτικὸν ἁπάσης γενέσεως. Plutarch *De Iside et Osiride* 372E; see also *Moralia* 1014D, 1015D, and 1023A; Plato *Timaeus* 49A, 51A.

9. Plutarch *De Iside et Osiride* 368C.

10. Jan Bergman, *Ich Bin Isis: Studien zum memphitischen Hintergrund der grieschischen Isisaretolgien* (Stockholm: Almqvist and Wiksell, 1968), 134 n. 1, 283–84.

11. See W. Speigelberg, "Eine Neue Legende über die Geburt des Horaz," *Zeitschrift für ägyptische Sprache und Altertumskunde* 52 (1917): 94–97. Hesiod (*Theogony* 213) had noted that Night gave birth to thirteen children although she had not slept with a male.

12. Herodotus 1.173.

13. Nicholas of Damascus *F Gr Hist* 90F103(k)=Stobaeus *Florilegia* 4.2.

14. Nymphis *F Gr Hist* 432F7=Plutarch *De mulierum virtutilous* 248D.

15. William M. Ramsay, *Cities and Bishoprics of Phrygia* (Oxford: Clarendon, 1895), 66, inscription no. 21.

16. *Journal of Hellenic Studies* (1892): 1; Ramsay, *Cities and Bishoprics*, 94–95.

17. Ramsay, *Cities and Bishoprics*, 94.

18. Eva Cantarella, *Pandora's Daughters: The Role and Status of Women in Greek and Roman Antiquity*, trans. Maureen B. Fant (Baltimore: Johns Hopkins University Press, 1987), 52–53.

19. Plutarch *Moralia* 374F; see also Philo *Who Is the Heir* 61.

20. Hippolytus *Refutation of All Heresies* 8.13.3–4; 14.5; 5.19.14; see Luise Abramowki, "Female Figures in the Gnostic *Sondergut* in Hippolytus' *Refutatio*," in *Images of the Feminine in Gnosticism: Studies in Antiquity and Christianity*, ed. Karen King (Philadelphia: Fortress, 1988), esp. 137, and n. 2.

21. Authentic Teaching NHC 5.23.22–26.

22. Tertullian *Against the Valentinians* 10; Irenaeus *Against Heresies* 1.2.4.

23. Hippolytus *Refutation of All Heresies* 5.1, *Ante-Nicene Fathers*, 5.50.

24. Authentic Teaching 6.322. 26–35.

25. Epiphanius *Panarion* 33.7.9 (Migne *PG* 41.568).

26. Clement of Alexandria *Excepta ex Theodoto* 78.2 (Migne *PG* 9.2.696). The Mithraic initiate prayed to "the first genesis of my genesis, the primordial beginning of my beginning." *Mithriac Liturgy* 1.6–7.

27. Gospel of Truth NHC 12.2.22.13–15.

28. The Teaching of Silvanus NHC 7.4.91.14–20.

29. Ibid., 7.4.92.11–14.

30. Irenaeus *Against Heresies* 1.21.5; Epiphanius *Panarion* 36.3.4 (Migne *PG* 41.636).

31. Epiphanius *Panarion* 33.8 (Migne *PG* 41.569).

32. Walter Burkert, *Homo Necans: The Anthropology of Ancient Greek Sacrificial Ritual and Myth*, trans. Peter Bing (Berkeley: University of California Press, 1983), 251.

33. Hippolytus *Philosophoumena* 5.8.40 (Migne *PG* 16.3. 3150–51).

34. Jane Ellen Harrison, *Prolegomena to the Study of Greek Religion*, 3d ed. (Cambridge: Cambridge University Press, 1922), 560–61.

35. See Catherine Clark Kroeger, "The Classical Concept of 'Head' as Source," Appendix 3, in *Equal to Serve*, ed. Gretchen Gaebelein Hull (Old Tappan, N.J.: Revell, 1987).

36. Didymus the Blind *On the Trinity* 3.41.3 (Migne *PG* 39.988C–989A). We have understood the lacuna in the text to read ε[τερο]διδάσκειν rather than ε[ν ταῖς ἐκκλεσίαις] διδάσκειν.

Chapter 10: Condemnation or Refutation? (2:13–14)

1. Irenaeus *Against Heresies* 1.11.1; see also 1.9.5, and Celsus *Against Origen* 5.62.

2. Irenaeus *Against Heresies* 1.30.6 (Migne *PG* 7.697–98); see also Epiphanius *Panarion* 25.2, 3 (Migne *PG* 41.321–22); Apocryphon of John 11.18–21; Reality of the Archons 86.29–87.4.

3. Epiphanius *Panarion* 36.5.3 (Migne *PG* 41.648).

4. Hans Jonas, *The Gnostic Religion: The Message of the Alien God and the Beginnings of Christianity* (Boston: Beacon, 1958), 93.

5. Elaine Pagels, *Adam, Eve, and the Serpent* (New York: Vintage, 1988), 66.

6. Ibid., 68; see also Clement *Protreptikos logos* 4.47.

7. Irenaeus *Against Heresies* 1.2.2–3ff.

8. Hippolytus *Refutation of All Heresies* 16.6.12–13 (Migne *PG* 16.3.3174).

9. Ibid. (Migne *PG* 16.3.3195).

10. Irenaeus *Against Heresies* 1.30.7 (Migne *PG* 7.698).

11. On the Origin of the World 113.33–34.

12. The Hypostasis of the Archons 2.89.11–16.

13. On the Origin of the World NHC 2.5.115.31–116.8.

14. Ibid. 2.5.113.25.

15. Ibid. 2.5.114.29.

16. Hypostasis of the Archons 2.4.88. 4–6.

17. Apocryphon of John 2.1.22. 32–23.2.

18. Bentley Layton, "The Riddle of the Thunder," in *Nag Hammadi, Gnosticism, and Early Christianity*, ed. Charles W. Hendrick and Robert Hodgson, Jr. (Peabody, Mass.: Hendrickson, 1986), 48.

19. Irenaeus *Against Heresies* 1.30.7 (Migne *PG* 7.699).

20. On the Origin of the World NHC 2.5.116.

21. Apocryphon of John NHC 2. 69.19–25.

22. Apocryphon of John 5.18, as quoted in Jonas, *Gnostic Religion*.

23. Henry A. Green, *The Economic and Social Origins of Gnosticism*, SBL Dissertation Series 77 (Atlanta: Scholars, 1985), 179.

24. Apocalypse of Adam 64.6–16.

25. Epiphanius *Panarion* 38.2.6; Apocryphon of John 23.35–24.25; On the Origin of the World 116.33–117.18; Reality of the Archons 88.17–30.

26. b. Yebamoth 103b; b. Abodah Zarah 22b; b. Shabbath 146a.

27. On the Origin of the World NHC 2.5.113.33–34; 115.33.

28. Testimony of Truth NHC 9.3. 47.1–4.

29. ὡς εὑρούσης τὸ βρῶμα τῆς γνώσεως ἐξ ἀποκαύψεως τοῦ λαλήσαντος αὐτῇ. ὄφεως. Epiphanius *Panarion* 26.2.6 (Migne *PG* 41.333).

30. Ibid. 37.3.1. (Migne *PG* 41.645).

Chapter 11: How an Important Bible Story Was Turned Upside Down

1. Tomas Hägg, *The Novel in Antiquity* (Berkeley: University of California Press, 1983), 112–13. Originally published as *Den Antika Romanen* (Uppsala: Bokförlaget Carmina, 1980), and revised by the author for the English edition.

2. For a discussion, see Hägg, *Novel in Antiquity*, 82–101.

3. Dennis Ronald MacDonald, *The Legend and the Apostle: The Battle for Paul in Story and Canon* (Philadelphia: Westminster, 1983).

4. Cicero *On the Nature of the Gods* 1.34.94; 3.

5. Dio Chrysostom *Discourses* 4.73–74. Apuleius's beautiful allegory of a soul coming to full salvation knowledge (as the ancient pagans understood it) is called an old woman's tale (*anilis fabula*). In the novel, the old woman tells her story to make a disconsolate young woman feel better. Apuleius *Metamorphoses* 4.28; 6.25.

6. Quintilian *Institutes* 1.8.9.

7. Lucian *The Lover of Lies* 9.

8. Strabo *Geography* 1.2.8.

9. Philostratos *Imagines* 1.15.

10. Flavius Philostratos *The Life of Apollonius of Tyana* 5.14.

11. Origen *Against Celsus* 6.34, 37; *De principiis* 2.4.3.

12. Plato *Republic* 350E; 377D; 378A, D; 381A, C.

13. Clement of Alexandria *Exhortation to the Heathen* 2.15.2.

14. Strabo *Geography* 1.2.3.

15. Horace *Satires* 2.6.77–78.

16. Cicero *On the Nature of the Gods* 3.5.12–13.

17. Strabo *Geography* 1.2.8.

18. Minucius Felix *Octavius* 20.

19. Horace *Satires* 2.6.77–78.

Chapter 12: New Stories for Old

1. Minucius Felix *Octavius* 20.

2. Eusebius *Preparation for the Gospel* 3 (prologue).

3. Quintilian *Institutes* 1.8.19–21.

4. Ibid., 19.

5. Ibid., 21.

6. See Euripides *Heracles* 339–47; *Ion* 437–51; *Antiope* 48.11–14 Kambitsis.

7. Clement of Alexandria *Stromata* 5.688.

8. See Eva C. Keuls, "The Happy Ending: Classical Tragedy and Apulian Funerary Art," *Overdnik mit Instituut de Mededelingen van het Nederlands te Rome* (Deel-XL, 1978): 83–91 (plates on 247–50).

9. Walter Burkert, *Structure and History in Greek Mythology and Ritual* (Berkeley: University of California Press, 1979), 6–7.

10. *Tragicorum Graecorum Fragmenta Papyracea Nuper Reperta*, ed. Arthur S. Hunt (Oxford: Clarendon, 1912), 6 Εὐριπίδου Μελανίππη lines 1–22.

11. κοὐκ ἐμὸς ὁ μῦθος, ἀλλ᾽ ἐμῆς μητρὸς πάρα. Frag. 484 Nauck.

12. ὁμολογεῖ οὖν τήν διδασκαλίαν τὴν ἀρχαίαν διὰ τῆς Μελανίππης. Dionysius of Halicarnassus *Ars rhetorica* 9.11. "It is possible that Melanippe's mother was familiar with an Orphic myth, since women were admitted to the Orphic mysteries. The term ἀρχαία διδασκαλία would suggest the archaic wisdom of the mysteries." Hans Liesegang, "The Mystery of the Serpent," in *Pagan and Christian Mysteries*, ed. Joseph Campbell, trans. Ralph Manheim and R. F. C. Hull (New York: Harper and Row, 1955), 15.

13. Plato *Symposium* 177A–B; Euripides *Helen* 513; Dionysius of Halicarnassus *Ars rhetorica* 9, 11, 8,10; Aristides 2.41; Philo *On the Change of Names* 152; *On Dreams* 1.172; Lucian *Hermotinus* 47; Horace *Satires* 2.2.2; Julian *Orations* 197C; *Satires* 358D, 387B.

14. The Roman poet Propertius (3.15) cried,

> Ah, how many times the queen tore her beautiful hair,
> Her pitiless hand drove into her soft face.
> Ah, how many times she burdens the slave with an unfair workload.
> and orders her to place her head upon the hard ground.
> Frequently she allows her to live in filth and darkness,
> frequently denies even brackish water to the starving woman.

15. See documentation in *Lexicon Iconographicum Mythologicum Classicum,* "Dirke," 25–28.

16. *LIMC* #3.

17. *Anthologia Palatina* 3.7. The story is shown twice in paintings at Pompeii, and in several mosaics throughout the Roman world.

18. Pliny the Elder *Natural History* 36.4.34.

19. ap. Athenaeus *Deipnosophistae* 13.597.

20. C. Müller, *Fragmenta Historicorum Graecarum* (Paris: Didot, 1841–70), 3:628–30.

21. Theo Smyrnaeus revealed that the fourth stage of initiation consisted in being the beloved of God. Aristotle pointed out that initiation was not so much what was said as what was experienced.

22. For documentation see Catherine Clark Kroeger, "The Nachleben of Euripides' Antiope: the Heroine's Transformation into a Mystagogue and an Element in the Justification of Zeus," unpublished Ph.D. dissertation, University of Minnesota, 1987.

23. E. R. Goodenough, "A Jewish-Gnostic Amulet of the Roman Period," *Greek and Byzantine Studies* 1 (1958): 71–80.

24. Birger Pearson, "Jewish Haggadic Tradition in *The Testimony of Truth*," in *Gnosticism, Judaism, and Egyptian Christianity* (Minneapolis: Augsburg/Fortress, 1990), 47.

25. See Douglas M. Parrot, "A Response to Jewish and Greek Heroines," in *Images of the Feminine in Gnosticism: Studies in Antiquity and Christianity*, ed. Karen King (Philadelphia: Fortress, 1988), 92ff.

26. Shabbath 2:6; Berakhoth 31a; Shabbath 31b, 32a; y. Shabbath 2:6; Genesis Rabbah 17:8; Shabbath 2, 5b, 34.

27. Life of Adam and Eve 3.1, 18.1. In *The Apocrypha and Pseudepigrapha of the Old Testament*, ed. R. H. Charles (Oxford: Clarendon, 1913), 2:143.

Chapter 13: Of Jewish and Gnostic Heroines

1. See E. R. Goodenough, *By Light, Light: The Mystic Gospel of Hellenistic Judaism* (New Haven, Conn.: Yale University Press, 1935), 14–23, 157–63, 201–11, 247–49.

2. Philo *On the Cherubim* 14.

3. Philo *Questions and Answers on Genesis* 4.145–46; *On the Cherubim* 12.

4. Philo *Questions and Answers on Genesis* 3.21.

5. ἡ ἐκ διδασκαλίας τελειουμένη ἀρετή. Philo *Questions and Answers on Genesis* 4.122. See also 4.6 and 3.29 and *On the Cherubim* 9.

6. Philo *Questions and Answers on Genesis* 4.97.

7. Ibid., 100.

8. Ibid., 9. See also 4.137.

9. Ibid., 116.

10. σοφίαν τῆς ἐπιστήμης. Philo *Questions and Answers on Genesis* 4.243.

11. πόθεν γὰρ ἄλλοθεν ἢ ἐκ τοῦ σοφίας οἴκου κοινωνὸν εὑρήσει γνώμην ἀνεπίληπτον, ἢ πάντα συνδιατρίψει τὸν αἰῶνα. Philo *On Flight and Finding* 10.52.

12. *On the Cherubim* 12, 13, 17–19.

13. Ibid., 42–48.

14. Philo *On the Cherubim* 57.

15. Ibid., 59–62.

16. Philo *On the Migration of Abraham* 89ff.

17. Philo *Allegorical Interpretation* 2.19, 71ff.

18. Birger Pearson, "Jewish Haggadic Traditions in the *Testimony of Truth* from Nag Hammadi (CG IX.3)," in *Ex Orbe Religionum: Studia Geo Widengren oblata* (*Numen* suppl. 21), ed. J. Bergman, K. Drynjeff, and H. Ringgren, 2 vols. (Leiden: Brill, 1972), 1:468; see also his "Gnostic Interpretation of the Old Testament in the Testimony of Truth," *Harvard Theological Review* 73 (1980): 317; "Some Observations on Gnostic Hermeneutics," in *The Critical Study of Sacred Texts*, ed. Wendy Doniger O'Flaherty (Berkeley: Graduate Theological Union, 1979), 244, and Henry A. Green, *The Economic and Social Origins of Gnosticism*, SBL Dissertation Series 77 (Atlanta: Scholars, 1985), 184.

19. Green, *Economic and Social Origins of Gnosticism*, 185.

20. For Gnostic commentaries on the proliferation of sects from Judaism see ibid., 113 n. 1.

21. Apion 2.145.

22. ὡς γοήτα καὶ ἀπατεῶνα. Josephus *Contra Apion* 2.145.

23. The Apocryphon of John 2.10.13.19–20, 22.22–23, 23.3, 29.6.

24. Epiphanius *Panarion* 26.6.1–2. See also Francis T. Fallon, *The Enthronement of Sabaoth: Jewish Elements in Gnostic Creation Myths* (Leiden: Brill, 1978), 81.

25. μῦθόν τινα παράπλήσιον τοῖς παραδιδομένοις ταῖς γραυσίν. Celsus *On True Doctrine*, ap. Origen *Against Celsus* 4.39.

26. W. F. Albright, "Recent Discoveries in Palestine and the Gospel of John," in *The Background of the New Testament and Its Eschatology*, ed. W. D. Davies (Cambridge: Cambridge University Press, 1956), 163; Green, *Economic and Social Origins of Gnosticism*, 186.

27. Pearson, "Jewish Haggadic Tradition in *The Testimony of Truth*," in *Gnosticism, Judaism, and Egyptian Christianity*, 47.

28. The Reality of the Archons 4.3.1ff; On the Origin of the World 116.12–117.15; Apocryphon of John BG 58.10–62; 3.28.25–31.13; 2.22.18–24; 4.34.25–38.3. Irenaeus *Against Heresies* 1.30ff.

29. Philo *Quis Rerum* 11.52.

30. Ξύλον ζωῆς ἐστι πᾶσι τοῖς ἀντεχομένοις αὐτῆς (Prov. 3:18). Note Hypostasis of the Archons 89.25, where Eve becomes a tree. Compare the laughter of Eve at the archons with the laughter of Wisdom at the foolish (Prov. 1:22b–26).

31. Philo *On Flight and Finding* 10.52.

32. Ἐπιλαβοῦ ἐμῆς παιδείας, μὴ ἀφῆς, ἀλλὰ φύλαξον αὐτὴν σεαυτῷ εἰς ζωήν σου.

33. Bentley Layton, "Hypostasis of the Archons," *Harvard Theological Review* 69 (1976): 55–58, nn. 57–69.

34. As translated by H. Freedman in Midrash Rabbah, Soncino ed.; text ed. Albeck (reprint ed., Jerusalem: Wahrman, 1965).

35. Genesis Rabbah 20:11.

36. Pearson, "Jewish Haggadic Traditions in the *Testimony of Truth*," 1:464. For the serpent as "the instructor," see Reality of the Archons 89.32, 90.6; Origin of the World 119.17; 120.2–3; see also Irenaeus *Against Heresies* 1.30.5; Hippolytus *Refutation of All Heresies* 5.16.8; Pseudo-Tertullian 2.1.

37. Hypostasis of the Archons 89 [137]3–11; Apocalypse of Adam 64. 6–12, 20–30.

38. Hypostasis of the Archons 89 [137]11–22; Apocalypse of Adam 64. 12–13.

39. Irenaeus *Against Heresies* 1.30.6.

40. Apocryphon of John 71.23–26.

41. See Jean Daniel Kaestli, "L'interprétation du serpent de Genèse 3 dans quelques textes gnostiques et la question de la gnose 'Ophite,'" in *Gnosticisme et Monde Hellénistique: Actes du Collque de Louvain-la-Neuve* (March 11–14, 1980), ed. Julien Ries, Yvonne Janssens, Jean-Marie Severin (Louvain-la-Neuve: Universitié catholique de Louvain, Institut orientaliste, 1982). See also R. P. Casey, "Naassenes and Ophites," *Journal of Theological Studies* 27 (1925–26): 383.

42. ⲈⲨⳆⲀ ⲚⲌⲰⲎ ⲈⲦⲈ ⲦⲢⲈⲨⲦⲀⲘⲞ ⲦⲈ ⲘⲠⲰⲚⳆ. On the Origin of the World NHC 2.5.113.32–114.4.

43. †ⲠⲚⲈⲨⲘⲀⲦⲒ[ⲔⲎ] . . ⲦⲢⲈⲨⲦⲀⲘⲞ. Hypostasis of the Archons NHC 2.4.89 [137]. 31–32; 90 [138].11–12.

44. Apocryphon of John BG 57.12; 60.17–18.

45. Irenaeus *Against Heresies* 1.30.7.

46. Ibid., 1.30.14.

Chapter 14: The Great Goddesses and Eve

1. B. Hrozny, "Une inscription de Ras-Shamra en langue churrite," *Archiv orientální* 4: 118–29, esp. 121. See also O. R. Gurney, *Some Aspects of Hittite Religion* (Oxford: Oxford University Press for the British Academy, 1977), 14.

2. *ANET*, 89 n. 152.

3. Gurney, *Some Aspects of Hittite Religion*, 18.

4. *ANET*, 393; see also 398.

5. *ANET*, 205, 206.

6. *ANET*, 123, 124.

7. *ANET*, 89, 205; Gurney, *Some Aspects of Hittite Religion*, 13.

8. Gurney, *Some Aspects of Hittite Religion*, 44–45.

9. Michael S. Moore, *The Balaam Traditions: Their Character and Development*, SBL Dissertation Series 113 (Atlanta: Scholars, 1990), 21.

10. For the pervasive influence of Egyptian religion on Ephesus, see Gunter Holbl, *Zeugnisse Aegiptischer Religionsvorstellungen für Ephesus* (Leiden: Brill, 1978).

11. Apuleius *Metamorphoses* 11.3, 4.

12. Plutarch *Moralia* 352A.

13.   ἐγώ εἰμι Κρόνου θυγάτηρ πρεσβυτατάτη
        ἐγώ εἰμι γυνὴ καὶ ἀδελφὴ Ὀσείριδος βασιλέως
        ἐγώ εἰμι ἡ ἐν τῷ τοῦ κυνὸς ἄστρωι ἐπιτέλλουσα.
        ἐγώ εἰμι ἡ καρπὸν ἀνθρώποις εὑροῦσα.
        ἐγώ εἰμι μήτηρ Ὥρου βασιλέως
        ἐγώ εἰμι ἡ παρὰ γυναιξὶ θεὸς καλουμένη . . .
        ἐγώ εἰμι πολέμου κυρία . . .
        ἐγώ εἰμι ἡ θεσμοφόρος καλουμένη.
Text from Bergman, 301–3.

14. Hippolytus *Refutation of All Heresies* 4.49 (Migne *PG* 16.3.3118).

15. b. Abodah Arah (On Idolatry) 43a.

16. Rose Horman Arthur, *The Wisdom Goddess: Feminine Motifs in Eight Nag Hammadi Documents* (Lanham, Md.: University Press of America, 1984), 116.

17. Thunder, Perfect Mind NHC 7.2.13, 16–20, 30–32; see also Bentley Layton, "The Riddle of the Thunder," in *Nag Hammadi, Gnosticism, and Early Christianity*, ed. Charles W. Hedrick and Robert Hodgson, Jr. (Peabody, Mass.: Hendrickson, 1986), 37ff.

18. Thunder, Perfect Mind NHC 7.2.13.

19. Ibid., 6.21.20–32.

20. Layton, "The Riddle of the Thunder."

21. Ibid., 41.

Chapter 15: The Veneration of the Serpent and Eve

1. Philo of Byblos F109 (814:23) apud Eusebius *Preparation for the Gospel* 1.10.45.

2. Valerius Maximus 1.3.2. *Cornelius Hispalus . . . Iudaeos, qui Sabazi Iovis cultu Romanos inficere mores conanti erant, repetere domos suas coegit* (Cornelius Hispalus forced back into their homes the Jews who sought to infect Roman beliefs with the worship of Jupiter Sabazios). For alternative view, E. N. Lane, "Sabiazus and the Jews in Valerius Maximus: A Reexamination." *Journal of Roman Studies* 69 (1979): 35–38.

3. See Helmut Koester, *Introduction to the New Testament*, vol. 1, *History, Culture, and Religion of the Hellenistic Age* (Philadelphia: Fortress, 1982), 186–87.

4. He was said to have been brought by a woman from Epidaurus to Sicyon in the form of a serpent. A statue of a woman riding on a serpent was supposed to be Aristodama, the mother of Asclepius's son. Pausanias 2.10.3.

5. Epiphanius *Panarion* 37.2.6 (Migne *PG* 41.644).

6. Origen *Against Celsus* 7.9.

7. Jerome *Epistle* 41.4 (to Marcella).

8. Pseudo-Tertullian *Against All Heresies* 7; Hippolytus *Refutation of All Heresies* 8.19.

9. Epiphanius *Panarion* 49.1.

10. Tertullian *On the Soul* 9.4.

11. Hippolytus *Refutation of All Heresies* 8.19.

12. Epiphanius *Panarion* 49.2.

13. Ibid., 49.3.

14. Origen *Catenae on Paul's Epistles to the Corinthians* 14.36.

15. Tertullian *On Fasting* 1.

16. Hippolytus *Commentary on Daniel* 4.20.

17. Hippolytus *Refutation of All Heresies* 10.25.

18. Theodoret *Compendium of Heretical Falsehood* 3.1.

19. Epiphanius *Panarion* 37.5.6–8.

20. Justin Martyr *First Apology* 27.

21. Formerly in the Lansdowne Collection, it passed into the William Randolph Hearst Collection and is now in the Los Angeles County Museum of Art.

22. *Monumenti inediti pubblicati dall' instituto di Corrispondenza archeologica* 5. 5. Rome 1849–1853, plate #28; Enrico Braun, "Trono d'Appolline e candelabro di bronzo," *Annali dell' instituto di corrispondenza archeologica* volume ottavo della serie nuova (23 of the entire series), 102–7, see also by the same author 117–27; A. H. Smith, ed., *A Catalogue of the Ancient Marbles at Lansdowne House. Based upon the Work of Adolf Michaelis with an Appendix containing Original Documents Relating to the Collection* (London, 1889).

23. Hippolytus *Refutation of All Heresies* 5.11 (Migne *PG* 31555B–C).

24. G. Sfameni Gasparro, "Interpretazioni Gnostiche e misteriosofiche die miti di Attis," in *Studies in Gnosticism and Hellenistic Religions Presented to Gilles Quispel on the Occasion of His 65th Birthday*, ed. R. van den Broek and M. J. Vermaseren (Leiden: Brill, 1981), 376–411.

25. Hippolytus *Refutation of All Heresies* 5.11.

26. Ibid., 5.11.9ff.

27. H. Vetters, "Der Schlangengott," in *Studien aus Religion und Kultur Kleinasiens. Festschrift für Friedrich Karl Dörner zum 65 Geburtstag am 28. Februar 1976*, ed.

S. Sahin, E. Schwertheim, and J. Wagner, *Études Préliminaires Réligions Orientals* 66.2 (Leiden: Brill, 1978), 2:967–79. Eichler, "Die österreichischen Ausgrabungen in Ephesos im Jahre 1962," *Anz Wien* 100 (1963): 54ff.

28. Inventory numbers 1590, 1591, 1592, Selçuk-Ephesus Museum.

29. Inventory number 1591.

30. Volker M. Strocka, *Forschungen in Ephesos*, vol. 8.1. *Die Wandmalerei der Hanghäuser in Ephesos*. Mit einem Beitrag von Vetters, H. (Vienna: Verlag der Österreichischen Akademie der Wissenschaften, 1977), 91ff.

31. Vetters, "Schlangengott," 975.

32. H. Vetters, "Ephesos": Vorläufiger Grabungsbericht 1980," *Anzeiger der phil.-hist. Klasse der Österreichischen Akademie der Wissenschaften* 118 (1981): 137–68; Machteld J. Mellink, "Archaeology in Asia Minor," *American Journal of Archaeology* 86 (1982): 569; Louis Robert, "Dans une maison d'Ephese, un serpent et un chiffre," *Comptes rendus de l'Academie des inscriptions et Belles-Lettres* (1982): 126–32.

Chapter 16: Considerations of Childbearing (2:15)

1. Mish. Shabbath 2:6.

2. They also commanded people to abstain from meat. The Naassenes, although they participated fully in the other rites of the Great Mother, did not castrate themselves. Nevertheless they lived a very ascetic existence and practiced sexual abstinence. Hippolytus *Refutation of All Heresies* 5.9 (Migne *PG* 16.3.3155).

3. An alternate text begins, "The man followed the earth, and the woman followed the man." On the Origin of the World 2.5.109.21–25.

4. The original text is not available to us, and we must depend upon the quotations given by Clement of Alexandria *Miscellanies* 3.45, 63–64 (Migne *PG* 8.1.1193).

5. Gospel of Thomas, saying 114.

6. First Apocalypse of James NHC 5.3.41.15–16.

7. The Gospel of Mary BG 1.9.15–50.

8. Trimorphic Tractate 78.3–12; Eugnostos 85.7–9; Sophia Jesus Christ 107.10–12, 118.15; Dialogue of the Savior 144. 17–22; Zostrianos 1.10–14; 131.5–8.

9. Gospel of Thomas, saying 22. The need for the two to be one is also expressed in sayings 4, 11, and 106.

10. 2 Clement 12:2–3 (Migne *PG* 1.345, 347).

11. Gospel of Thomas, saying 56.

12. Hippolytus *Refutation of All Heresies* 5.8.22 (Migne *PG* 16.3.3146).

13. Ibid., 5.8.19 (Migne *PG* 16.3.3150).

14. See Stephen Benko, "The Libertine Gnostic Sect of the Phibionites According to Epiphanius," *Vigiliae Christianae* 21, 2 (1967): 103–19.

15. Epiphanius *Panarion* 26.13.2–3 (Migne *PG* 41.352–53).

16. Ibid., 26.13.4–6; see also 26.13.2–3 (Migne *PG* 41.353).

17. Ibid., 26.5 (Migne *PG* 41.340).

18. Zostrianos 8.1.131.5–8.

19. See Walter Bauer, William Arndt, F. W. Gingrich, and F. W. Danker, *A Greek-English Lexicon of the New Testament and Other Early Christian Literature* (Chicago: University of Chicago Press, 1979), "διά" 3.1.c.

Appendix 1: Could *Authentein* Mean Murder?

1. Apollonius of Rhodes *Argonautica* 4.479.

2. Euripides *Iphigenia at Aulis* 1190.

3. Clement of Alexandria *Exhortation to the Heathen* 3.42.9 Stahlin; Scymnos Chius *Periegesis* 861; Pausanias 7.19.1–6, 8.53; Tatian *To the Greeks* 29.1.

4. Migne *PG* 114, 770.

5. Euripides *Iphigenia among the Taurians* 1458–60.

6. Anton Bammer, *Das Heiligtum des Artemis von Ephesos* (Graz, Austria: Akademische Druck-u. Vergsanstalt, 1983), p. 159.

7. For a detailed discussion see Richard Seaford, "Dionysiac Drama and the Dionysiac Mysteries," *Classical Quarterly* 31, 2 (1981), esp. 267.

8. Plutarch *De anima* 7.2 frag. 178.

9. Minucius Felix *Octavius* 23.1.

10. Clement of Alexandria *Exhortation to the Heathen* 1.4; 2.12, 16.

11. Ibid., 2.60 (Migne *PG* 8.77).

12. Philostratus *Life of Apollonius of Tyana* 4.2.

13. Apuleius *Metamorphoses* 11.5.

14. Scriptores Historiae Augustae, *Commodus* 9.6.

15. Plutarch suggests that this was done with poison.

16. Callimachus *Hymn to Artemis* 266–67.

17. Strabo *Geography* 10.3.11.

18. Flavius Philostratus *The Life of Apollonius of Tyana* 4.2.

19. Elmar Schwertheim, "Mithras, Seine Denkmaler und sein Kult," *Antike Welt* 10 (1979), illustration #29, 38ff. and 73. A similar trick sword is described by Achilles Tatius in *The Adventures of Leucippe and Clitophon* 3.20.7.

20. Le Roy A. Campbell, *Mithraic Iconography and Ideology* (Leiden: Brill, 1968), 297; M. J. Vermaseren, *Mithraica I: The Mithraeum at S. Maria Capua Vetere* (Leiden: Brill, 1971), 25–26.

21. Ambrioaster *Questions on the Old and New Testament* 114.11; Tertullian *De corona* 15.

22. Achilles Tatius *The Adventures of Clitophon and Leucippe* 7.12.2–30.

23. Ibid., 2.13.1–5.

24. Reinhold Merkelbach, *Roman und Mysterium in der Antike* (Munich: Beck, 1962).

25. A. D. Trendall and Alexander Cambitoglu, *Red Figured Vases of Apulia* (Oxford: Clarendon, 1982), 2:762, plate 284.

26. Plutarch *Lives of Demetrius and Antony* 24; Clement of Alexandria *Exhortation to the Heathen* 2.19.

27. Hippolytus *Refutation of All Heresies* 5.9.8–9.

28. Firmicus Maternus *De errore profundo* 18.1.

29. Hippolytus *Refutation of All Heresies* 5.4.

30. Ibid., 5.4.5.

31. Ibid., 5.3.

32. Origen *Against Celsus* 4.10.

33. Ibid., 6.34.35.

Appendix 2: A Lesson in Greek Grammar

1. In Luke 23:53, three negatives are strung together. If we were to translate all of them into English, we would have something to the effect that Joseph of Arimathea buried the

body of Jesus in a tomb where no one never yet had not been laid. Other triple negatives occur at Mark 5:3 and 14:25. This is impossible English but perfectly respectable Greek. These so-called redundant negatives often occur after verbs of prohibition, hindering, and denying.

2. "In Greek this merely strengthens the first negative if the second is a compound form like οὐδέ, μηδείς, etc. . . . But when the second negative is a single negative, it retains its force." A. T. Robertson and W. Hersey Davis, *A New Short Grammar of the Greek Testament*, 10th ed. (Grand Rapids: Baker, 1977), 391. "When a negative is followed by a compound negative (or by several compound negatives) in the same clause, the negation is strengthened." William W. Goodwin, *Greek Grammar*, rev. Charles Burton Gulick (Boston: Ginn and Co., 1930), 342, #1622.

3. *Didaskein* occurs with an expression of indirect discourse at Mark 8:31. For a discussion of *didaskein* being used with either infinitive or ὅτι, see A. T. Robinson, *A Grammar of the Greek New Testament in the Light of Historical Research* (Nashville: Broadman, 1934), 1035–36.

4. οὐ often remains when followed by ἀλλά. James Hope Moulton, *A Grammar of New Testament Greek* (Edinburgh: T. and T. Clark, 1908–63).

5. Literally, "I am not convinced that none of these things escaped his notice"; "I did not decide to know anything among you save Jesus Christ and him crucified."

6. For a discussion of the infinitive as complement of a verb, see Friedrich Blass, Albert Debrunner, and Robert W. Funk, *A Greek Grammar of the New Testament and Other Early Christian Literature* (Chicago: University of Chicago Press, 1961), #392, especially sect. 2.

7. We are grateful to Professor Philip Sellew for pointing out the possibility of this construction.

8. In Revelation 2:14 *didaskein* takes a dative object, "Balaam who taught Balaak." This raises the possibility of rendering 1 Timothy 2:12, "I certainly do not permit teaching a woman that she is orginator of man." Aesop too used *didaskein* with a dative object. Aesop 210c (*Aesopi Fabulae*, 2 vols., ed. E. Chambray [Paris: Les Belles Lettres, 1925], vol. 1); Plutarch *Marcellus* 12.4.

9. See, e.g., Hippolytus *Refutation of All Heresies* 5.49 (Migne *PG* 16.3.3118): ἐδίδασκε φιλοσοφεῖν; also *Iliad* 5.51–52.

Appendix 3: Sex Reversal and Female Dominance

1. Diodorus of Sicily 2.45.1.

2. Ibid., 2.46.1.

3. Callimachus *Hymn to Artemis* 3.237–47.

4. Diodorus of Sicily 3.52.4–54.7.

5. Arrian *Anabasis* 1.23.7; Diodorus of Sicily 17.24.2.

6. William M. Ramsay, *Cities and Bishoprics of Phrygia* (Oxford: Clarendon, 1895), 94.

7. Simon Pembroke, "Women in Charge: The Ancient Idea of Matriarchy," *Journal of the Wartburg and Courtauld Institutes* 1, 30 (1967): 1–35, and "Last of the Matriarchs," *Journal of Economic and Social History of the Orient* 8, 3 (1965): 217–47. See Robert Flacelière in *Histoire mondiale de la femme I: Préhistoire et antiquité* (Paris: Nouv. Libr. de France, 1965).

8. Strabo *Geography* 11.5.3.

9. For first-century attestation, Nicholas of Damascus *F Gr Hist* 90 F 103 (k); Plutarch *Moralia* 248D.

10. Arrian *Expeditio Alexandris* 1.23.

11. Herodotus 7.68–70, 89–96,100–101.

12. Ibid., 8.88.

13. Ibid., 8.95; Flavius Philostratus *The Life of Apollonius of Tyana* 4.21.

14. Diodorus of Sicily 4.31.4–8.

15. Athenaeus 11.11; Servius *ad Aeneid* 1.658.

16. Athenaeus 12.11.516a.

17. Plutarch *Lives of Demetrius and Antony* 3.3; Ovid *Heroides* 9.55ff.

18. Lucian *Dialogues of the Gods* 237.

19. Naples Museum 299/6406; D. K. Hill, *Catalogue of Classical Bronze Sculpture in the Walters Art Gallery* (Baltimore: Walters Art Gallery, 1949), 50, plate 23.

20. Pliny the Elder *Natural History* 29.30.

21. Tacitus *Annals* 3.61.

22. L. R. Farnell, *Greek Hero Cults and Ideas of Immortality* (Oxford: Clarendon, 1921), 141; Jane Ellen Harrison, *Themis: A Study of the Social Origin of Greek Religion* (Cambridge: Cambridge University Press, 1912), 506.

23. Sophocles *The Trachinian Women* 248ff.; Apollodorus 2.127ff.

24. Diodorus of Sicily 3.55.3.

25. See especially Eva C. Keuls, *The Water Carriers in Hades: A Study of Catharsis through Toil in Classical Antiquity* (Amsterdam: A. M. Hakkert, 1974).

26. Hippolytus *Refutation of All Heresies* 5.21.

27. Herodotus 2.35; Sophocles *Oedipus at Colonna* 337–41.

28. *Oxyrhynchus hymn*, papyri 11.1380.214–16.

29. Diodorus of Sicily 1.27.1.

30. Pseudo-Heraclitus of Ephesus *Epistle* 9.6–12; Flavius Philostratus *The Life of Apollonius of Tyana* 4.2.

Appendix 4: Sex and Death in Ancient Novels

1. Photius *Bibliotheca* 2.94 Henry; Reinhold Merkelbach, *Roman und Mysterium in Antike* (Munich: Beck, 1962), 107.

2. Walter Charleton, *The Ephesian Matron* (reprint ed., Los Angeles: William Andrews Clark Memorial Library, University of California, 1975). The tale is also told by Aesop, *Aesopica*, ed. Ben E. Perry (Urbana: University of Illinois Press, 1952), # 543 (Phaedrus App. 15).

3. Petronius, *Satyricon*, trans. J. P. Sullivan (New York: Penguin, 1977), 122.

4. *Apollonius of Tyre*, trans. Paul Turner (London: Golden Cockerel Press, 1956), 34.

5. Achilles Tatius 5.21.3–4.

6. Ibid., 5.19.4.

7. Ibid., 5.11.5.

8. Ibid., 5.11.2.

9. Ibid., 5.14.4.

10. Ibid., 5.15.6–16.3.

11. Ibid., 5.26.3.

12. Ibid., 5.26.1–3.

13. Robert Fleischer, *Artemis von Ephesos und verwandte Kultstatuen aus Anatolien und Syrien* (Leiden: Brill, 1973), 99–100, 276ff., 288ff.

14. Longus *Daphnis and Chloe* 3.17.

15. Ibid., 3.18.

16. Ibid, 3.17–19; 4.40. For a view of the Lykainion episode as mystic initiation, see H. H. O. Chalk, "Eros and the Lesbian Pastorals of Longus," *Journal of Hellenic Studies* 80 (1960): 32–51.

17. In each case, the man or men slain have been making erotic advances to the woman who slays them. Semiramis, heroine of the *Ninus Romance,* is said to have slain her lovers after she had slept with them.

In the *Aethiopica* of Heliodorus, another heroine, Charicleia, along with her father and fiancé, is captured by pirates. The leader wishes to marry her, but she gains time by asking leave to dress for the nuptials. She reappears arrayed as Artemis herself and, in a manner reminiscent of the goddess's own action, uses her ornamental bow and arrow to deadly advantage. The beach is soon littered with dead pirates. At one point in the novel Charicleia claims to hale from Ephesus, though she is in fact a priestess of Artemis's brother, Apollo.

In a novelette inserted in a longer work, an Amazon follower of Artemis slays a persistent lover who begs her to kill him if he may not share her bed. The Amazon, Nicaia, also described as *androphonon* (man-slaying), complies with his request and thereby arouses the indignation of the other gods. Dionysos rapes her as she sleeps. The unfortunate Nicaia awakes to find that her virginity is gone and that she can no longer present herself to Artemis, but in due time a daughter is born, Telete (initiation). Thus the murder as well as the sexual encounter ultimately leads to initiation.

Artemis herself would brook no courtship and had slain several would-be suitors. Actaeon paid with his life for having surprised her in her bath. The poet Callimachus warned that any who wooed her might suffer death as did Otus and Orion (Callimachus *Hymn to Artemis* 264–65).

18. Achilles Tatius 7.5.

19. Pausanias 4.31.8; Strabo *Geography* 11.5.1. See F. M. Bennet, *Religious Cults Associated with the Amazons* (reprint ed., New York: AMS, 1967), 30–39.

20. Herodotus 4.118.

21. William M. Ramsay, *Letters to the Seven Churches of Asia* (reprint ed., Grand Rapids: Baker, 1963), 326.

22. *Forschung in Ephesos* 3 (1923): 44.

Appendix 5: The Curse Tablets of Cnidus

1. Iris Love was later to suggest that this was in fact the head of the famed Cnidian Aphrodite which had somehow been transported to the sanctuary of Demeter. Iris Cornelia Love, "A Preliminary Report of the Excavations at Knidos, 1971," *American Journal of Archaeology* 76 (1972): 401, esp. n. 3.

2. Athenian women are known to have used such lamps as votive offerings. Pausanias 2.22.4.

3. Karl Preisendanz, "Fluchtafel," *Reallexikon für Antike und Christentums,* 17 vols. (Stuttgart: Hiersemann, 1950), 8, 19, 1.

4. Plato complained of the barbarous Carian songs which professional female mourners sang at Athenian weddings. *Laws* 8.801.

5. Plato *Republic* 364C.

6. David Jordan, "Two Inscribed Lead Tablets from a Well in the Athenian Kerameikos," *Mitteilungen des Deutschen Archäologischen Instituts.* Athenische Abteilung. Band 95. 1980, 226.

7. Or, "consumed with fever."

8. Charles T. Newton, *Halicarnassus, Cnidus, and Branchidae* (London: Trustees of the British Museum, 1863), no. 81; Augustus Audollent, *Defixionum Tabellae* (Paris, 1904), no. 1.

9. Plutarch *Moralia* 768B–E; 257E–258; also Polyaenus 8.39.

10. William M. Ramsay, *Historical Commentary on St. Paul's Epistle to the Galatians* (New York: G. P. Putnam Sons, 1900; reprint ed., Grand Rapids: Baker, 1965), 88.

11. Tatian *To the Greeks* 8.

12. H. Collitz, *Sammlung der griechischen Dialekt-Inschriften*, 4 vols. (Göttingen: Vandenhoeck und Ruprecht, 1884–95), no. 3502.

13. Newton no. 82; Audollent no. 2.

14. Herodotus 5.89.

15. Newton no. 83; Audollent no. 3A.

16. Newton no. 84; Audollent no. 3B.

17. Newton no. 85; Audollent no. 4A.

18. Newton no. 86; Audollent no. 4B. The text is eroded at several points and the reading difficult. The emendation of Audollent reads:

> Agemone dedicates to Demeter and Kore and all the gods and goddesses the bracelet which I lost in the gardens of Rhodocles. May it be lawful and permissible for the one who brings it back to receive a reward for the lost property, for the woman who restores it to me or the man who returns it. And if the one who refuses to return it is by any chance already sold anywhere, may it be a special concern to Demeter and Kore. I further consign to Demeter and Kore [anyone who may have caused me] to pay more than was right for the weight which I requested. Already sold, may it be a special concern to Demeter and Kore. Mistress Despoina, be gracious to me! I further dedicate to Demeter and Kore the one who has unsettled my house, now both him and his belongings, but may it be lawful and permissible for me to . . .

19. According to Pausanias (8.37.6), this name might not be used by the uninitiated. It might, however, have been used quite safely by an initiate when the text was rolled up and fastened securely away from the view of the curious. It occurs elsewhere as a title of Persephone and also of Hecate.

20. Newton no. 87; Audollent, no. 5.

21. Strabo *Geography* 8.1.2.

22. Newton no. 88; Audollent no. 6A.

23. Newton no. 89, Audollent no. 6B.

24. Newton no. 90; Audollent no. 7.

25. Newton no. 90; Audolent no. 7.

26. Newton no. 91; Audollent no. 8; *SIG* no. 1179.

27. Newton no. 92; Audollent, no. 9; *SIG* no. 1199.

28. Newton no. 93; Audollent, no. 10; *SIG* no. 1180.

29. Newton no. 93A; Audollent no. 11.

30. Newton no. 94; Audollent no. 12B.

31. Newton no. 95; Audollent no. 12B.

32. Ronald Stroud,"Curses from Corinth," *American Journal of Archaeology* 77 (1973): 228.

Appendix 6: Gnostic Use of Sex

1. Hippolytus *Refutation of All Heresies* 5.3.

2. Ibid., 5.5.

3. Epiphanius *Panarion* 26.9.6–8.

4. Ibid., 38; Irenaeus *Against Heresies* 1.31.2. For the continuing custom of invoking a divine name before intercourse in the only surviving Gnostic group, see E. S.

Drower, *The Mandaeans of Iraq and Iran, Their Cults, Customs, Magic, Legends, and Folklore* (Oxford: Clarendon, 1937), 34.

5. See Appendix, "La Seduction des Archontes," in F. Cumont, *Recherches sur le Manicheisme* (Brussels: H. Lamertin, 1912).

6. Hippolytus *Refutation of All Heresies* 6.24.

7. Irenaeus *Against Heresies* 1.21.3, *Ante-Nicene Fathers* 346.

8. Ibid., 1.18, 346.

Appendix 7: Alternative Versions of the Creation Story

1. Philo *On the Cherubim* 59–62. We are grateful to Professor Greg Riley for checking the three Coptic translations, and for his helpful advice. We also appreciate the helpful suggestions of Dr. Richard Cervin with regard to Greek grammar and syntax.

2. A break in the text leaves the meaning in doubt. It may be that a more correct rendering is "she spent the night with them."

3. ⲧⲣⲉϥⲧⲁⲙⲟ

4. I.e., the Adam of light.

5. The Adam of light.

Index of Authors
and Subjects

Index of Scripture, Apocrypha, and Pseudepigrapha

Manufactured by Amazon.ca
Bolton, ON